SATURDAY PEOPLE, SUNDAY PEOPLE

**ISRAEL
THROUGH
THE EYES OF
A CHRISTIAN
SOJOURNER**

LELA GILBERT

ENCOUNTER BOOKS • *New York* • *London*

First American edition published in 2012 by Encounter Books, an activity of Encounter for Culture and Education, Inc., a nonprofit, tax exempt corporation. Encounter Books website address: www.encounterbooks.com

Manufactured in the United States and printed on acid-free paper. The paper used in this publication meets the minimum requirements of ANSI/NISO Z39.48 1992 (R 1997) *(Permanence of Paper)*.

FIRST AMERICAN EDITION

LIBRARY OF CONGRESS CATALOGING-IN-PUBLICATION DATA

Gilbert, Lela.
Saturday people, Sunday people : Israel through the eyes of a Christian sojourner / by Lela Gilbert.
p. cm.
ISBN 978-1-59403-639-2 (hardcover : alk. paper) -- ISBN 978-1-59403-652-1 (ebook)
1. Israel--Description and travel. 2. Christian Zionism. 3. Gilbert, Lela--Travel. I. Title.
DS107.5.G55 2012
956.9405'4--dc23
2012020853

For my father, Caryle Keith Hamner,
In his memory and in gratitude for his faith.

CONTENTS

Prologue *vii*

Chapter One: In Search of the Unexpected *1*

Chapter Two: War and Peace *19*

Chapter Three: Days of Awe *37*

Chapter Four: Digging for Truth *55*

Chapter Five: Fighting Apartheid *73*

Chapter Six: Unsettling Misconceptions *91*

Chapter Seven: Ancient Rivalries *109*

Chapter Eight: Gaza Disasters *131*

Chapter Nine: Blind Spot *149*

Chapter Ten: Jewish Nakba *167*

Chapter Eleven: Anne Frank of Baghdad *185*

Chapter Twelve: A Second Exodus from Egypt *201*

Chapter Thirteen: Beyond Bethlehem's Calm *223*

Chapter Fourteen: Natural Allies in a Dangerous World *239*

Epilogue *263*

Acknowledgments *271*

For Further Reading *273*

Index *279*

A flag displayed at an anti-Israel demonstration during the First Intifada. Reiterating an oft-repeated slogan of radical Muslims, the Arabic text reads, "On Saturday we kill the Jews. On Sunday we kill the Christians."

PROLOGUE

The view from the King David Hotel's terrace is one of the most memorable in Jerusalem. In the foreground, flags snap in the wind, and just beyond the aquamarine pool and manicured garden is a sweeping panorama of the Old City, one of the world's most historic landmarks. In late afternoon, the limestone walls are bathed in Jerusalem's famous rose-gold light, contrasting pale limestone against a sapphire sky. Late in the day, a breeze often accompanies the first hints of sunset.

On just such an afternoon one September day, some American friends and I were sharing a bottle of wine on the terrace and catching up on life. Although I'd been seated at that same table many times before, the view still filled me with wonder. Somewhere in the distance church bells were ringing. Birds chirped, a siren whined and a muezzin called the Muslim faithful to a faraway mosque. Our conversation stopped as we absorbed these breathtaking moments.

Suddenly, one of the men turned toward me, and his familiar questions shattered the spell. "So, Lela, why are you in Jerusalem? What exactly are you doing here?"

Those are fair questions. My friends and relatives know that I'm a Southern California native, and that my two 30-something sons, my daughter-in-law and my grandson still live there. And they know that I'm not Jewish. There's every reason to inquire. Yet each time it happens, I feel a little perplexed. On the one hand, Israel now feels very much like home. On the other hand, it really isn't. So I always start by trying to explain why I traveled to the "Holy Land" in the first place.

For one thing, I came to fulfill a personal aspiration—it had been my father's dream to visit Israel before he died. He didn't make it, but I had long shared his fascination with the place. So I came on my own, and in his memory.

And I came to gain perspective and understanding. I've worked for years on books about both Christianity and Islam. Israel is the only place in the Middle East where Christians, Jews and Muslims live more or less side-by-side, shop in the same stores, eat in the same cafes and share the same streets and sidewalks. I imagined that living in a country where these religious groups were represented—even amidst tension and occasional terror—would give me a more intimate and direct experience of that reality.

And I came on a pilgrimage. The holy places of Judaism and Christianity represent road signs and revelations in my own spiritual journey. I suppose I wanted to find out if Jerusalem's air still glimmered with traces of ancient glory, if only now and then.

It's true that these purposes continue to enliven my days, but all of them might well have been fulfilled in a few weeks' time. Yet my visit stretched unexpectedly from four months to more than six years. The best explanation for that is that the women, men and families I met and got to know charmed and captivated me. This connection with people was also unexpected, because when viewed from afar, Israel doesn't really seem to be about people at all.

To read about Israel in international media is typically to meander through an assortment of abstract discussions, some about politics, some about religion; about Jewish history and Palestinians' rights, about armed conflicts, resistance movements and terrorism; debates about grudges, betrayals and injustices; descriptions of holy sites, and the various meanings of innumerable religious texts. In fact, the endless stream of words too often amounts to little more than cold categorizations, especially of Israelis—labels that can rob the warm-hearted, smart, savvy and lively people I have come to know of their decency and humanity. All these things provide little, if any feel for the actual Israeli way of life. And it is that, above all things, that I hope to portray in these pages.

Still it is inevitable that Israel's people and their way of life are greatly affected by politics and conflict. In fact, although it was unplanned, I arrived in Israel in the midst of a war. That also gave me a greater sense of what Israel is all about. During my first two weeks, as the group I was with made its way around the country, we faced the very real threat of Katyusha artillery rockets striking the cities, hotels and highways where we traveled. Israel's northern population centers absorbed literally thousands of rocket and mortar attacks. Over half a million Israeli civilians were displaced, while innumerable others huddled in bomb shelters for more than a month. Yet I soon came to see that even when Israel is under the constant threat of war, the real substance of the land and its people is not compromised.

One of the questions non-Israelis—relatives, friends, and acquaintances—most often ask me is "Aren't you afraid of the violence?" Like my Israeli neighbors, I am well aware of the possibilities. Thankfully, besides the hidden hand of Providence, the Israeli Defense Forces, who are skilled and practiced in the arts of war also protect us. But, by far, most other Israelis—nearly all of them IDF veterans and reservists—focus their full attention on far different arts: those of creativity, and of building up their land, and of peace.

In my Old Katamon neighborhood, I am blessed with a beautiful garden surrounded by tall old trees, populated by an assortment of cats, song-birds and, incongruously, a flock of green parrots. I often sit there in the warm months—particularly on the Sabbath—to read, pray, think or simply absorb the tranquility. I especially love the ever-changing shadows of sunlit leaves and the quiet breeze that stirs them. In those idyllic moments, I don't pray for the peace of Jerusalem. I thank God for it, however long it may last.

Of course there are violent incidents from time to time. And there is more than enough to be read about Israel's disputed place in the world. But what appears in print rarely captures the noisy, bustling marketplaces, the informality of neighborhood conversations, or the vibrancy of shop- and café-lined streets, and festive gatherings for birthdays, baby showers or reunions. Little reading material evokes the familiar rhythms of everyday life, the humor and heartaches of ordinary parents and grandparents, school children and soldiers, and the strong pulse of faith that beats relentlessly beneath the surface. After some time in Israel, it seems important to convey that experience to others.

As it happens, I am a writer. For decades I've written poems and novels, songs and children's books and non-fiction. And while in Israel, I have also become—at least in part—a journalist. When I turned my attention toward the myriad people, places, vistas and ideas that swirled around me, poems weren't exactly what appeared on my computer screen, but at times the words flowed from a similar place inside me. People have long declared that there is poetry in the very air of Jerusalem. Maybe that's why.

All the same, I had a more urgent, disquieting concern than that of writing pretty words: the women, men and children, the circumstances and events I was becoming acquainted with in Israel were often shamelessly distorted in the eyes of the world. Again and again I wondered how the simplest realities could become so factually skewed, grossly exaggerated, misrepresented or, perhaps worst of all, overlooked altogether. "Fair is foul and foul is fair," I heard myself muttering on more than one occasion. Surely these stories and situations deserved a closer look, or at least a second look from a different angle. That's what my articles were about.

The first couple of pages I wrote in late summer 2006 roughly captured the beginnings of my Jerusalem journey. I titled the piece, "Expecting the Unexpected." Through the good graces of a new friend, it was published in the *Jerusalem Post* (more about that in Chapter Two). Many others followed.

I never cease to marvel at the kaleidoscopic impressions of everyday life in Jerusalem. From time to time, I have recorded those glimpses for others or myself. Putting those snapshots together now, I return to the more expansive format with which I am most familiar—a book. In the pages that follow are reflections and recollections interwoven with segments of my articles. I have also tried to juxtapose moments of exploration and discovery with insights from my entirely unmapped and untested spiritual journey.

Not only was my spiritual journey uncharted, but my earthly learning curve was also much greater than I could have guessed. There are certain political and religious issues that inevitably arise in conversations about Israel, and my own ideas about many of those concerns were formed or reformed by very concrete experiences. A few examples: a trip to Jerusalem's Mamilla Mall and conversations with a Christian South African and adamant opponent of apartheid—who had to flee his homeland because of his controversial views—helped me see the absurdity of apartheid accusations against Israel. Visits to bomb shelters—in both the north and south of Israel—and talks with those who live in rocket range of Gaza allowed me to appreciate the seemingly endless state of war as seen through the eyes of parents, children and the elderly. And similarities between Israel, my home state of California and the free and democratic American experience are many, but they end abruptly with this hard fact: Americans do not live with ongoing terrorist alerts and threats of annihilation.

My discovery of the "Forgotten Refugees" was perhaps the greatest surprise of all. Of course, like everybody else, I'd heard about the Palestinian refugees who abandoned their homes during Israel's War of Independence. But I did not know that even more Jews were forced to flee Arab and Muslim lands by the hundreds of thousands between 1948 and 1970. Nor had I heard the radical Muslims' slogan, "First the Saturday People, Then the Sunday People," which has now become reality for millions of Christians, who are presently subjected to Muslim hostility in the same countries the Jews once fled.

And as a last example—this book contains many others—I came to see that Israel is not only meant to be a safe haven for Jews after the catastrophe of the Holocaust. It is also a place where the Jewish people have found a new dignity in providing security for themselves, while building their own way of life in the land of their fathers. As the national anthem Hatikvah puts it, "...to be a free people in our own land." Life for Israel's Jews is not focused on death and destruction, but on life and construction. And what a wonderful country they have built—and are still building.

Perhaps my words will inspire readers who are entering a new season of life to live it to the utmost in accordance with Irenaeus' vision, "the glory of God is man fully alive." I hope Christian and Jewish readers alike will not only be intrigued by a portrait of Israel today but will also consider the very essential and even urgent reasons for finding common ground with one another. Finally, these pages may offer to friends and loved ones a reasonable explanation of my lengthy stay abroad. And they are lovingly intended as a tribute to my beloved Israeli friends, who may be curious to learn how their country looks through the eyes of a Christian sojourner.

CHAPTER ONE

IN SEARCH
OF THE
UNEXPECTED

It was a stifling and dusty Thursday afternoon. My face was dripping with grimy sweat, and I was standing on a dun-colored hill overlooking Gaza. On my right soared a sleek, grey surveillance tower. On my left, Israeli Defense Forces artillery pounded away, the constant, earsplitting thunder shaking the earth beneath my feet, sending deadly rounds across the infamous security barrier. Beyond the "fence," Gaza City stretched out in a monochromatic sprawl, broken up by random antennas, assorted minarets and a sad-looking collection of scraggly trees. Somewhere, hidden among Gaza City's buildings, automatic weapons answered each other in bursts of fire and chatter. Smoke and dust plumed upward here and there as the IDF shells homed in on their targets.

It was August 3, 2006—my third full day in Israel. My lifelong dream of visiting the Holy Land had finally come true, albeit not quite in the way I had imagined.

First of all, I had arrived in the middle of a war.

Second, I was not exactly "visiting" the country. For better or worse I had rented an apartment in Jerusalem that I'd only seen on the Internet, and had committed myself to living there for four months.

Third, the closest thing to a "holy site" on my immediate itin-erary was the Tel HaShomer Medical Center outside Tel Aviv—a rehab center where battered young soldiers were arriving from the north, their wounds freshly stitched and bleeding through their bandages. Dazed and depressed, these 18- to 20-year-olds were facing a world of hurt minus an arm or a leg, or trying to adjust to the awful reality of having neither feeling nor function from the waist down.

"What are they fighting over this time?" a perplexed relative had asked me just before I left the US. "It's always something. Jews and Arabs will never stop killing each other. So why do you have to get into the middle of it?"

My friends and family had expressed varying degrees of support, fear and frustration as I prepared for my journey—particularly after the latest round of fighting broke out on July 12 and turned into a war. In California, news about the conflict was hardly concise; it had to be pieced together from websites. In mainstream media reports, the fighting was primarily blamed on Israel's allegedly disproportionate response to a couple of minor military skirmishes. Among pro-Israelis, the war was perfectly justified, triggered by the kidnapping of three soldiers, along with mortar and rocket attacks along two fronts, Gaza and Lebanon.

In any case, on July 31, when my British Airways flight touched down at Tel Aviv's Ben Gurion Airport, Katyusha rockets were hailing by the hundreds into the northern third of Israel, Kassams were blasting into Sderot, and sections of Beirut and southern Lebanon lay in smoldering ruins. As for my own little piece of the action, my biggest fear was that Israel's sole commercial airport would be closed to incoming flights before I could get my feet on the ground. I had over-nighted in London, where I'd heard that Tel Aviv was being specifically targeted by Hezbollah for a long range missile attack. Was that a serious danger? Did Hezbollah have that kind of firepower? If so, would they launch it? Who knew?

In reality, the conflict seemed to have made no appreciable difference at the airport. My Boeing 777 not only landed safely, it was actually on time.

I had anticipated a rush of tears when I finally set foot on the land, but I found myself unmoved and, instead, tensed for trouble. Over the years I had disembarked—a woman alone—at more than my share of foreign airports, everywhere from Hong Kong to Entebbe to Moscow to Sydney. Tel Aviv was no less challenging. As always, I tried to summon what remained of my sleep-deprived mental resources. In a matter of minutes I had to determine which line I was supposed to stand in for passport control, whether my five battered red bags had arrived, how to hoist them all onto one flimsy cart, what kind of luck I would have finding a trustworthy taxi driver, and what kind of luck he would have finding my hotel.

"And why were you in Egypt in January?" the immigration officer inquired, examining my passport and studying my face carefully as I answered.

"I was traveling with friends."

"Oh, so you have friends in Egypt?" he asked, his eyes narrowing slightly.

"No, they were American friends."

"Do you have any friends in Egypt?"

"No."

"Are you in touch with anyone in Egypt?"

"Nope."

He looked me up and down, paused for a few seconds as he stared at his computer screen, then stamped my passport. War or no war, I was in Israel. I had finally made it to the Promised Land.

Now, three days later, I was still buzzed by jet lag, caffeine, sugar, new faces and surreal surroundings. After watching the battle blazing in Gaza City for awhile, we moved on. Soon we were standing at the Gaza/Israel border, at the Karnei Border Crossing, where at that time 200 trucks a day were transporting food and supplies into the Palestinian territory. In a system that operated much like locks in a canal, pallets of food, soft drinks, and other necessities were delivered into warehouses. Once everything was unloaded and the truck pulled away, massive steel doors on the

Israeli side were locked down and secured. Then identical doors on the Gaza side were unbolted and lifted open. The pallets were reloaded onto trucks and delivered to Gaza.

A young lieutenant explained to us that this entire production was necessary for just one reason: it prevented Palestinian terrorists from crossing into Israel, specifically suicide bombers. Rather than cutting off the food supply to Gaza, the IDF operated the Karnei Crossing at a cost of millions of dollars a week. To my eyes it was more of a fortress than a border crossing, as carefully guarded as a prison, equipped with formidable surveillance capabilities and armed to the teeth. As we toured the facility, more artillery fired sporadically, deafeningly close.

A year later, when Hamas took over the Gaza strip in 2007, the functioning transfer mechanisms on the Palestinian side of Karnei were unexplainably destroyed. The entire terminal has been closed since then; at the time of this writing, supplies are delivered from Israel to Gaza through the Kerem Shalom and Sufa Crossings.

Slightly dazed, and trying to understand the alien world I had entered, I next found myself in a little civilian community of 20,000 called Sderot. The only reason Sderot is "on the map" is because in the last dozen years it has been struck by thousands of rockets, fired from Gaza. As we looked and listened that day, our little group was well aware that a rocket could tear into us at any moment, no matter where we stood or walked or sat. The good news was that we could and would leave Sderot after an hour or so. Not so the local residents.

Behind the Sderot police station is a collection of exploded rockets. I held in my hands the remains of one of hundreds of Kassams that have been retrieved, marked, catalogued and piled up there. We listened as a local rabbi reported the community's situation. The rockets we saw were mostly low-tech and home-made, crudely fashioned in Gaza garages and workshops, and because they have limited trajectory and no guidance systems they often explode without harm in unpopulated areas. Recently, more sophisticated, Iranian-manufactured missiles have been added to Gaza's arsenal. And even the Kassams are loaded with shrapnel that pierces metal, shatters glass and mutilates human flesh. Just a couple of months before our visit there, one of the rockets had struck near a Sderot nursery school. Two people were killed, one of them a four-year-old boy walking to school with his mother, who was critically wounded. Ten others were also wounded.

Gaza City. Karnei Crossing. Sderot. I hadn't had time to adjust to a new time zone, culture, language or climate before setting foot in these unfamiliar, controversial and hazardous places. Taken together, they raised myriad questions, all of them beginning with the same word: Why? Why rockets and missiles? Why civilians? Why kidnappings? Why "disproportionate"? Why mortar and artillery? Why such bad neighbors? Why centuries of violent history? Why debates, dialogues and useless diplomacy? Why death instead of life? As the war continued, a never-ending stream of "why" questions were raised in the press, bandied about in endless conversations, and echoed in my own mind.

At the same time, among the dozen or so American Jewish travelers I had joined up with in Tel Aviv, there were also questions about me. My new acquaintances asked them as politely as possible. My friends at home had been raising them for months: What was I doing in Israel? Why did I leave California and move into a war zone? Why would a Christian woman choose to live in a Jewish nation?

In Search of the Unexpected

One morning the winter before, after an overnight rain shower had chilled the California air and the Pacific Ocean was an intense shade of indigo, I was standing on a sea-front balcony explaining to a friend my plans for summer and fall. He was trying to understand my eccentric decision to leave a Dana Point beach house and move halfway around the world into a tiny Middle East apartment. It wasn't all that easy to explain it to him, perhaps because I hadn't completely explained it to myself.

South Orange County is a scenic locale, part holiday resort and part opulent bedroom community. Although its homes, food and wine are world class, to me it has always seemed quite removed from the people and places that populate the global headlines. The more writing and traveling I've done, and the more my interest in international affairs has deepened, the more Orange County has seemed to be light-years away from the "real" world.

But if there is a "real" world, where is it? I've always loved the energy of cities like Washington D.C., Rome and London. Still, in my imagination, the center of the world—the "navel" of the earth as it's sometimes called—has always been Jerusalem.

A fascination with Israel was woven into my consciousness early on by my Christian parents. In the 1960's my mother, an indefatigable Bible teacher, somehow constructed a model of the ancient Hebrew desert tabernacle—pomegranates, cherubim and all—and stored it in our family garage. Meanwhile, against her frugal better judgment, my father faithfully sent $15 each and every month to some now-defunct Zionist organization, his way of helping "build a stronger Israel." As for me, Israel's against-all-odds triumph in the 1967 War still remains far clearer in memory than the shock of John F. Kennedy's assassination.

Decades have since passed. I no longer cling to some of the social aspects of my parents' self-described Christian "fundamentalism." Meanwhile, less benign varieties of religious fundamentalism have entered the world's stage. Osama Bin Laden's heir Ayman al-Zawahiri is a Sunni Wahabist. Mahmoud Ahmadinejad is the President of Shi'ite Iran. They and their "fundamentalist" followers may disagree on the finer points of Koranic dogma, but they are attuned in their calls for the eradication of the "Zionist entity," the Great Satan, and a general assortment of other random intolerable infidels. They save their fieriest diatribes of death and damnation for Jews and Christians alike—wherever they may be found.

At the same time I have discerned a gradual unraveling of friendship's cords between some Americans, the Jewish people, and Israel. Politically liberal, mainstream Christian groups are demanding that their Protestant denominations divest from corporations that do business with Israel because of perceived human rights abuses. Middle-of-the-road tourists shrug off the vision of a spiritual pilgrimage, heading for Venice, Vienna and Vietnam rather than braving the unpredictable "surprises" that might ruin their Holy Land holidays. Even some Bible-believing evangelicals have stopped talking about the miraculous re-gathering of the Jewish people in the Land of Promise. 1948 was, after all, a long time ago.

In spite of all this, or perhaps because of it, I fully intended to visit Israel someday. I planned to go with my father, but he died too soon. The writing assignments that would have provided all-expenses-paid trips never presented themselves. By the year 2005 I had written numerous books, some on subjects that no longer interest me, and had traveled extensively—but never to the Holy Land.

In January 2006, I was in Egypt. My son Colin and I were standing on a beach at a Gulf of Aqaba resort called Nuweiba. It was a gorgeous sun-drenched day, crisp and cool. Colin took a spectacular photograph of a white camel and his rider splashing through the surf, with the mountains of Saudi Arabia clearly visible behind them. We were only about 40 miles from the Egyptian-Israeli border—it was somewhere on the horizon just ahead. In fact, a few decades earlier we would have been in Israel, before the Sinai Peninsula was returned to Egypt. As I stood there, a kind of excitement stirred in me, something that I can only describe as a personal epiphany. I knew in an instant that I was going to Israel; somehow I needed get myself there, and the sooner the better.

For months my two sons, both in their twenties, had been encouraging me to "do something different." Maybe I was looking for surprises, searching for the unexpected, hoping for an end to preconceived notions. I still don't know exactly why, but instead of taking a pre-packaged two week "Holy Land" tour, to everyone's astonishment including my own, I rented the little flat in Jerusalem sight unseen. I could do my work there, come and go, and discover what a few months as a Jerusalemite might teach me.

Changing Times, Changing Tactics

When the Lebanon War caught fire in northern Israel I obsessively followed the news, and it wasn't just because I was on my way to the Middle East. For me, hearing about Hezbollah day after day had an unpleasantly familiar ring to it. In the 1980s I had coordinated an international prayer campaign for the American hostages who were held in Lebanon. Their captors were a gang of terrorists called Hezbollah. At the time their "spiritual leader" was a cagy ayatollah from West Beirut named Mohammad Hussein Fadlallah. Today Hezbollah is inspired by the firebrand cleric Hassan Nasrallah. Then as now, everybody close to the situation knew that Iran was the financier of the kidnappings, assassinations, bombings and Hezbollah's other various and sundry brutalities.

After their release, a couple of the American hostages told me about the severe deprivation of their captivity. They spoke of peeking out from under the blindfolds they wore for months, eyeing the moldy bread, stale olive oil and dry cheese they were given to eat. They described the hours and days and months of imprisonment they endured—the boredom, the acute loneliness, the deep fears, the false rumors of imminent release. They sometimes alluded to severe physical pain and emotional horror they suffered at the time of their abduction, as well as during bouts of interrogation and intimidation. They were all deeply, probably permanently, traumatized.

But they also told me about the Christian worship they carried on in what they wryly described as "The Church of the Closed Door." Terry Anderson and the late Father Martin Lawrence Jenco were Roman Catholics; Thomas Sutherland and David Jacobsen were Protestants. Together they managed to carry out a Eucharist service every Sunday, sharing scraps of hoarded bread. They prayed and sang together. For the first time in 25 years, Anderson "went to confession," sharing his past sins with fellow-hostage, Fr. Jenco. And they all read from the Bible their captors had given them.

Today, as unspeakable atrocities increasingly appear in full color videos, and calls for the death of Jews and Christians are repeated in mosques and on websites around the world, it appears that times and tactics have changed. Yesterday's Hezbollah kidnappers would probably be looked upon as moderate Muslims today. In the present Middle East climate, for such blatant Christian observance, those four Americans might well have been beheaded—on YouTube.

Following the destruction of the World Trade Center towers in New York on September 11, 2001, and the subsequent bombings in Bali, Madrid and London, the Western world appears to be on a collision course with a vicious and virulent form of Muslim holy war. From their vast treasuries of oil money, from jihadist epicenters in Saudi Arabia and Iran, both branches of Islam—Sunni and Shi'a—finance terrorist organizations around the world. So-called holy warriors target infidels in general, western Christians and Jews in particular, and, unfailingly, the nation of Israel. At the same time, a resurgence of anti-Semitism is casting long and ever-darkening shadows across Western Europe. French and British Jews are immigrating to Israel in record numbers.

Meanwhile, it's no coincidence that world opinion continues to frown upon Israel. In July 2006, after being attacked by Hezbollah, Israel was accused of brutality, human rights violations, and killing civilians even as, day in and day out, hundreds of rockets were launched from Lebanon at Israeli civilian population centers. Distortion and dishonesty by major news organizations, both in reporting and photography, were unprecedented. My fourth day in Israel, on a blog post, I read these unsettling words by Victor Davis Hanson:

Our present generation…is on the brink of moral insanity. That has never been more evident than in the last three weeks, as the West has proven utterly unable to distinguish between an attacked democracy that seeks to strike back at terrorist combatants, and terrorist aggressors who seek to kill civilians…. In short, if we wish to learn what was going on in Europe in 1938, just look around.

Symbols of Solidarity

Is Hanson right? Are the deadly currents of 1938's anti-Semitism washing across the world again? Mahmoud Ahmadinejad first called for the extermination of Israel just weeks after becoming Iran's president in August, 2005. It wasn't a new idea, of course. But it was now being declared by the head of a sovereign state, a member of the United Nations.

That same fall, I visited Holland to complete a book project on the persecution of Christians for an international Evangelical ministry. As I left the Netherlands, on my way to Schiphol Airport, my hosts impulsively took me to visit the ten Boom "safe house" in Haarlem, where hundreds of Jews had been temporarily sheltered from the Nazis. Two young sisters, Betsie and Corrie, were eventually swept up in a Nazi raid for their part in an underground railroad network helping move hundreds of Jews from one safe house to another until they were out of harm's way. I was amazed to learn that the ten Booms even provided Kosher food for their "guests." For their good deeds, the two sisters ended up at Ravensbruck concentration camp, where Betsie died, leaving Corrie to tell the tale; she died in 1983. The house still stands, and visitors can explore the cleverly designed secret compartment that served as a hiding place.

The sisters' old father Willem ten Boom did more than shelter Jews. When his Jewish friends were required by the Third Reich to put on the notorious yellow armband, marked with the Star of David, Willem wore the armband too. And despite their frantic insistence that he save his own skin, he refused to take it off. He said that if his friends were mistreated for being Jews, he would be mistreated with them. And so he was. He died in a jail cell, awaiting his own transfer to Ravensbruck.

Hearing about the ten Boom sisters' and the old man's bravery made me ask myself whether I possessed such courage. I could only answer, *I don't know, but I hope so.* In the months that followed, I gradually began to think that living among Israel's Jews, sharing the dread and the danger, might amount to something far less dramatic, but at least similar. Given the opportunity, it was the best I could do.

During those first days in Israel, a shopkeeper on Jerusalem's Ben Yehuda Street seemed to confirm my notion. Even though it was the high tourist season, the man's little souvenir shop was empty when I went in to buy T-shirts for my sons. The war had robbed him of his usual summer customers. He welcomed me to Jerusalem and asked me what kind of work I did.

"I'm a writer," I said absently, examining the shirts.

"What do you write?"

He was a cordial character and seemed eager for conversation, so I tore my attention away from shopping. "I write all sorts of things, but mostly books."

"What kind of books?" he persisted.

"Mostly non-fiction." I chose not to mention my shelved novel.

The man seemed to think writing books was a wonderful business. "What are they about?" he asked enthusiastically. "Have I read any of them?"

I hesitated. "Um…probably not…a lot of my writing has been done for the Christian market…"

"So you're a Christian?"

"Yes."

He stared at me for a moment and I felt a rush of embarrassment, sure that I had offended him. Then he shook his head in disbelief. "I can't believe you'd come here, especially during a war, if you're not Jewish."

With that he scurried across his shop, opened a drawer and pulled out a small, silvery Star of David. He walked over and put it in my hand. "I want you to have this. It's my way of saying thank you for being with us." At my request, he attached it to my bracelet. It finally broke and fell off, but a similar star remains there today.

A couple of days later, our group returned to Tel HaShomer rehab center, this time to attend a birthday party for some of the wounded soldiers. The occasion provided an excuse for everyone—patients, their families and friends, and the rest of us—to celebrate during a very gloomy time. One young man, who looked about 20 years old, had lost a leg in the Lebanon War. His whole family was sitting outside with him, smoking and laughing together. They had even brought the family dog along.

As a few of us stood around him, he explained that he had been wounded when a rocket-propelled grenade demolished his tank. His leg had been blown to bits, but he had somehow found the strength to crawl out of the wreckage, pull himself across a field on his belly, and get picked up by another tank that was also under fire. Almost miraculously, the tank commander had managed to keep fighting while also getting the wounded soldier into a Medivac helicopter before he could bleed to death.

The boy—and he was only a boy—was still a little dazed but glad to be alive. He seemed excited to have his dog curled up in his lap while he chatted with a few visitors from overseas. For some reason, one of the women in our group told him I was a Christian. He frowned and shook his head, clearly puzzled. Then he remembered, "Oh yeah, I think I met a 'Christian Zionist' while I was at Rambam." Rambam Hospital in Haifa is the primary trauma center in Northern Israel where most of the war's serious casualties were taken for emergency treatment.

I wasn't sure I wanted to categorize myself in quite those words, but it would have taken a while to explain why. So I said, "Yeah, I guess that term more or less describes me."

"But why are you a Zionist if you are a Christian?" he asked. For him, the term was an oxymoron.

I tried to explain that many Christians who believe the Bible also believe that the Jews' return to the Land and the founding of the nation of Israel are among the greatest miracles of our time.

"I never knew such people existed," he said, shaking his head. All at once his eyes flooded with tears. Needless to say, so did mine. "Thank you for coming here," he smiled, reaching across his wheelchair to shake my hand. "You didn't have to come and you did anyway. That's amazing."

Christians, Jews and Common Ground

Such warm welcomes were a pleasant surprise to me. I'd read and heard that some Israelis mistrust Christians in general, and so-called Christian Zionists in particular. They suspect that foreign Christians—especially Americans—who come to live in Israel have an ulterior motive: proselytizing to Jews. There is another related theory that Christians want to convert Jews so that Jesus will come back. More than a few Israelis—particularly among the ultra-Orthodox—seem to hold a bad opinion of Christians in general. Considering a few centuries of pogroms, the Inquisition, and at least in the minds of some, the Holocaust itself, I guess it's understandable.

Meanwhile, for years I had been naïve enough to think that all Christians loved and respected the Jewish people and applauded the re-birth of Israel. That false impression was quickly corrected when I started reading histories of the Jews and, more recently, when I tried to talk to some Christians about my plans to live in Israel. Their recoil was, on a couple of occasions, visible.

In practice if not in doctrine, it appears to me that more Christian denominations worldwide mistrust, disapprove of or utterly reject Jews than embrace them. And as for Zionism itself, meaning the support and development of the state of Israel as a safe Jewish homeland? Suffice it to say, a word that once carried the promise of a haven for the abused has now become a pejorative, itself implying abusiveness and, for more than a few, something akin to Nazism.

One of my ideas for making good use of my time in Israel had been to explore Christian-Jewish relations and write about them. The complexities of that idea became very clear to me when my Jerusalem landlady, Nomi, innocently asked, "So...what is a Christian anyway?" One visit to the Church of the Holy Sepulcher with its quarrelsome custodians—Roman Catholic, Armenian, Greek Orthodox, Coptic, Ethiopian and Syriac—made Nomi's question both relevant and difficult to answer in less than 500 typed pages. And that's without a word about Protestants.

But my earliest experiences in Israel raised a similar point: What is a Jew? Which Jews would tolerate me and which wouldn't? What kind of Jews had been so kind to me? I couldn't figure out the categories. Some of the men wore a kippah, others didn't. A few women covered the hair, but most were stylishly coiffured. Some of my new friends kept kosher and observed Shabbat, others did not. Clearly, there's no short answer for the "What is a Jew?" question, either. But my first view of Israel's Jews was multicolored, moving, and, as I later discovered once the Lebanon War was over, maybe a little on the optimistic side.

Tisha B'Av—the ninth of the Hebrew month of Av—marks the destruction of the Jewish Temple in Jerusalem. Both the first temple (Solomon's) and the second (Herod's) are said to have been destroyed on the same day. In memorial of these historic tragedies, and of so many other losses over the centuries, on Tisha B'Av Jews from every nation arrive in Jerusalem. They all gather at around 9:00 PM at the Western Wall—the last remains of the second temple. And they remember.

It was my good fortune that Tisha B'Av, 2006 fell on my first day ever in Jerusalem. And in a way, it was fortunate for me that it happened during the war, when the community was of one heart and one mind. I arrived with the group I'd met up with in Tel

Aviv—a mission planned by an LA-based Israel advocacy group called StandWithUs. The organization's founder, Roz Rothstein, made a special point of guiding me around the Western Wall that night, making sure I understood what was taking place.

I looked in amazement at thousands of Jews of every race and color and attire—Middle Eastern, African, Eastern European, American—as artful in composition as a living tapestry, vivid and vivacious. What struck me was how young most of the people were, many appearing to be less than 25 years old. And whatever they wore, however they expressed their devotion, whether they stood or sat, read or recited, they were all repeating ancient words from the book of Lamentations.

I wandered away from the others and went to the Wall alone. The women's section was completely packed. A small group of girls was singing. But what touched me the most were the young female soldiers—there must have been 25 or 30 of them scattered among the crowd. Some of them clung to each other in small clusters, guns slung across their backs, faces wet with tears. Some sobbed deeply. There was weeping all around. The waves of emotion that washed over me there were relentless—I had never been to such a place.

Later, our group regathered and we made our way to the southern side of the ruins. There you can clearly see the massive stones that crashed down from the temple into the pavement below. A small Conservative Jewish congregation was gathered there, men and women worshipping together. A few of us sat on the stones and joined them.

Everyone was singing quietly when all at once the muezzin's call to prayer from the Al-Aqsa Mosque, located just above us, blasted into our ears. The nasal, metallic sound was jarring, and it all but drowned out the singing. Not long after it stopped, the rabbi prayed a blessing on the families of the soldiers who have died in Lebanon. He prayed for the injured, for courage and for peace. Then the congregation stood and after a few moments of silence, someone began to sing Hatikvah, and everyone around me joined in the song.

> *As long as the Jewish spirit is yearning deep in the heart,*
> *With eyes turned toward the East, looking toward Zion,*
> *Then our hope—the two-thousand-year-old hope—will not be lost:*
> *To be a free people in our own land,*
> *The land of Zion and Jerusalem.*

Hope for the Jews—for us all—resonates in a verse from the book of Lamentations that is read every year at Tisha B'Av. "It is of the Lord's mercies that we are not consumed. They are new every morning. Great is Thy faithfulness…"

Life, Love and Death Threats

A couple of weeks after Tisha B'Av, I experienced *Erev Shabbat*—the Friday night that begins the Sabbath—in my first Jerusalem apartment. I was still adjusting to a new home, a new city, and a new way of life. My Baka neighborhood seemed light years removed from the seaside California housing development I'd left behind. I sat on my small balcony with a glass of Galilee wine, weary but content, transfixed as the light faded, stars appeared, and a luminous blue haze of tranquility fell across the city.

That's when I first noticed the music. All evening, it drifted from one family to another as they breathed their worship into the evening air. Intentionally or not, their voices blessed the entire neighborhood. I'd first heard people singing together at Tisha B'Av. This time they were welcoming Shabbat.

I quickly learned, however, that the music in my neighborhood wasn't just about religious observance. The next week, as I walked to the post office and market, through an apartment window I heard the diligent practice of piano exercises; through a house's open shutters came the tentative sounds and squeaks of a flute. Someone was singing here, or playing a clarinet there. Sometimes my closest neighbors added to the symphony—a young man next door had acquired a taste for black Gospel music, while the genial sexagenarian downstairs was partial to Bobby Vinton and Elvis.

But the sound of music is only one vibrant sign of life in Jerusalem. Another is the children, who can be heard at most hours of the day or night—playing, laughing, wailing. There always seems to be a newborn baby somewhere nearby, whose cry brings back memories of my own babies, three decades ago. While walking one afternoon, I saw a little boy of no more than five, arms wide open and kippah dangerously askew, rushing with glee to embrace his little sister. She shrieked with joy at the sight of him.

To this day, other lively impressions touch my senses as well. Tireless, prowling cats. Occasionally frantic dogs. Good smells of neighbors' cooking. The hammering and drilling of new construction. The trash truck. The ceaseless horns, car alarms and sirens; televisions, arguments, laughter and animated half-conversations on mobile phones.

Lovers stroll, arm and arm, eyes only for each other. Mothers push baby carriages. Families walk to synagogue, fathers carrying little ones on their shoulders. Friends talk across fences. Phones ring, doorbells buzz, knuckles knock on doors. Everywhere I look, people of every age and appearance and attire seem to be living life to the fullest and loving one another in the process. Then as now, I couldn't help but love them in return, even though we are still strangers.

But there is another reality, too. I remember getting up one morning, making my coffee and half-consciously opening the newspaper. "Death to the Jews!" I read, and quickly found myself wide-awake, confronted with the visage of Iran's Ahmadinejad. "Wipe Israel off the Map!" Yes, I'd heard it all before. But the words now pounded against me like a body blow.

"The Jews" he was cursing were the people next door, the people across the street, the people I met for lunch or dinner. "Israel" comprised those who had helped me in every conceivable way to be welcome, comfortable, at ease in their country. They searched for my packages at the Post Office, tolerated my horrendous attempts at Hebrew, and gathered to pray, sing and weep at the Western Wall.

In *Reading Lolita in Tehran*, author Amir Nafisi describes her 1970s college days in the US when she joined other protesting students in their rebellious cries of "Death to America." Some years later, when she found herself in the midst of the Iranian Revolution, she saw with her own eyes the brutal deaths of her countrymen, including acquaintances and colleagues. "Death to America" or any place else could never again be a cheap slogan for Nafisi, because Death had become a reality. The mullahs' insane bloodbath was splattering against the threshold of her house.

I continue to doubt that anyone beyond Israel's borders takes such threats as Ahmadinejad's seriously. A handful of my friends in America and England do, but who knows about the rest of the world? What I do know is that since I moved to Jerusalem, I am certainly paying close attention myself. Why? Because the threats aren't just against some controversial little "Zionist entity" across the ocean. And they aren't only against my new neighbors and friends. These days "Death to Israel" is a threat against me, too.

CHAPTER TWO

WAR AND PEACE

T he scorching days that preceded that first, peaceful Shabbat Eve in Jerusalem were hectic and exhausting. After several weeks of roaming the earth like an international bag lady with a quintet of overstuffed suitcases, I finally arrived in my upstairs apartment. The former tenant was out, and, thankfully, I was in. But getting my belongings into the place was a huge production. I paid a cab driver extra to help drag everything up the steep stone steps in 95+ heat—he was soaked in sweat by the time he finished. For that matter, so was I.

The work, however, had only begun. The tenant—an American medical doctor from Florida whose young daughter had been living with him—was most helpful in communicating, doing his best to make sure I had everything set up in advance—Internet, phones, heating/air conditioning information and whatever else he could think of. But he didn't know me, so he couldn't think of everything. Once he and his daughter actually left, there was still much to be done as far as livability was concerned—much more than I expected.

I spent the first full day trying to put things in order, which, to put it mildly, didn't happen all that quickly. I sorted through stacks of varicolored and mostly unmatched "linens," paper plates, disposable knives, spoons, and forks, two-handled plastic cups for ceremonial washing, dairy plates, meat plates; ditto cutlery and pans, and myriad bags of unfamiliar snack foods. I made the beds, moved furniture, rearranged shelves, opened creaky shutters that had been closed for a very long time, and bought food, coffee, wine and a manageable corkscrew. I asked the Sri Lankan cleaning man, Saman, who more or less came with the property, to sweep the layers of pine needles and bird droppings off the front balcony. This also entailed the eviction of a free-loading cat that had been sleeping in a planter destined for red geraniums. The cat was ugly, with a ragged ear and a pathetically skinny body. As a peace offering I provided it with nauseatingly fishy cat breakfasts.

In the intense summer heat, I found myself carrying plastic bags full of supplies for several blocks from the shops and up the stairs. I also had to do everything the old fashioned way. I was a spoiled and pampered American suddenly on my own without a car, dishwasher, garbage disposal or clothes dryer. To further complicate matters, some of the conveniences installed in the apartment didn't seem to work so well, at least not at first.

Nonetheless, despite my lack of Hebrew language skills, notwithstanding my geographical handicaps that found me lost on strange streets at odd hours, and despite my lack of mechanical know-how, problems got resolved. With every accomplishment came a sense of satisfaction—I seemed to be moving from strength to strength, even though I felt mostly weak.

Before long my computer was up-and-running-on-line 24/7, the stove flashed and flared with blue flames, the solar water heater—with a little help from its electric boiler—spewed out scalding water around the clock, the mysterious German washing machine with no instruction booklet produced undamaged laundry, and the air conditioner was competing with the refrigerator for producing critically frigid air.

Day of Rest

In the midst of all this, I was introduced to an unfamiliar rhythm of life. Israel marches, as they say, to a different drummer. Life is spontaneous, serendipitous, and sometimes capricious. Most unusual for me, and punctuating every week, is the communal preparation for Shabbat—the Sabbath. By mid-afternoon on Friday, the streets are teeming with shoppers, dashing from store to store with braided challah and wine in one hand, and colorful, fresh-cut bouquets in the other. A sense of anticipation charges the air. By two o'clock Emek Refaim—the busy, cosmopolitan street that runs through Jerusalem's German Colony—has the feeling of a soon-to-arrive national holiday. The atmosphere reminds me of the day before Thanksgiving in America, when breathless, last minute, don't-spoil-the-day-for-Grandma preparations absolutely must be made before the stores close.

Housewives sweep their stoops and steps, take out the trash, and bring in the laundry from the clothesline. Men of the house water their gardens, wash off their cars, and hose down their driveways. The fragrances of roasting meat and baking delicacies pervade the neighborhood. Big, noisy street-sweeping machinery roars by, making one last pass at the pavements, while busboys stack chairs and merchants slam down shutters. Everyone seems to be in a hurry, keeping one eye on the sky and the other on the clock, determined to finish before for sundown.

Somewhere around five in the afternoon, I heard the long, clear wail of the city siren: Shabbat had officially begun. Not long afterward, as one writer describes it, "... the first stars appear on Friday evening, [and] a luminous blue covering of tranquility falls across Jerusalem." By now businesses were closed, buses had stopped running, and only a few cars—mostly Arab-operated taxis—remained on the streets. The workaday world had ceased. As shadows lengthened, I began to notice a change in the air's temperature—for the first time the late afternoon breeze was rather chilly as it stirred the trees. Unexpectedly, autumn was breathing cold air across the still-warm streets. Before long I saw families dressed up and walking somewhere together: Synagogue, I guessed. Impulsively, I rummaged through a drawer and found a couple of candles—I lit one for me, and one for my children. I prayed for our safety, peace and wisdom.

The next morning dawned to an unearthly stillness. Even in the midst of a war, there was pure peace—at least in my neighborhood. No car engines, no horns, no dogs barking, not even a cat mewing. I was determined to try to observe the sacred day, if for no other reason because it is said to be a day for "being" instead of "doing," something I definitely need to learn more about. I reminded myself that God really had a great idea with his keep-the-Sabbath-holy commandment. How strangely overlooked it is by many Christians.

Unfortunately, my pious idea of remaining idle that Saturday was squelched some time just after noon, when I realized there was nothing in the house to eat. I'd been people watching but not following their good example of stocking up on supplies. Devotionally speaking, a Sabbath rest was one thing, but fasting was quite another. Thankfully, Aroma coffee shop on Emek Refaim was, at the time, open on Saturdays. I glanced inside, noticed it was wall-to-wall with people, and that the posted menu was only in Hebrew.

I opened my bag for the guard—after far too many suicide bombings in restaurants and other public places, security guards are ubiquitous in Israel's cities; they examine purses, shopping bags and backpacks, while giving everyone a quick visual once-over. Once inside, I found a menu in English (promising myself that I would sign up for an immersion Hebrew language class as soon as possible), ordered an "omelet" sandwich and a cappuccino, located a place to sit at the counter, and settled myself on a red plastic stool.

There was nothing left to do but to watch the TV that was squarely in front of me, and, naturally, broadcasting news about the war. Even though the commentary was in Hebrew, I could tell by the images in the background what incidents were being revisited, yet again, by the talking heads.

A handsome, twenty-something young man next to me, whose eyes were startlingly pale blue, was watching the news, too.

He mumbled something to himself, including at least one censorable English word I recognized. He was soon talking to me about the Israeli government's poor performance and dishonesty during the war. By that time, Ariel Sharon, the old warrior-turned-Prime Minister, had been in a stroke-induced coma for eight months. Despite his highly controversial and unpopular decision to unilaterally "disengage" from Gaza, Sharon's powerful presence seemed to be sorely missed by some Israelis. Others, who could not forgive him for forcing 8,000 Israelis to walk away from their long-time homes, gardens and livelihood, simply spoke of a generic leadership vacuum.

I asked the young man—his name was Yossi—what he would do if he could take charge of the country right then and there. His face was sorrowful. He was silent for a few moments, and then he shrugged his shoulders slowly and eloquently, both hands opened toward heaven. He sighed deeply before he answered, "If I could, I would wake up Sharon."

Yossi's response resonated with another conversation that took place a few weeks afterwards, this with a taxi driver. Avi, who had driven a cab in Jerusalem from time immemorial, was an extrovert, more than happy to share his political views, in thickly accented English. He ranted non-stop about the lack of leadership in Israel, both political and military, saving the deadliest dose of his venom for Prime Minister Ehud Olmert and Defense Minister Amir Peretz. He also made several asides about certain rabbis whose names I didn't recognize.

Finally I asked him who, specifically, he had in mind to resolve the dilemma. Avi assessed me for a few seconds in his rear view mirror, apparently weighing my taste for the supernatural. I was fully expecting him put his money on Benyamin Netanyahu, but I was wrong. When he finally answered, he spoke solemnly and without amusement. "Do you know about Messiah?"

Both the war and the Sabbath were nearly over by the time I left the restaurant. I wandered home thoughtfully, feeling both out of place and glad to be settled, well aware that I was in an unusual situation during an unusual time. Was I crazy? Maybe, but a little surge of excitement rippled inside me anyway. Someone had told me, "Shabbat is not a time for creativity, because God stopped creating on Day Six." Nonetheless, something creative happened anyway. A nearly forgotten Muse passed through my soul for the first time in recent years and an idea formed in my mind, coming into my consciousness, taking the form of a poem.

> *Jerusalem wind,*
> *Breath of September,*
> *Gently but without delay*
> *Hurries through the pine trees beside my little balcony,*
> *Stirring the eucalyptus in the neighbors' garden,*
> *Rustling, murmuring, busily sweeping away the week,*
> *the month, the many years,*
> *Rushing to complete the task before the sun—*
> *Still burning against my face—*
> *Descends into a still blue twilight.*

> *Jerusalem wind,*
> *Breath of heaven,*
> *Rushing to be done*
> *before the stars appear, one after another,*
> *Heralding, in crystalline silence*
> *Another Shabbat,*
> *Another season, to be sure,*
> *And this life of mine:*
> *Faint star among blazing constellations,*
> *Lit anew.*

Kiryat Shmona: Paying the Price

By Tuesday, August 22, 2006 the Lebanon War's ceasefire had held for more than a week. I was eager to see with my own eyes what had happened in northern Israel, so along with new StandWithUs friends, I visited Kiryat Shmona—one of the cities hardest hit during the war. If you look at a map, you'll find Kiryat Shmona very close to Israel's northern border with Lebanon. It is a small city, with a population of 24,000. During the conflict it endured more than 1,000 of the 4,000 total Katyusha rockets that struck Israel in about a month's time. The rockets were launched by Hezbollah, and their targets were civilian. That was obvious, even for a newcomer like me. As a result, around 2,000 homes were damaged in Kiryat Shmona alone, 150 people wounded and twelve killed.

Our first stop was at the office of the city's mayor, Haim Barbibay, who proudly told us that he sees Kiryat Shmona as the "Northern Gateway to the Jewish State." When we met him the dust had barely settled and he was exhausted. Everyone in the municipal offices had dark circles under their eyes. They were all running on empty. The mayor had been to hell and back, and his comments seemed fitting not only to his city, but to his country. "For every house that was destroyed, we will build ten more. For every tree that was burned we will plant ten more. This is the Israeli way." In Mayor Barbibay's startlingly optimistic view—and in what is typically the spirit of the country after wars, terrorism and other forms of destruction—it was time to clean up the war's damage, rebuild, replant and move forward. And if he had his way, Kiryat Shmona would someday be among the first fruits of lasting peace. Its citizenry would welcome Lebanese visitors to his city with open arms, setting a good and humane example for the rest of Israel and the world beyond. That was his vision.

Meanwhile, the mayor's public relations representative, Susan Peretz, who was from New Jersey (and apparently was no relation to the then-Minister of Defense; I doubt that she would have admitted it in any case) was also exhausted, and measurably less sunny: "We lived in an inferno for four weeks. It was a nightmare—I've been through six wars in Israel and this was worse than all of them. Parts of the city were reduced to cinders. We know that this war was not, in actual fact, between Israel and 1,000 Hezbollah guerrilla fighters. We know that we were facing the armies of Iran and Syria."

Susan said what many others had already told us. "Our people would have voluntarily stayed in the bomb shelters—hot, cramped and miserable as they were—for weeks longer, for as long as it took," to allow the IDF to complete their disarming of Hezbollah in Southern Lebanon. The UN-brokered ceasefire had aborted the Army's efforts, however. And it seemed to me that everybody everywhere expressed the same conclusion in so many words: "It's just a matter of time, months if not weeks, before the fighting erupts and the rockets start blowing the city apart again."

At the local high school, which had been hit several times by Katyushas, we spoke with Yaakov Cohen, a physics teacher. Yaakov showed us the three different areas on the campus that had been damaged by rockets. There was shattered glass everywhere, bent metal, burned walls, and one metal pillar that was entirely shredded, not by the explosion itself but by the shrapnel inside the rocket, intended for human devastation. Plants were torched and dead, but no students had been injured thanks to their summer holiday schedule.

Yaakov shook his head, "School is supposed to reopen September 2, and there is much to be done for that to be possible." I later learned that workers somehow succeeded in meeting the deadline. The school had opened on time.

As we drove away from the high school, we noticed a ruined house. We pulled over and walked toward the door. The owner, Maurice Mamann, was willing to talk to us and show us around the damaged structure. "My wife and kids and I were able to leave when the bombing started," he told us. "We were lucky because we had someplace to go. That wasn't the case for a lot of people, but we had friends in Jerusalem who let us stay with them."

While the Mamann family was in Jerusalem, like everyone else they were constantly glued to the news. One night they saw their devastated house on television. The hit it took was dramatic and made for good footage—at least in Israel. They rushed back to find nearly half of their home in ruins. We walked, very carefully, around the interior and saw for ourselves the sorry remains of the kitchen, laundry area, and children's bedrooms. A little girl's dresser and mirror, with a red, heart-shaped box containing tiny bottles of cologne, nail polish and hair spray was ruined, scorched and covered in ashes. We also looked into the outbuilding where the Katyusha was still firmly embedded in the floor—it had made a direct hit on the house, then ricocheted into the outside storage building.

We visited a mini-mall in another part of the city that had taken a Katyusha strike through the roof. The room most damaged was a classroom, used for training government employees. It was littered with demolished window shutters and shards of glass. Of a double-doorway into the inner part of the building, only one section of broken glass remained, bearing just half the image of the Israeli government's symbolic menorah. It seemed iconic to me, representing the physical, emotional and spiritual damage not just to the community of Kiryat Shmona, but to the nation of Israel itself.

Our last stop was at an apartment complex, where we found our way into a couple of bomb shelters. There were no longer families hiding in them, but the bunk beds were still neatly made up with colorful quilts, and children's art was taped to the walls—innocent drawings of happier times, including sunshine, trees and smiling stick figures. The heat inside was insufferable, and evidently only a small plastic fan, still in place, had stirred the heavy air.

Somehow these families, like countless others, had attempted to retain some semblance of "normal life," even under incessant bombings. The Lebanon War's trauma to ordinary families and especially children—the intentional targets of the rockets launched into Israel during the war—remains incalculable. Nonetheless the mayor of Kiryat Shmona said more than once, "The hand of God saved us, and we will rebuild. We have always wanted peace, and to be good neighbors to the Lebanese. Someday it will be so . . ."

Realities on the Ground

As a news junkie—at least I was then—I can attest that there wasn't a word about this weary man or his point of view on any international broadcast I heard. I didn't see him on SkyNews, BBC, or CNN. He certainly didn't appear on Al-Jazeera.

Instead the world saw the collapse of a building in a Lebanese town called Kfar Qana, where some sixty children were said to have died. In fact, on a layover in London on my initial flight into Israel, I saw the same footage endlessly looped on enormous plasma screens behind the reception desk at the Heathrow Hilton: over and over again the same Arab men carried the same dead children in their arms. If true, it was a horrible tragedy. But in the days that followed there were contradictory body counts—reduced by around half; revelations of staged and falsified photographs; queries about why none of the children appeared to have been wounded; unanswered question of why civilians remained in the building after warning leaflets had dropped in advance of the operation. Before long Kfar Qana was revealed to be an international "fauxtography" opportunity thanks to some not-so-proficient Photoshop edits, intended to demonstrate that a bloodthirsty and brutal Israeli army intentionally murders innocent civilians—and particularly children.

A week later, thanks to a new acquaintance, I had a chance to view declassified Israel Defense Forces footage in which Hezbollah fighters were launching rockets just steps away from a civilian house. Scattered among the men launching the rockets were children— some of them appearing to be very young. Once the Katyusha was fired, the men all ran frantically away. Eight or ten of them piled into an ambulance, clearly marked with the Red Crescent, which quickly careened off the scene. The IDF is not authorized, according to Israeli military doctrine, to attack a medical rescue vehicle, so the Hezbollah fighters were perfectly safe.

There were other images as well. There were freeze-frames of weapons—RPGs, automatic rifles, and hand grenades—stockpiled in the living room of a family residence; a stronghold hidden within a Lebanese home. It reminded me of footage I had seen a year or so before. It had been shot in Fallujah, Iraq, during another violent and controversial battle against Muslim insurgents. I saw the interior of a Fallujah mosque, piled floor to ceiling with armament, crammed full of every imaginable sort of conventional weapon. I learned from the person who showed me the footage that more than sixty other Fallujah mosques had been similarly equipped, untouchable "holy sites" that served as impregnable fortresses for international terrorists.

It's true that no one suffers more in times of war than children. Although it wasn't a widely publicized story, I had already learned something about the difficulties Israeli children faced during the war. During the StandWithUs "Mission," we had helped pass out pizza to kids who had been transported from northern Israel to an amusement park near Tel Aviv. Several American Jewish organizations had cooperated in raising funds to hire buses, buy t-shirts and food, and provide hundreds of children with a day of fun, removed as far as possible from the bomb shelters and danger they had lived in for nearly a month.

We had also toured a seaside "Tent City" large enough to house 6,000 evacuees from the north. A wealthy Russian-Israeli, Arkady Gaydamak, whose shady reputation seemed, at the time, only to be eclipsed by his generosity, had assembled the entire complex on a beach 24 hours after the war began. It contained a dining area where 900 people could eat at a single sitting, a full service laundry, an outdoor café, a sheltered game area for children, and a synagogue.

On the surface, the site looked like a festive beach campground that might be enjoyed by Club Med types. But the conditions inside were not so vacation-like, with 300+ people sleeping in each large tent. Most of the occupants were seriously traumatized—especially the children. They had lost their homes and left behind their friends, pets and belongings. There were cries in the night. There were panic attacks. There was bed-wetting. Volunteer counselors were working around the clock, trying to soothe fears, offer hope, and alleviate suffering. The refugees were mostly low-income Jewish Israelis, although we later earned that displaced Arab families were sheltered there too.

The Lebanon War lasted just over a month. As long as it continued, a majority of Israelis stood behind the military conflict, and more precisely, they stood with their soldiers. All 18-year-old Israelis are required to enlist in the military—the exceptions are the ultra-Orthodox, who are exempt, and a few draft-dodgers. Most Orthodox Jews serve.

Just about every adult Israeli I have talked to has, indeed, served in the IDF, and nearly everyone seems to have lost a friend or loved one in one of the major battles the country has fought since the War of Independence in 1948. In fact, there are still some elderly veterans of the 1948 war who will gladly share their experiences and their losses with a willing listener.

The Lebanon conflict did not end with the power and glory the Israelis, and maybe the rest of the world, anticipated. The Israeli Defense Forces had achieved extraordinary victories in 1948, 1967 and 1973. Their courage and valor are legendary. Likewise, Mossad, the Israeli intelligence apparatus, is envisioned as wily and virtually omniscient. As the days and weeks rolled by, Israelis held their breath, hoping the phone wouldn't ring with bad news while keeping an eye on the TV, waiting for the 2006 miracle.

It wasn't that easy. The conflict ended with a whimper, not a bang. The initial air assault was dramatic and left parts of Lebanon in ruins, but failed to stop the Katyushas. Subsequently, the belated ground operation was given neither time nor preparation to successfully complete its bunker-by-bunker attacks of Hezbollah terrorists.

When peace was declared, at the behest of the international community, another war immediately broke out in the Israeli press—a battle of ideas, insults and accusations. All previous solidarity, all unity of mind and spirit vanished, and in its place surged more than enough mud to sling, and a surfeit of blame to go around. All the second-guessing brought forth more questions than answers: What did the war accomplish? Who actually won? What was the point? Who was at fault? What will this do to the deterrence factor? When will it start up again? What does this bode for the future?

Friends and Neighbors

My journey to Kiryat Shmona had begun before sun-up. It ended after dark. As I tried to find my way up the unfamiliar steps to my apartment without much light, a "Hello!" interrupted my progress. I looked across the vine-covered stone wall that separated my building from the neighbors', and saw two people who had stopped on their way up their own stairs to greet me.

"We were hoping to meet you. Are you living in Nomi's apartment now?"

I noticed a glint of gold in her hair, a glimmer of silver in his beard, and welcoming smiles on both their faces. At first glance they looked faintly Bohemian to me. Or maybe they were just stylish. As it turned out, they were an artistic and attractive family and I was right on both counts.

I introduced myself and we talked for a minute or two. The woman said, "Well, Lela, welcome to Jerusalem. Why don't you come over and have a glass of wine with us?"

I hesitated, plagued by the kind of shyness that can ruin a perfectly natural conversation. Then I remembered my California neighbors and their vague attempts at hospitality: "We really *must* get together for a drink one of these days." In two years time, it had never happened.

"I'll be right over."

I told these new friends, Bridget and Israeli Hadany, that I'd visited Kiryat Shmona that day and we talked a little about the war, but it seemed to me that the Hadanys had no interest in dwelling on it. They told me about living for decades in Abu Tor, a mixed Arab-Israeli neighborhood less than a mile away, where they had long intermingled with their neighbors and had thought of them all as family. When the jihadist tide began to rise, however, their friendships with their Arab neighbors had chilled. One troublesome incident after another had added up to a list of good reasons to move, and they had reluctantly done so just a few years before. Like many artists, their political point of view had always been left of center. Since the Second Intifada, the Gaza disengagement and now this latest war, they had observed enough to alter their position a little. Still, their reality-based change of mind seemed to sadden them both.

My hospitable neighbors made me feel at home mostly because our conversation was open-ended—we all knew it wasn't finished. I left feeling elated, and by the time I got home I had to remind myself about Kiryat Shmona, and the destruction I'd seen there. I was so grateful to have spent time with them. Somehow I felt as if I'd crossed over a bridge and arrived on the other side of an impasse: How could I acquaint myself with people in Jerusalem? Now it didn't seem so hard.

Before leaving California, I had emailed a woman who uses the pen name Bat Ye'or. She is a scholar and historian in Switzerland and has written some of the world's most influential books about *dhimmitude,* the inferior status of Christians and Jews ("People of the Book") in Islamic societies under Shari'a law—the official Muslim legal system. Bat Ye'or and her husband had welcomed me, along with a couple of other friends, to their home six years before, just as the Second Intifada began. Since that time I had been impressed by her exhaustive work, so I'd written to inform her about my plans to live in Israel for a while.

In response, aware that I am a Christian, Bat Ye'or had given me the name and phone number of a German Christian woman in Jerusalem, an ordained Lutheran minister, suggesting that I contact her. Although I certainly wanted to meet people, I found it difficult to telephone complete strangers, so I hadn't yet made the call.

The next morning, after meeting the Hadanys, I headed for the post office, hoping to pick up a package from home. As I walked, I saw that notices had been posted along our street. I'd tried to learn some basic Hebrew before arriving in Israel, but all I could decipher on this flyer was the time of day: 8:30 to 12:30. There was also a logo that might have represented flowing water. I was studying it helplessly when someone said "Good morning" in English. I turned and saw a petite, dark-haired woman with a radiant smile.

"Oh, good" I responded. "You speak English. Can you help me read this sign?"

She glanced at it and said, "Oh, it's just letting us know that the water will be turned off from 8:30 until noon on Thursday." We talked a few moments about who I was, where I lived and what kind of work I planned to do in Jerusalem. "I'm a writer," I explained. "I'm finishing up a couple of projects here. And I'm interested in Jewish-Christian relations…"

"Are you Jewish?"

"No, I'm a Christian."

"Well, so am I," she nodded. "I'm actually an ordained Lutheran minister." She extended her hand. "My name is Petra Heldt."

Instantly I remembered Bat Ye'or's email, and tried to remember the name of the woman she had mentioned. I couldn't quite recall. "Do you happen to know a woman…in Geneva?" I asked rather awkwardly. "A scholar by the name of Bat Ye'or?"

Petra beamed. "You know Bat Ye'or? How wonderful! She's been my friend for 28 years!"

A shiver of amazement rippled down my spine, a welcome spiritual confirmation that I was precisely where I was supposed to be. "Where do you live?" I asked.

"Right here," she said, pointing toward the apartment directly across the street from mine.

I didn't see Petra again for a few weeks. When we first met, she was on her way to Germany, with her husband, scholar and linguist Malcolm Lowe. But I hadn't seen the last of her—that was clear to both of us. That story continues, as I'll explain in later chapters.

Whatever our imaginations may tell us about living in foreign lands, or exploring international issues, or having "adventures" in faraway places, it is the people we meet that breathe life into our dreams. In a matter of days, I had met interesting neighbors whose company I enjoyed, who had reached out to me in friendship, and who lived just steps from my new home.

And there was one more, introduced to me in an email message from a friend in Washington DC. I met Ruthie Blum, who was at the time a too-busy journalist for the *Jerusalem Post*, just about a week later. At the time she and her family also lived within a stone's throw of my apartment, though both she and I have since moved. When we met, we were both single mothers. Ruthie is a surprisingly spiritual woman with sparkly earrings and an even-more-sparkling sense of humor. She was the reason my articles began to appear in the *Jerusalem Post*, unexpectedly adding "journalist" to my writing credentials. But most notable was the conversation between the two of us, which began in my earliest days in Israel. We haven't stopped talking since.

More quickly than I'd dared hope, I had found friends who read, thought about issues, remembered the past, reflected on the present, and wondered about the future. They were bright, generous and hospitable. Suddenly my neighborhood—which so far had been populated by whispering trees, wayfaring cats and songs in the night—was also rich in wonderful people.

I never really found time to ask them the litany of questions I had rattling around in my head, because without missing a beat, more changes began to unfold. Even though Israeli newspapers and websites were still mired in tiresome analyses, contradictions, official and unofficial inquiries into what had happened in Lebanon, there was already a new promise in the air—something that would surely lift our spirits, something everyone seemed to be frantically preparing for, something more important than a whole string of Shabbats in a row.

The High Holy days were to begin on September 22, which also happened to be my birthday. If there was anything Israel needed in fall 2006, besides, in many people's opinion, a new government, it was a *New Year*. And as the war tried to beat a hasty retreat out the back, Rosh Hashanah—New Year's Day—was knocking at the front door. Ready or not, we were all about to enter the year 5767.

CHAPTER THREE

DAYS OF AWE

...My years do not depart with December solstices
Nor arrive with January celebrations;
My years are marked, as summer burns away,
By the rising September moon.

I wrote those words as a moonstruck teenager. Yet even today, the word "September" remains laden with expectation for me, it is my birthday month and forever a season of renewed hope. It was no surprise that the first days of September in Jerusalem were especially stirring. They arrived with a chilly wind that chased away the oppressive heat and set the leaves trembling with change.

I was continually fascinated by my surroundings—all sorts of things captured my curiosity. Now that the war was over, and I was more or less used to a new routine, new people, new foods, new ways of dressing and speaking and, at times, behaving, I was eagerly looking forward to yet another new experience, the Jewish High Holidays. My idea that the New Year should begin in September was actually coming true. Along with a new year, a new decade of my own life was beginning as well, and all on the same day.

Rosh Hashanah, the Jewish New Year, is celebrated on the first and second days of the Jewish month of Tishri, which falls in September or October. It initiates a ten-day period called the Days of Repentance or Days of Awe. These end with Yom Kippur, the Day of Atonement and the most sacred of all Jewish holidays. During these days, Jews reflect on their sins and moral failings, and seek forgiveness from anyone they have wronged during the past year. Rosh Hashanah is the "Day of Judgment," but although God's judgment is passed on that day, it is not finalized—made absolute—until Yom Kippur, when it is sealed in the Book of Life. Yom Kippur's observance includes a strict 25-hour fast, during which the faithful neither eat nor drink anything, including water. In prayer, fasting and asking forgiveness, and through God's mercy, Rosh Hashanah's initial judgment can be altered. One Yom Kippur greeting is *khatima tova*—"may you have a good seal..." in the Book of Life.

But why should a Christian be interested in Jewish holidays? St. Paul described Christians as wild olive branches engrafted into the ancient Jewish olive tree: "If some of the branches have been broken off, and you, though a wild olive shoot, have been grafted in among the others and now share in the nourishing sap from the olive root, do not boast over those branches. If you do, consider this: You do not support the root, but the root supports you."

If St. Paul is correct, perhaps Christianity would benefit by sitting at the feet of the Jewish faithful, listening carefully to what our "elder brothers," as he called them, can teach us. Maybe that is why those first High Holy Days in Jerusalem were especially meaningful to me, because I had so much to learn. I didn't really observe them in a religious sense—I didn't know any Jewish people well enough to be included in their family plans, and I was too unsure of cultural dos and don'ts to venture into a synagogue alone. Instead, like a child with her nose pressed against a window, I watched and listened and wondered, perhaps the mirror image of the Jewish child staring in curiosity at the neighbors' Christmas tree.

On the morning of Rosh Hashanah, I walked to the Western Wall. It was a warm, quiet day. Tourism was still slow, partly because summer was over, but mostly because people had changed their travel plans due to the war. The Old City's Arab Quarter merchants were desperate for business. I hadn't yet learned to simply ignore their attempts to entice me into their shops:

"Madame, Look! This way! I want to show you something...."

"Madame, may I ask you a question? Please—I just want to ask you one question—look, here! Here!"

"Please, you look so very beautiful. Please talk to me! Madame...I want to know where you bought your beautiful earrings."

"Yes, I'm the one you have been waiting for! Come in my shop and see—I know just what you're looking for!"

I was perhaps overly self-conscious about being tall, blonde and not looking like a "local." And, of course, I was alone. The whole situation made me uneasy. Should I pay no attention to the assertive merchants at the risk of acting like the classic ugly American? Or should I mumble "No, thank you" a thousand and one times? Or should I set my face like a flint, frown and look incredibly grumpy in hopes that they would leave me alone? To this day, I'm not sure what is best. One of my friends had suggested that I get to the Western Wall by turning right at the Jaffa Gate, walking around the perimeter of the Old City and making my way through the Armenian quarter. This spared me running the gauntlet through the Arabic shuk. I took his suggestion gladly.

After a couple of detours, and an unfortunate side trip into an Armenian garden where I was not made to feel particularly welcome, I found my way down to *HaKotel*, the Western Wall. As it always does, the very sight of it stopped me in my tracks. A montage of gold-hued blocks of stone, massive at the bottom, growing smaller toward the top, the Wall is punctuated here and there by tufts of brush, and by birds that perch alone or in pairs. Some of them seem to be nesting—making themselves very much at home, recalling Psalm 84:

How lovely is your dwelling place,
O LORD Almighty!
My soul yearns, even faints,
for the courts of the LORD;
my heart and my flesh cry out

for the living God.
Even the sparrow has found a home,
and the swallow a nest for herself,
where she may have her young—
a place near your altar,
O LORD Almighty, my King and my God.
Blessed are those who dwell in your house;
they are ever praising you.
Selah (v 1-4 NIV)

I walked past the women's section, stood back a few feet from the opening into the men's area, and viewed the scene. I'd had high hopes of hearing a shofar trumpeting the arrival of the New Year but wasn't sure whether it would be sounded only once, early in the morning, or throughout the course of the day. I watched a few dozen black-hatted, black-coated worshippers, an equal number informally dressed modern Orthodox with varicolored yarmulkes, a few devout gentlemen in mink hats and medieval garb, and a scattering of tourists awkwardly outfitted in cardboard yarmulkes. It wasn't long before my shofar question was answered: from a distance I could see a steady stream of men moving into place and blasting in the New Year (they were of varying talent, I might add).

I later learned about a ruckus at the Wall that took place early the next morning. It was caused by a shofar, or more specifically by a 20-year-old worshipper who refused to obey police commands that he stop playing the shofar. He and his friends were dragged off none-too-gently to the local precinct. The Israeli police had been summoned by an Arab woman who had complained that the sound of the shofar was disturbing her children. According to a local news service, some of the Old City Jewish Quarter's residents found the incident puzzling and distressing. "The loud Arab weddings and the early prayers by the muezzin over a loudspeaker at 4:30 am disturb our sleep every night!" one resident complained.

The incident was particularly worrisome to older Israelis who still recalled their joy and celebration following the 1967 War. Despite promises to respect Jewish religious observances, the Jordanian government had strictly forbidden them. After decades of silence, there had been great excitement when the shofar was once again (legally) heard at the Western Wall on Rosh HaShanah. Was it destined to fall silent again?

As for hearing the sound of the shofar for myself, I needn't have walked so far. By early evening my street was alive with the sound of countless children laughing and playing their own little shofars, like so many tiny bleating lambs.

Days of Repentance

The Days of Awe leading up to Yom Kippur seemed relatively ordinary to me except for the New Year's greeting *Shana Tovah!*—"Have a good year!"—which was repeated in shops and cafes around our neighborhood. There seemed to be a lot of extra people on the streets. Most of them sounded American; in fact, I was hearing more English than Hebrew on Emek Refaim. The Neuman bakery on the corner was packed with customers, sharing the richly prepared baked goods on the shelves with a small but frantic swarm of bees with an aggressive sweet tooth. So packed was the grocery store that it was not maneuverable when I ventured there, and the sidewalks bustled with people congregating around kiosks of gifts and food, where they smoked, chatted and answered their cell phones. Some shops were dark and locked up, their handmade signs explaining in Hebrew scribbles that they were closed for the holidays.

A couple of days before Yom Kippur I was invited to two homes on a single afternoon. Both offered food for the body as well as for thought. First I joined a group of seven or eight Christians, many of them new to the city, for a barbecue. These friends came from Pentecostal/Charismatic Christian traditions, and their conversation was sprinkled with interpretations of ancient Hebrew prophecies. A couple of them were applying certain scriptures, verse by verse, to recent newspaper reports. They were scared, and anyone who connected the dots the way they did would also have been apprehensive. From their point of view, a brutal and bloody end of the world was at hand. The encroaching darkness of "End Times" had all but blotted out their joy and hope. One couple actually wondered aloud if they should flee. This was not, by the way, the kind of apocalyptic talk that dooms Jews to a bloody end if they reject Jesus. It was an equal opportunity doomsday scenario in which we were all destined for slaughter together.

It wasn't entirely clear to me why these folks were in Jerusalem. My impression (and it was admittedly a first impression, and brief) was that they were primarily interested in the well-being of their Christian enclave, but were otherwise in a sort of bunker mode—fearful of the Muslims who were arrayed against Israel, while feeling like defenseless aliens within a not-always-hospitable Jewish State. There were, of course, interesting people there. One German woman had for years been involved with caring for elderly Holocaust survivors. A young British man was devoted to prayer on the Temple Mount—something he does every week, walking around the Al-Aqsa Mosque and the Dome of the Rock, praying quietly but fervently for the peace of Jerusalem.

I left there with a shadow of gloom and doom trailing behind me. Even without the apocalyptic spin, the news around town wasn't all that good. I rushed off to see an elderly Israeli couple who had befriended me. Both of them were in their late seventies and network news was too much for them; "We just don't think about it," they told me. Instead they wanted to discuss something uplifting. My hostess, a lively woman with a sunny smile, couldn't stop talking about the New Testament. That day she said to me, her eyes shining, "I remember the first time I ever read the Gospels. It was so beautiful! I ran to one of my friends and said, 'Look, have you seen this?' She said to me, 'Shhh! Don't talk about that!'"

She sighed and shook her head. "So, I'm just quiet about it now…"

As the conversation went on, the old couple told me how they had been evangelized by well-meaning Christians who wanted them to "accept Jesus." Their Christian friends had, however, overlooked the fact that Jesus was a rabbi, that his mother and siblings were Jewish, that his disciples were Jews, that his early followers met in synagogues, and that his entire recorded story took place in and around modern-day Israel.

"Accept Jesus?" my friend concluded. "What's to accept? He is my brother! I sometimes think Christians have pushed Jews away from Jesus. Anyway, he said he would be with us always, and I believe he is."

I was surprised by her words. Did that mean she believes in the resurrection? Rather than press the point, I let it rest. I silently reflected on one big question among the earliest gatherings of Christians—recorded in the New Testament book of Acts. It wasn't whether Jews could accept Jesus as Messiah. It was whether Gentiles could accept Jesus as Messiah without first becoming Jews.

Before I left, the old man read aloud from the 84th Psalm—my favorite—in Hebrew, and then translated it into English so I could understand it.

Sunrise, sunset, and the next thing I knew it was the eve of Yom Kippur. By early afternoon, our local shops and restaurants were shuttered, buses had stopped running, and the streets were emptied of cars. Garbage was collected, sidewalks were swept, and omnipresent street sweepers took one last, noisy pass at the pavements. As darkness fell, as on the eve of Shabbat, I could smell delicious food cooking on countless stovetops; and once again I heard families singing together, *Baruch Atah Adonai, Eloheinu…* "Blessed are You, LORD, our God…" In a last-minute burst of holiday good will, the downstairs neighbor's grandson charged up to say "Shalom" to me. After I took his picture in his new shirt and matching kippa, he hurriedly explained that he was five years old, that he speaks Hebrew, English and French, and that his name was Yoav. Then off he raced, clattering down the steps. Minutes later I heard the blessing being sung by his family.

The next day, on Yom Kippur, I made my way toward the Old City, thinking deeply as I walked. Wherever I had gone, whomever I had talked to in recent days seemed to be wrestling with fear. The possibility of another military conflict—perhaps even a major one against Iran and Syria—was more than an undercurrent. Newspapers and websites were fountains of bad news about smuggled weapons, broken treaties, weak-kneed politicos and raging mullahs, all spilling forth into rivers of blame and shame. Endless news stories and editorials forecast death, destruction and annihilation.

How do you live, I asked myself again and again, *when everyone around you wants you dead, or at least gone?*

I had learned before my trip that it is frustrating to keep an eye on the Middle East in places like California. You have to carefully search the media to figure out what's happening. Even then, reports need to be taken with a grain of salt, especially if they come through mainstream outlets like CNN, BBC, or Reuters. By contrast, the constant bombardment of threats in the Middle East press is mind-numbing. In the midst of ongoing peril, people of every sort—overtly religious, private believers, hard-core doubters, or those who smile and say "No, I'm not religious, although I'm a *very* spiritual person"—all seemed to have hesitantly turned their eyes toward heaven, quietly hoping for a miracle. What a time to be in Jerusalem.

I walked toward the Western Wall, finding my way fairly easily on the new route. I did manage to get lost in the Jewish Quarter, ending up in a back alley with a garbage dump and a couple of stray cats—this because some children were singing somewhere and I was trying to move closer to their music. In fact, there was singing everywhere I walked that day.

I finally arrived. This time I had my book of Psalms in hand. I made my way to the women's section and found a chair in the shade. I stayed an hour or so, reading Psalms, thinking, praying and listening to the men singing across the way. There weren't a lot of people there because on Yom Kippur even the least observant Jews go to synagogue.

When I glanced at the text a woman seated near me was reading, I couldn't help but smile: First Corinthians. How many of the women at the wall on Yom Kippur were Christians? Maybe we had inadvertently gone to "church" together. Maybe like me, the others were also trying to shovel away Christian cultural rubble that has, at times, nearly buried our faith alive. Maybe we were like so many spiritual archeologists digging for rare coins or gems or royal seals.

At times I grow weary of church and churches, which comprise the most difficult aspect of Christianity for me. It has little to do with my personal faith and is probably is the result of myriad life complications that needn't be inventoried. That is undoubtedly one of the reasons I spent so much time peacefully seated in the shadow of the Western Wall, letting my surroundings and the book in my hands speak for themselves.

History Written in Stone

The remnants of the ancient Jewish Temple serve as a sanctuary for Judeo-Christian believers, its traditions rooted more deeply in the bedrock of God's Word than any other holy site on earth. Sitting there on Yom Kippur it occurred to me that there is a rock-hard foundation even beneath the single most divisive issue that separates Christians and Jews. Judaism cherishes and exalts above all else the revealed, written and remembered Word of God, the Torah. Christians believe that the Jewish Messiah came as "the Word made flesh." Both Jews and Christians build their faith on the "solid rock" of Holy Scripture.

In these days of multiculturalism, it is not uncommon to hear protestations that one particular holy place is no more significant than another. And it is generally true that our inner belief—

subjective awareness—is what recognizes and responds to tangible symbols, sites and shrines. But we do live in space and time, and try though we may to transcend them, we still find ourselves in a real world with a real history, and a Biblical narrative that quite literally has been written in stone.

Some Christians who are less-than-enthusiastic about Israel voice their concern about "living stones" being overlooked. This is an implicit message that visitors to Israel should be more concerned about the region's current residents (they are usually referring to Arabs, not Jews) than about touring the ruins of old civilizations. It is true that the New Testament says believers, like living stones, are being built into God's spiritual house. But gazing at the Western Wall, I wondered, are the two mutually exclusive? Surely traces of glory remain in antique stones that have been trod upon by holier feet than mine. There are sacred lessons to be learned among the stony remains of the past—pilgrim places that have for centuries been washed by the tears of the faithful. And to this day, the ruined Temple remains a threshold into another reality. It is a heavenly portal at which King Solomon prayed, millennia ago, for the likes of me:

> Also concerning the foreigner who is not of Your people Israel, when he comes from a far country for Your name's sake (for they will hear of Your great name and Your mighty hand, and of Your outstretched arm); when he comes and prays toward this house, hear in heaven Your dwelling place, and do according to all for which the foreigner calls to You, in order that all the peoples of the earth may know Your name, to fear You, as do Your people Israel, and that they may know that this house which I have built is called by Your name (1 Ki. 8:41-43, NASB).

Lifting my face toward what's left of Solomon's great house of prayer, I reflected once again on Psalm 84, which had repeatedly come to my mind and attention in recent days. I was moved by one particular passage: "For one day in Your courtyards is better than a thousand [elsewhere], I prefer to stand exposed at the threshold of my God's house than to dwell securely in the tents of wickedness." Again, the ideas of atonement and redemption came to mind. I later recorded my thoughts,

How lovely is your dwelling place, Lord of All.

My heart yearns, aches, draws me
to the ruins of your sacred house,
where even today nesting birds flutter among the ancient stones.

I hear the dove's call,
I hear the sound of singing just across the way,
stronger and stronger it grows;
I hear the voices of former rains and latter rains
surging, roaring, flooding, rushing away the years
not by tears alone, but with showers of blessing, living waters,
A merciful, cleansing deluge.

And so I stand, wet face pressed against the golden wall,
blemished, shamefully exposed in the pure light,
unholy feet on holiest of ground,
yet mysteriously, miraculously safe
just one step inside the threshold.

How lovely is your dwelling place, Lord of All.

Fasting and Feasting

In Jerusalem, Yom Kippur is not only a day of fasting, of denying oneself water and food, but it also involves ample time for contemplation. I'd read an article in the *Jerusalem Post* by my friend Ruthie Blum, about children riding bicycles on Yom Kippur in

Jerusalem. The story surprised me, but the truth of it turned out to be one of the nicest things about the day. More silent than any Sabbath, there were no cars (and hence no horns), no radios or TVs, no hammering, no drilling, no shouting, no work of any kind. A complete shutdown of the city is enforced, and the wonderful by-product of this is almost complete silence. I say "almost" because, as Ruthie predicted, all was not solemn. The streets were full of colorfully helmeted kids on bikes—riding fearlessly and frenetically because there was no traffic.

Some people—I later learned that they were Sephardic Jews from North Africa—dress entirely in white to celebrate Yom Kippur. I walked past them as they sat in circles like huge white flowers on the park's grass, chattering and laughing. And of course musical chants emanated from synagogues everywhere I walked. These cheerful sights and sounds seemed like prescient glimpses: the sought-after Atonement would surely be fulfilled. The cup of redemptive blessings was spilling over into the streets, unable to contain itself until sunset, until the three stars' appearance, and the final blast of the shofar. The children, the singers, and the people in white already seemed to know—their sins would most certainly be forgiven, cast away by their Redeemer's hand as far as the East is from the West.

It was nearly sunset when I walked to the Haas Promenade, a park with a spectacular view of the Old City not far from my apartment. As I surveyed Abu Tor, the Kidron Valley and the Old City, yellow streetlights were beginning to illuminate the roadways. All seemed muted. Even the muezzins' call to prayer sounded distant and less piercing than usual. The only other noise I noticed was the caw-cawing of raucous and disheveled-looking ravens that flocked around the hilltop.

Daylight faded to black and just as I was leaving the Promenade, I heard the city siren's prolonged whine, announcing the holiday's end. Minutes later, I found myself near the corner of Hebron Road and Yehuda Sreet, standing outside a synagogue where the Yom Kippur service was still going on. There were several dozen women and children talking and laughing in a crowded outside courtyard—it was packed with people of all ages, including a few men. I stood off to the side where I could watch, unnoticed, through a window and between some leaves. The men inside, garbed in prayer shawls, chanted and *davened*, bowing rhythmically as they prayed. Less than a minute later the shofar sounded and soon the men filed out of the synagogue, gathered their wives, children and friends and went off in every direction, laughing and talking as they headed toward what, in my religious past, was usually categorized as "food, fun and fellowship."

I walked on, noticing that the streets were quickly beginning to surge with families streaming out of all sorts of little *shuls* in the area, unmarked synagogues that I didn't even know were there. At about the same time, cars rematerialized on the streets and, unavoidably, horns once again began to honk.

I was starving by then. I hadn't officially fasted, since I drank water all day. But I hadn't eaten, so I rushed home and heated up some leftover pasta in the microwave. Not the most traditional fast-breaking meal but it was more than welcome.

Building a Goodly Heritage

Just days later, I was on a plane again, heading for London to finish a book about Baroness Cox, the uniquely gifted, globe-trotting and devoutly Christian British peer who was for years a Deputy Speaker of the House of Lords. She has spent the past three decades being, as she and I eventually titled her story, *Eyewitness to a Broken World*. Knowing Caroline Cox and working with her had, in many ways, increased my awareness of the harsh realities that surround us all—now more than ever.

At the same time I had been reading extensively about the Jewish repopulation of the Holy Land during the 18th, 19th and 20th Centuries. I had received, as a gift, a lovely and well-worn used book titled *This Goodly Heritage* by Avraham Yaari. This, along with a collection of Jewish poetry dating from Biblical times until the 20th Century, articulated for me the Jewish people's passionate quest to return to their homeland. Through these books and several others, I was introduced to the unquenchable longing for the Land of Israel that had burned in the hearts of the Diaspora for 2,000 years, centuries before the birth of modern Zionism.

In those pages I met heroes whose names are unknown to most Americans, and perhaps have even been forgotten by some American Jews. They were pioneers and trailblazers in a locale more formidable than the Wild West; they had scraped together enough money to purchase often barren scraps of land from local Arabs and with sheer determination, hope, skill and little else, to develop it into fields, gardens and orchards. Here was biography, literature, biblical faith and history, drawn from personal journals, printed articles and poems. Within the texts I could feel the pulse that still pounds beneath the flesh of modern Israel. One unforgettable passage comes from Judah Halevi's Ode to Zion, written in the early 12th Century:

If only I could roam through those places
where God was revealed to your prophets and heralds!
Who will give me wings, so that I may wander far away?
I would carry the pieces of my broken heart over your rugged
mountains.
I would bow down, my face on your ground;
I would love your stones; your dust would move me to pity. ...
I would weep, as I stood by my ancestors' graves ...
The air of your land is the very life of the soul,
the grains of your dust are flowing myrrh,
your rivers are honey from the comb...
Happy is he who waits and lives to see your light rising,
your dawn breaking forth over him!
He shall see your chosen people prospering,
he shall rejoice in your joy when you regain the days of your youth.

Halevi's vision has come to pass—to a point. Yes, the Light has risen and the chosen people are prospering in their land. But their prosperity has come with heartache as well as with joy.

As our British Airways 777 rattled down the runway and roared into the air, I stared out the window, lost in thought. Tel Aviv's skyscrapers gleamed beside the sea, and then diminished into flat, sprawling suburbs. Beyond the suburbs were fields. And beyond the fields were farmlands, carefully laid out, meticulously tended and irrigated.

I recalled a recent train journey from Tel Aviv to Jerusalem, which revealed a similar scene from a different perspective. The train had wended its way through farmlands and orchards, past cement plants and factories and small communities. It meandered between hills and then gradually began to climb upward through forests and craggy rocks. I was absently enjoying the sight of a stream surging alongside the railroad tracks, shadowed by dense conifers, when it suddenly dawned on me that every tree in that forest had been placed in the soil by human hands, all within the last 100 years. In fact, more than a billion trees have been planted in Israel since 1900, making it the only country in the world with more trees in the 21st century than it had at the beginning of the 20th.

The flight attendant interrupted my reverie by handing me a menu. It was in English and Hebrew. Since I was in a historical mood, that brought to mind one Eliezer ben Yehuda, the brilliant linguist who revitalized and modernized the ancient Hebrew language. Although Biblical Hebrew had never died out in religious studies, ben Yehuda was convinced that the re-gathered Jews needed to speak Hebrew, for the sake of their Jewish history, cohesion and identity, as they established new lives in the Land. He worked tirelessly to fulfill his dream. Trying to make sense of the back-to-front Hebrew side of the menu, I smiled to myself. Well, Ben Yehuda certainly was successful. In an extraordinary case of reviving an ancient language that virtually no one spoke, today's

Israelis have recovered the language of their patriarchs, breathed modern vocabulary into it, and it is now their own. They speak it so well that, to this day, I can hardly figure out what they're talking about and have to, shamefacedly, ask them to please repeat themselves in English.

I glanced out the window as the plane banked and once again Tel Aviv's skyline reappeared, now a bit farther away. In my apartment there are several early photographs of Israel. One, titled "Tel Aviv Inauguration," was taken in 1909, just a year after my devotedly Zionist father was born, when Tel Aviv was officially founded. It reveals a cluster of perhaps a hundred people standing stiffly, their backs to the camera, surrounded by sand dunes that stretch as far as the eye can see, utterly barren of vegetation. By 1909, a committee of Jaffa businessmen had purchased untold acres of sand from the Arabs, and had managed—not without seemingly endless delays—to acquire building permits from the Turkish authorities. Avraham Yaari wrote of the committee's subsequent accomplishments...

By the end of summer, the first houses were ready, and about the beginning of November several dozen families moved in. Since the sand lay deep in places, carts could not make their way to the suburb. For weeks, therefore, long strings of camels and donkeys could be seen transporting the settlers' furniture and other household goods to their new homes...

Another photo is entitled "Tel Aviv, 1925." Now, across the sandy beach, box-like buildings have appeared, and a few structures are under construction in the foreground. They are, indeed, bisected by a caravan of camels laden with necessities, with Jaffa Harbor as a backdrop. Recalling those old photographs, I felt a rush of emotion. So quickly Israel's desert has blossomed as a rose—and just as quickly, a cluster of tiny dwellings has burst into a dazzling array of skyscrapers—all in my own father's lifetime. Yet how agonizing the cultivation has been.

Whether constructing Tel Aviv and other towns, establishing kibbutzim, draining malarial swamps or defending their villages, immigrants from Europe, American, Asia and North Africa faced indescribable challenges. Against all odds they did it. Somehow they hung on by their fingertips, fought off bloodthirsty aggressors, survived diseases and overcame despair. Thanks to them and through them, never-forgotten biblical prophecies were fulfilled, and an ancient nation was, from the soil to the sky, resurrected. That late September afternoon, I watched it sparkle along the shores of the Mediterranean Sea like a thousand gemstones. Israel had become a thriving reality, vibrant with life. *They did it!* I told myself again. And, even though today's Israel is perpetually in a state of war with deadly enemies, wrestling with unending anxiety and uncertainty, they are still hard at it.

The building and rebuilding of Israel has never really stopped; all around the country projects great and small are so prevalent that some smart alecks claim that the construction crane is the "national bird." In fact, that very week I had heard the noise of new workmanship in my neighborhood. It was nearly midnight, the night of Yom Kippur, and I was very close to falling asleep when the sound of hammering began reverberating on both sides of my apartment. Why? I soon discovered that the very people who had piously halted any and every kind of labor during that holiest of holidays were now burning the night oil, getting a head start on the next one. My neighbors were nailing together their "booths" for *Sukkot*, the Feast of Tabernacles. Another week of holidays was just around the corner.

CHAPTER FOUR

DIGGING FOR TRUTH

...the ministering angels had gathered
As was their custom
In choruses of Holiness
To sing the song of dawn.
And they opened the windows of the firmament
And inclined their heads toward the Temple Mount
To see if the Temple doors were opened
And if the cloud of incense smoke ascended.
And they saw, and behold the Eternal, the God of Hosts,
Ancient of Days, sitting in the morning twilight over the desolation!
His garment was a pillar of smoke
And His footstool dust and ashes;
His head bowed low between his arms
And mountains of sorrow on His head.
Silent and desolate, sitting and gazing at the ruins,
His eyelids darkened with the rage of all the worlds
And in His eyes congealed was the Great Silence.
—Hayyim Nahman Bialik, 1873-1934.

During the early autumn days between Yom Kippur and Sukkot, Jerusalem neighborhoods are transformed. Balconies are festively adorned in palm fronds, decorated with glittery garlands and sparkling baubles, and in some cases sided with thin white fabric, enclosing the "booth" on all sides except for the roof. That is left open to the sun, moon and stars.

Restaurants with patios are similarly arrayed, and some cafés even add outside tables so they too can become *sukkot*, the "booths" commemorating the temporary dwellings the ancient Israelites lived in during their desert journey from Egypt to the Land of Promise. According to the Jewish calendar, the Sukkot holiday begins five days after Yom Kippur, which places it in September or October. Historically, the seven-day feast was one of three pilgrimage festivals during which the earliest Jewish people traveled, ascending Mt. Zion to the Jerusalem Temple, before it was destroyed, rebuilt, and destroyed again.

Feasts, Celebrations and Parades

Sukkot is often called the Feast of Tabernacles by Christians—I had first heard about it in childhood, during discussions about the Bible. The Jewish Feasts are of particular interest to some prophetically-minded Protestants who, like my parents, believe that every feast has been "fulfilled"—in the sense of messianic foreshadowing—during Jesus' ministry except for one, the Feast of Trumpets, part of Rosh Hashanah. That still unfulfilled event is said to await the arrival of Messiah, which to Christians means the return of Jesus.

This event will be heralded by, among other things (depending on who you talk to), the blast of heavenly *shofarim* and a major earthquake with its epicenter at the Mount of Olives. I question how this rather specific prediction about the Feast of Trumpets correlates with Jesus' own comments about his second coming: "No one knows the day or the hour..." As with most things of a "last days" nature, there seem to be more than enough answers.

The Christian understanding of the Feast of Tabernacles' fulfillment is recorded in the book of John, chapter 7. During a water-drawing ritual in the Temple, on the last day of Sukkot, Jesus cried out, "'If anyone is thirsty, let him come to me and drink. Whoever believes in me, as the Scripture has said, streams of living water will flow from within him.' By this he meant the Holy Spirit, which those who believed in him were later to receive…."

A modern-day Christian celebration of the Feast of Tabernacles takes place each year in Jerusalem, with thousands of Christians arriving from all over the world to celebrate. This Christian Feast includes an enormous gala opening night featuring dance, drama, music, prayer and preaching. It concludes with a colorful parade through the streets of Jerusalem, when tens of thousands of celebrants, Jews and Christians alike, virtually shut down the City Center for hours.

I've never made it to the Sukkot parade. But one year, after the Feast ended, I decided to return to the Western Wall. As I made my way to the Jaffa Gate I heard the sounds of a noisy crowd. At first I was a little worried—there had been Arab rioting on the Temple Mount the day before over what sounded to me like necessary repair work. I needn't have worried. This was something altogether different—neither Arab nor a riot. It was a parade, too, but one of a different kind. I had arrived just in time for a local synagogue's *Simchat Torah* procession.

During Simchat Torah, which falls at the end of Sukkot, religious Jews conclude a year's reading through the Torah. Before they start over again at the beginning, they celebrate. In Jerusalem, many congregations take their synagogues' Torah scroll to the Western Wall. As I watched that day, a rabbi carried the scroll under a canopy fashioned of a prayer shawl, supported by four young men and accompanied by a happy throng. Without being noticed, I walked along with them as they sang, clapped and at times danced their way from Jaffa Gate to the Wall. Their joy was contagious, and it was an unexpected pleasure to be with them.

No Temple on the Temple Mount?

Christians and Jews—those who believe the Bible as well as other historic records regarding Jerusalem's history—have a deep attachment to the sacred space once occupied by the Jewish Temple. This is true because of the events that have unfolded there across the millennia, but also because of the Presence of God believed to have dwelt there in the Temple days gone by.

When the Jewish fast day of Tisha B'Av takes place, the destruction of the first and second Jewish Temples is ritually commemorated, and the history surrounding them is recalled. This day of remembrance does not pass without dispute, however. With increasing stridency, an Arab outcry accompanies Tisha B'Av's prayerful mourning and observance. For example, in August 2011, the Palestinian news site *Al-Hayat Al-Jadida* reported,

> Since Monday morning, groups of extremist Jews have been roaming the courtyards of Al-Aqsa mosque [i.e., the Temple Mount] one after the other, under heavy police protection, on the occasion of the so-called "destruction of the Temple"... This Sunday, the occupation's police handed the shop owners in the Market of the Cotton Merchants... which leads to the blessed Al-Aqsa Mosque, an order forcing them to close their shops on Monday afternoon [i.e., the eve of the anniversary of the destruction of the Temple, Tisha B'av], in order to facilitate the arrival of the settlers to the Market, for the sake of holding special Talmudic rituals on the occasion of the destruction of the *alleged* Temple. [Emphasis added]

A visit to the Temple Mount Plaza is revealing and, honestly, a little shocking. Despite the fact that it is the holiest Jewish site in Jerusalem, it feels like a spiritual no-man's land—some sort of a Saudi Arabian outpost. Tour guides inform their groups that all non-Muslim prayer is forbidden. After passing through two security checks, a quick survey of the plaza reveals no vestige of Judaism. This is nothing new. In 1217, Spanish pilgrim Judah al-Harizi was deeply distressed when he arrived on the Mount. "What torment to see our holy courts converted into an alien temple!" he wrote.

I can relate to his outcry. Christianity doesn't fare much better. In fact, for those who believe that Jesus is God's Son, crucified for the sins of the world and later resurrected, the writing is quite literally on the wall—the wall inside the Dome of the Rock.

In Arabic calligraphy dating from the 7th Century, the text declares,

O People of the Book! Do not exaggerate in your religion or utter aught concerning God save the truth. The Messiah, Jesus son of Mary, was only a Messenger of God, and His Word, which He conveyed unto Mary, and a spirit from Him. So believe in God and His messengers, and say not 'Three'—Cease! [it is] better for you! —God is only One God. Far be it removed from His transcendent majesty that He should have a son. His is all that is in the heavens and all that is in the earth.

From the moment the army of Titus, son of Roman Emperor Vespasian, destroyed the Second Jewish Temple and massacred the citizens of Jerusalem in 70 AD, until June 7, 1967 when Jerusalem was retaken by Israel in the Six Day War, the Temple Mount was never once under Jewish authority. It has always remained, however, the ultimate destination in the land of Abraham, Isaac and Jacob.

"Praiseworthy is the man whose strength is in You, those whose hearts focus on the paths leading upward," says Psalm 84:6. Ibn Ezra, an 11th Century scholar, identifies "those whose heart focus on the paths leading upward," as "those who embark on pilgrimage to the Holy Temple." 19th Century Rabbi Hirsch goes on, "Even when physically unable to visit the Temple, they ascend the paths leading to God in their hearts." To see the Temple rebuilt one day remains a sacred hope for many Jews.

Christians, too, have an attachment to the Temple Mount based on Jesus' words and deeds as recorded in the Gospels. It seems outrageous that Jews and Christians are not permitted to read their scriptures or pray aloud on the Temple Mount. But even that is not the greatest scandal.

During the Camp David Accords, PLO Chairman Yassar Arafat denied that any Jewish Temple had ever existed on the Temple Mount. Former Middle East envoy Dennis Ross described the incident, in an interview with Brit Hume,

> ...at Camp David [in the summer of 2000] we did not put a comprehensive set of ideas on the table. We put ideas on the table that would have affected the borders and would have affected Jerusalem. Arafat could not accept any of that. In fact, during the 15 days there, he never himself raised a single idea. His negotiators did, to be fair to them, but he didn't. *The only new idea he raised at Camp David was that the Temple didn't exist in Jerusalem, it existed in Nablus... This is the core of the Jewish faith...he was denying the core of the Jewish faith there.* [Emphasis added]

President Bill Clinton, a Baptist Christian, was reportedly aghast at Arafat's statement. As for me, when I first heard this story, I thought it was an exaggeration—some sort of an urban legend. It didn't take much research on my part to find that it is entirely true. It represents, in fact, a form of historical revision that increasingly permeates Muslim politics as well as Islamic religious teachings. Although Jerusalem is not mentioned by name in the Quran, the Jews certainly are. And the Temple Mount itself has been, more and more, disputed territory since the Muslims conquered Jerusalem in the 7th Century.

Along with many other sites in the land of Israel and the Palestinian Territories, Islam has its own version of Biblical people and places and their significance—accounts that abrogate the Judeo-Christian Scriptures. Still, this relatively new declaration of Temple Denial literally took my breath away.

A Conversation with Gabriel Barkay

Fortunately, thanks to my friend Petra Heldt, I was able to track down a prominent Israeli archeologist, who knows a great deal about the Temple Mount. Dr. Gabriel Barkay, professor at Bar-Ilan University, is one of the world's most respected Biblical archeologists. He is perhaps best known for making one of the 20th Century's great findings in an area of Jerusalem near today's St. Andrew's Scottish Guest House, dating from the 7th Century BC. The Center for Biblical Hebrew reports the find:

> In 1979 two small rolled pieces of silver were discovered in a burial cave in Jerusalem, Israel. When the little scrolls were carefully unrolled, researchers found words from the Book of Numbers inscribed into the silver, written in characters from an ancient Hebrew script. The scrolls contain the text of the Priestly Benediction, which appears in Chapter 6 of Numbers, and which is still recited today by Jews in synagogue prayer throughout the world.

The priestly benediction is not only spoken in synagogues. It is the prayer with which Jewish parents often bless their children. And it is often spoken or sung as a benediction in Christian churches as well:

> *The LORD bless thee, and keep thee:*
> *The LORD make his face shine upon thee, and be gracious*
> *unto thee:*
> *The LORD lift up his countenance upon thee, and give thee peace.*

The Beginning of Temple Denial

Happily I was able to schedule an appointment with Dr. Barkay about the Temple Mount controversy. I went to his home, set in a quiet residential neighborhood on the outskirts of the city, one Sunday morning.

He was then, and remains today, in the midst of the project of a lifetime—sifting through tons of rubble that was illicitly dug up on the Temple Mount by the Muslim Waqf—official custodians of the Temple Mount under Israeli authority—and stealthily dumped into a landfill. The truckloads of debris contain immeasurable historical treasures.

"So what is the background of Temple Denial?" I asked Professor Barkay. "When did it begin? How did it become popularized?"

He shook his head, and took a deep breath. "This idea of Temple Denial," he began, "this denial of the historical, the spiritual, the archeological connections of the Jews to the Temple Mount is something new. There was always talk about the temple of Solomon in Jerusalem—called the 'praise of Jerusalem'—in Arabic literature, in Islamic literature. This new idea of Temple Denial is due to the Arabic fear of Jewish aspirations connected to the Temple Mount. It is part of something I call the 'Cultural Intifada.'"

Dr. Barkay went on to explain to me that the Temple Mount has been under the rule of Islam since 638, when the Caliph Omar and the Prophet's armies conquered Jerusalem a short time after Mohammad's death. Other than during a brief period of Crusader rule, during the last of the 11th and part of the 12th century, the Temple Mount remains under Muslim rule until this very day.

"I have here," he motioned toward a shelf of books, "Muslim booklets published from the first half of the 20th century, by the Islamic Trust. They mention the existence of the Temple upon the Temple Mount. Perhaps they stress the Islamic history of the Temple Mount. But they do not deny the existence of the temple."

Barkay explained that a change took place not so long ago in the 1990s, "...in the think tanks surrounding President Bill Jefferson Clinton in Washington DC." He said that in the years leading up to Arafat's denial of the Temple's existence, there were certain scholars in America that "...understood that the Temple Mount is the crux of the problem of the Middle East conflict. They thought that if they could find a way to work out a future agreement on the subject of the Temple Mount, then the entire 'Hercules Knot' (the Middle East conflict) could be solved, and the question of 'Whose is Palestine?' could be answered."

These think tanks decided that if there could be "split sovereignty" on the Temple Mount then split sovereignty could also be achieved over the entire land of Palestine. "So they suggested that in a future agreement, the Temple Mount would be split horizontally," Barkay continued with a wry smile, "That is to say that whatever is above ground, the part that includes the shrines of the Muslims, that would be under Palestinian sovereignty. Whatever is underground, which would include the remnants of the Temple of the Jews, would be under Israeli sovereignty."

He paused briefly and took a sip of water. Then he continued,

It's a brilliant idea, an excellent idea, but totally idiotic from the point of view of practicality. You cannot have a building standing with its foundations in another country. You cannot have a building with the infrastructure and the plumbing in another country. And you cannot have sovereignty on the sub-ground without having accessibility to the sub-ground because the accessibility is from above ground. The whole thing was stupid. But this idea, which was leaked to the Islamic Waqf, led them to carry out excavations in different parts of the Temple Mount and to clear many of the subterranean cavities.

The Temple Mount is honeycombed with more than 50 different cavities, holes, passageways and cisterns. Some of them have been explored, others have not. They are filled with earth that is literally saturated with very valuable archeological materials. But in the 1990s, illicit building activities—"I wouldn't call them excavations," Barkay remarks—did enormous damage. "The fear, the fear of anything representing a Jewish presence on the Temple Mount drove them mad," he concludes.

While Dr. Barkay took a phone call, I glanced around and noticed that I was facing a fanciful depiction of the Prophet Mohammad seated upon a very elegant horse, soaring above the Jerusalem landscape, a rendering of the Prophet's mythological journey to heaven—the *Miraj*—during which he passed through Jerusalem. The Persian engraving would be, of course, a scandal in the eyes of many Sunni Muslims today, an unholy image of the Prophet Mohammad. Nonetheless it illustrates the Muslims' justification for possessing the Temple Mount, which they call the "Noble Sanctuary."

In Sura 17:1, the Koran says, "Glory be to Him who made His servant [Mohammed] go by night from the Sacred Mosque to the farthest [or remotest] Mosque." There has always seemed to be wide agreement that the "Sacred Mosque" is located in Mecca. The farthest, or most remote Mosque wasn't so easily identified, at least not at first.

Some Muslim scholars initially thought that the "farthest mosque" was in Medina. A few years later, it was said to be in Jerusalem. Today, as the story goes, Mohammed—perhaps in a dream or vision, or perhaps in a real journey—traveled to heaven on a winged horse named Buraq (or Barack). Along the way they stopped at the Jerusalem mosque where a ladder was lowered from heaven to take Mohammad to a meeting with Abraham, Isaac, Joseph, Moses and Jesus. Afterwards horse and prophet returned to Jerusalem. There, Mohammad's footprint is said to remain on the stone of Mount Moriah, where, according to the book of Genesis, Abraham bound his son Isaac and prepared to sacrifice him. Muslims, of course, say it wasn't Isaac who was rescued from sacrifice in the first place. It was his half-brother Ishmael, the Arab Patriarch.

In any case, Mount Moriah is, today, enclosed beneath the Dome of the Rock. Only Muslims have access to it. Jews and Christians are prohibited.

I remembered my visits around the Plaza, walking across the broad pavement crowned by the golden Dome. Whatever glimpse of glory may have appeared there in days gone by, in light of today's

religious restrictions and the constant surveillance, little sense of
the sacred remains today. The area incorporates a few scattered
Muslim worship-related sites, such as fountains for ritual washing,
and the rather drab Al-Aqsa Mosque.

I only recall seeing a few people, mostly veiled women and unsmiling policemen, framed by scattered trees and bushes. Nowhere
did I see a third edifice, which I'd heard about—the al-Marwani
Mosque. I later found out that I hadn't seen it because the gigantic
structure, located in the southeast corner of the Temple Mount
Plaza, is subterranean. Today, the al-Marwani Mosque is said to
accommodate more than 7,000 people.

Illegal Excavations, Hidden Treasures

Dr. Barkay provided background information about the Al-Aqsa
structure, which Muslims claim was a mosque before the time
of the Crusaders. He explained that its origins lie in the Second
Temple period. Herod the Great built the Temple Mount platform
on a series of vaults supported by pillars. The terrain beneath the
Dome of the Rock is solid stone. But the southeast area is hollow
and has suffered extensively during seismic events. The last large-
scale restorations there took place under the Fatimids, who ruled
from Cairo, after a series of earthquakes in the 11th Century.

"There are quite solid hints in the literature of the existence of
an early Christian church there, marking the place where St. James
was killed in the 1st Century. The place is more Christian than
Muslim. I don't understand why Christians aren't more interested."

The Al-Aqsa building was called "Solomon's Stables" by the
Crusaders, who stabled their horses there. Barkay points out with
a slight grin, "It was not built as stables and it was not built by
Solomon. Otherwise the name 'Solomon's Stables' is okay."

In 1996, the Muslim Waqf began a huge and highly controversial reconstruction project, digging out and enlarging the
al-Marwani Mosque beneath Al-Aqsa. Then, in November 1999,
the Waqf asked permission from the Israeli government for an

emergency exit leading from the al-Marwani Mosque.

"The Prime Minister at that time was Ehud Barak, and as usual he didn't consult with anybody else," Barkay recalled. "He gave them permission. But instead of an emergency exit they created a main entrance to the building—a monumental entrance. For that entrance they dug a pit 40 meters in length, 12 meters in depth. They carried it out with bulldozers in the most destructive manner possible—that of an elephant in a china store. The work on that place should have been done carefully, not with bulldozers. They removed 400 truckloads of earth."

"And that's what you began to sift through?" I asked him. "How did that project begin?"

"It is a simple story. I was here in my home, sitting at my dining table when one of my students appeared. He poured out on the dining table some finds that were collected from that rubble. And he asked me, 'What do you say about this?' That's what drove me to get interested in the subject. But at first we couldn't get a license from the Israeli Antiquities Authority. That took a few years."

Thousands of Archeological Findings

According to Barkay, the sifting of the material from the Temple Mount is very significant because it amounts to a black hole in archeological history. Israel is one of the most excavated places in the world, and it has been researched and studied continuously since the 1850s. But although the Temple Mount was surveyed by British explorers Charles Wilson and Charles Warren between 1867 and 1870, it was never excavated. No archeological findings have been published about the Temple Mount. Therefore, ironically, the destructive digging and wanton removal of earth from the Temple Mount in the 1990s has provided a new and rare opportunity.

"At least it enables us to look at the soil," the archeologist shrugged, "although everything comes from a very disturbed context. But we know it comes from the Temple Mount. And we have tens of thousands of finds."

These finds have altered the historic understanding of the area's history—unprecedented discoveries that cover approximately 15,000 years. The volunteers who have been sifting through the debris have found Stone Age flint implements. They have discovered pre-Israelite material. Bronze Age pottery. Two Egyptian scarabs. And several seals and seal impressions.

One very significant find is that of a *bulla*, a clay lump with a seal impression upon it, which is about 2,600 years old and dates from the First Temple Period. It bears the name of an official, Gadaliyahu son of Immer. The Immer family is recorded in the Bible, in the 20th chapter of the book of Jeremiah, verse 1. Barkay says, "Most probably the brother of Gadaliyahu is mentioned, a priestly man named 'Pashur son of Immer.' He is introduced as the man in charge of the Temple."

Findings from the time of Solomon's Temple until the 20th Century illuminate the raging conflicts of passing civilizations. Barkay goes on to say,

> We have enormous quantities of war artifacts: we have lead slingshots of the Seleucid armies in the battles of Judas Maccabaeus, we have arrowheads of the army of Nebuchadnezzar, who destroyed the first temple. We have arrowheads of the Hellenistic period. We have one arrowhead bearing distinguishing markings of having been shot by a catapult machine. Those machines were only used by the armies of Titus in 70 AD in the destruction of the 2nd Temple. We have stone slingshots, we have spearheads, and we have medieval arrowheads from the Crusader conquest of the Temple Mount. We have all different kinds and types of war artifacts. There are even bullets from both the Turkish army and the British army in the First World War.

Other findings on the Temple Mount—jewelry, coins, pottery shards and architectural fragments—provide specific details of human life spanning several millennia. Some of these materials date back to the 10th century BC, the time of David and Solomon and the reign of the Judean Kings. There is abundant material from the early Christian days. This is very significant, according to Barkay, because most historical texts state that the churches moved to the Church of the Holy Sepulcher after it was built (it dates back to at least the 4th Century), and thereafter the Temple Mount was neglected and became a garbage heap. But these recent finds reveal a new history, based on archeological evidence.

"We have fragments of capitals from church buildings," Barkay describes the Christian artifacts. "We have remnants of chancel screens that separated the presbytery from the nave of the church. We have large bronze weights for weighing gold coins from the Christian era. We have to rethink: What was the role of the Temple Mount in the time of early Christianity? Was it a garbage heap? Or is that biased history? I think that history was ideological."

Of particular interest to archeologists are bones, and Barkay reports that large quantities of animal bones have been found on the Temple Mount. "Bones are very important. We have pig bones, which had to have come from pagan or Christian times." One example of these bones' importance lies in a famous Jewish tale. Dr. Barkay explains, "We also have bones of foxes. And that is interesting because in the Talmud we have a story about foxes on the Temple Mount, which until recently I thought was a legend...."

In Defense of History

Foxes or no foxes, and despite the masses of evidence to the contrary, Temple Denial seems to be a growing phenomenon. It continues to spread in Europe and America, led by seemingly strange bedfellows—revisionist, hard-left academics and Islamist political activists. Barkay is appalled by "...the very tragic harnessing of politics in order to change history. It is not a different interpretation of historical events or archeological evidence. This is something major. This is part of what I call the Cultural Intifada.

Just as we have armed attempts of terror there is also cultural terror. Cultural terror attempts to erase any historical or religious or other cultural linkage between non-Muslims and this land. And that certainly includes the Temple Mount." He concludes,

> Temple Denial in general is something more dangerous and more serious than Holocaust denial. Why? Because for the Holocaust still today there are living witnesses. There are photographs, there are archives, there are the soldiers who released the prisoners, there are testimonies from the Nazis themselves. There were trials, a whole series of them, starting with Nuremberg. There are people who survived the Holocaust still among us. Concerning the Temple there are no people among us who remember. Still, you have to dismiss the evidence of Flavius Josephus, you have to dismiss the evidence of the Mishnah, of the Talmud, you have to dismiss the writings of Roman and Greek historians who mention the Temple of Jerusalem, and you have to dismiss the Bible. That is, I think, too much. It is too much.

Like the Archangel Michael warring with the Prince of Persia, a mighty struggle continues between truth and lies, between yesterday and today, between inspiring religious vision and strong-armed political manipulation. The battleground in question is a tiny, bloodstained wedge of soil—the nation of Israel—and perhaps the most salient symbol of that nation is the Temple Mount Plaza, where the celebrated Temples—constructed by Solomon and Herod—once reigned as the House of God, and thus the holiest sites in Judaism. This life-and-death wrestling match is unlikely to be finished until the End of Days.

In practical terms, a large portion of Israel's Jewish population seems not to be particularly concerned about the Temple Mount. More than a few rabbinical edicts since 1967 have declared that religious Jews should avoid the entire Plaza for reasons of ritual purity. These serve as a caution to many who long to pray openly there, or more drastically, hope to rebuild the Temple. Some religious Jews, however, persist in praying on the Temple Mount anyway—especially during such observances as Tisha B'Av. They do so as a statement of their respect for the historic sacred space as well as their right.

Meanwhile, the groups who focus on the construction of the Third Temple have already created recreated precise reproductions of the Biblical worship implements necessary for the resumption of ancient rites of worship, including animal sacrifice. These faithful zealots seem outnumbered by other believers, however, who are convinced that the Third Temple will be made possible only by the Messiah's appearance—or for Christians, his re-appearance. In fact, biblical Christians can be found in both camps.

The leftist secular community has long feared the explosiveness of Muslim-Jewish confrontations regarding the Temple Mount. Some would just as soon be rid of the Temple Mount as have to deal with it. Meanwhile, conservative secular Jews are disgusted by what they see as political capitulation to the Arab Waqf's demands, and to the insistence that the site is holy only to Muslims. Religious or not, for these Zionists, refusal to demand freedom of worship on the Temple Mount is just more evidence of appalling fecklessness on the part of successive Israeli governments.

But Temple denial is another matter. The idea that there was never a Jewish Temple on the Temple Mount would be laughable to most informed observers if it weren't of such unholy intention. Amusement quickly gives way to flashing eyes and angry words. Even those Jews who have no interest in visiting the Temple Mount are incensed by Muslim attempts to rewrite history, which aim to deny all Jewish connections to the land of Israel. The Temple Mount debate has become a microcosm of those escalating efforts.

This issue, and innumerable others, find the average Israeli suspended between the past and the present, death threats and the embrace of life, outrageous lies and belief in ultimate truth.

A glimpse into the conflicted hearts of those who bear the scars of grave losses while clinging to hope is captured by the modern Israeli poet Yehuda Amichai (1924-2000) in his poem "Lying in Wait for Happiness."

On the broad steps leading down to the Western Wall
A beautiful woman came up to me: You don't remember me,
I'm Shoshana in Hebrew. Something else in other languages.
All is vanity.
Thus she spoke at twilight standing between the destroyed
and the built, between the light and the dark.
Black birds and white birds changed places
With the great rhythm of breathing.
The flash of a tourist's camera lit my memory too:
What are you doing here between the promised and the forgotten,
between the hoped for and the imagined
With your lovely face like an advertisement for God
And your soul rent and torn like mine?
She answered me: My soul is rent and torn like yours
But it is beautiful because of that.
Like fine lace.

CHAPTER FIVE

FIGHTING APARTHEID

ate fall 2006, and the evening breeze grew colder with
each passing week. I'd been in the country only a few
months, and no one had warned me about the Jerusalem chill that penetrates to the bone. My apartment, so
pleasantly cool even in the summer's heat or during the *Sharav*—a
dust laden, scorching desert wind—was now difficult to keep warm.
Built of stone, with little or no insulation and high ceilings, the old
structure wasn't easy to heat, and the corner where I worked was
unlivable without the help of an ancient red-hot space heater that
always smelled like it was about to burst into flame.

Two entirely unrelated things became more or less ubiquitous
in early December: rows of beautifully frosted donuts appeared, as
did Jimmy Carter's somewhat less-appealing profile. The donuts
were a wonderful surprise to me. I had actually found myself in a
nation that celebrated a religious holiday with, among other things,
jelly-filled donuts! Their real name is *sufganiyot,* and they herald
the arrival of Hanukkah in bakeries, markets and even in restaurants. The ones I sampled were marvelously fresh and juicy. As yet,
their connection to the Festival of Lights remains unclear to me,
but I wholeheartedly approve.

As for Jimmy Carter's omnipresent profile, it appeared in the
windows of bookstores all around town, heralding the arrival of his
best-selling book *Palestine: Peace Not Apartheid*, which he was pro-
moting on a widely publicized—and much discussed—book tour.

The first I heard about Carter's book was in an email from a
Jewish-American woman who was a great friend of the Palestin-

ian people, and who would describe herself as an avowed leftist. She had conducted extensive interviews with women in the disputed territories, had lived in Israel for prolonged period over many decades, and had long been on the "peacenik" side of Israeli politics. However, she wrote that she had found herself unexpectedly defending Israel at her women's book club, so strident were the attacks in Carter's narrative. She wrote, "I know that his accusations are unjust and that he is not telling the truth when he uses the word 'apartheid.' He also fails to acknowledge the damage the 2nd Intifada has done to Palestinian-Israel relations."

Not long after I read her rather surprising email—I would have guessed that she agreed with Carter—I heard from two other Jewish friends of mine, one in America and one in England. They also related how disheartening the book was, how depressed they felt seeing its accusatory title on display in bookstores, and how angered they were about its inaccurate and distorted message.

At the time I hadn't read the book. Carter was a politician for whom I had voted, then had pitied, then finally had come to thoroughly dislike. The title of his book had surprised me in its exaggeration, but otherwise I hadn't paid a lot of attention to what seemed to be yet another of his attacks on Israel's demand to defend itself. But before long, his misuse of the hot-button word "apartheid" was gaining serious traction among book reviewers.

Hanukkah Festivities

At a Hanukkah gathering at the Foreign Press Club I was reintroduced to a man I'd barely met before—David Parsons, the editor of the *Jerusalem Post's Christian Edition*. He, his wife and son were at the party and Parsons asked me if I would like to attend another event later that evening. "There's a candle lighting ceremony at the International Fellowship of Christians and Jews," he told me. "Rabbi Eckstein and Malcolm Hedding with be there…"

"Who is Malcolm Hedding?" I couldn't place the name.

"He's the Executive Director of International Christian

Embassy at Jerusalem—the ICEJ," David Parsons explained. "It would be good for you to meet him."

As I walked back to my apartment from the Foreign Press offices, I realized that I knew less about Hanukkah than any of the other Jewish holidays. Somehow I'd always had the impression that Hanukkah was a sort of latter-day Jewish alternative to Christmas. That, it turned out, was far from accurate. In fact, I was surprised to learn that Hanukah's history goes back to the Second Century BC.

The story behind the holiday took place at the time of a Jewish revolt against the Seleucid Empire and its despised dictator Antiochus Ephiphanes, who then ruled over the land of Israel. The revolt was occasioned by Antiochus' attempt to forbid the practices of Judaism. The revolutionaries, led by the family of Judas Maccabeus, succeeded and managed to restore Jewish independence and control of the 2nd Temple.

An unexpected miracle occurred when Judas Maccabeus cleansed and rededicated the Jewish Temple, which had been desecrated by Antiochus when he sacrificed a pig on the altar.

At the time of the rededication, because of the war's upheaval, there was just enough sacred olive oil left for one day's use; it would take eight days to prepare more. Hanukkah is called the Festival of Lights because that tiny supply of consecrated oil miraculously burned for eight days—it lasted until more was pressed and blessed. The hero of the story, Judas Maccabeus, called for an eight-day celebration—the Festival of Lights—because of the miracle of the oil.

As I walked, I noticed harp-shaped arrangements of blue lights bedecking Jerusalem's largest streets including King David and Emek Refaim. Thanks to those lights, along with the frigid night air blowing in my face, I couldn't help but hear "It's beginning to look a lot like Christmas…" playing in my mind. In actual fact, there was no sign of Christmas anywhere, although merchants displayed small gift items on tables outside their shops, the wine store offered tastings of Israeli wines, and people seemed to be in a celebratory mood.

Later that evening I arrived at the reception, which was exceptionally elegant. It was held in Rabbi Eckstein's opulent headquarters, and was well supplied with excellent hors d'oeuvres. And of course there were sufganiyot by the dozens, piled on silver trays in small tempting towers. This seemed to be remarkably in keeping with Jewish historian Flavius Josephus's description of the first Hanukah holiday in his account, *Jewish Antiquities XII*.

> Now Judas celebrated the festival of the restoration of the sacrifices of the temple for eight days, and omitted no sort of pleasures thereon; but he feasted them upon very rich and splendid sacrifices; and he honored God, and delighted them by hymns and psalms. Nay, they were so very glad at the revival of their customs, when, after a long time of intermission, they unexpectedly had regained the freedom of their worship, that they made it a law for their posterity, that they should keep a festival, on account of the restoration of their temple worship, for eight days. And from that time to this we celebrate this festival, and call it Lights. I suppose the reason was, because this liberty beyond our hopes appeared to us; and that thence was the name given to that festival.

Most of the people at the reception knew each other. One of the more interesting characters in attendance was Eli Moyal, the then-mayor of Sderot—the small Israeli city with the unfortunate situation of having been the closest target of literally thousands of mortars and short-range rockets fired from the Gaza Strip. Since I'd visited Sderot during my first days in Israel, I was fascinated to hear him relate the story of his introduction to rocket fire from Gaza in 2002.

Not long after taking office he'd heard an explosion, followed by the sound of sirens. Minutes later a rocket crashed into his garden. There had been some 4,000 attacks since then. Moyal was an engaging personality, familiar to anyone who followed the Israeli news, and he embodied the story of his small town. Three years later, he famously resigned as mayor because the Israeli government had refused to take action against the rocket-launching terrorists. "I don't want to be around when a rocket hits a kindergarten and kills 20 children," he told Voice of Israel Radio. "I have been losing sleep over such a scenario for years."

I later found out for myself that he wasn't the only sleepless person in rocket range, as we'll see in the pages that follow.

During the reception, David Parsons introduced me to his colleague Malcolm Hedding. I realized that I'd seen him before, during a gala Feast of Tabernacles event in Ein Gedi, by the shore of the Dead Sea, but we hadn't met. I discovered that he was from South Africa, and had spent most of his life there.

"So what do you think about Jimmy Carter's book?" I asked. "You must know something about apartheid."

"I know a great deal about apartheid," he replied with a steely glint in his eyes, "I had to flee South Africa because I was the pastor of a church with a partly black congregation."

"I can only guess that you don't think of Israel as an apartheid state?"

"No, it most certainly is not!" he said firmly, his jaw tightening. "It's a far cry from it."

"I'd like to know more about your situation—about having to flee South African because of apartheid. Have you written about it?"

He shook his head. "No, I haven't told that story yet."

Thinking of Jimmy Carter's profile in every bookstore window, I asked him if perhaps it wasn't time he did. He agreed to an interview.

A couple of days later, I found my way to the Christian Embassy's headquarters in the German Colony. I was greeted by a stately Arab-style mansion, with Israeli flags fluttering in the wind and a solid security gate. We walked to a recording studio—complete with a technician and professional equipment—and began to talk about Malcolm Hedding's perspective on apartheid and Israel. He had organized his thoughts carefully, and he started out by speaking about his father.

Reflections on an Apartheid State

Guy Usher Hedding, Malcolm's father, came from a long line of British émigrés to South Africa, and had managed a gold mine. He grew up on a trading station in the Eastern Cape, and his first contact with society was with the Xhosa-speaking tribal community. He learned their strange-sounding "click" language and could speak it fluently; with an ear for African languages, he went on to master many others as well.

Most of the miners who worked for him were black Africans, and because Guy Hedding could speak so many tribal languages, he was able to communicate better than the other white supervisors, and thus he rapidly rose to become a mine manager. Soon he was in charge of all the African mineworkers. They esteemed him because he always treated them with dignity and respect. In fact, he was so beloved by the blacks that they twice crowned him—literally—an African King.

After World War II, the Nationalist Party swept to power in South Africa and apartheid was galvanized into a political system. The architect of apartheid, in its Calvinist Nationalist Party form, was a religious man—a Dutch Reformed Minister, Daniel Francois Malan. He had the dubious distinction of being South Africa's first Apartheid Prime Minister.

Hedding explained,

The Dutch Calvinists' platform was a false notion, a deviant form of Replacement Theology based on the biblical injunction that Christian believers ought to keep themselves separate from the heathens. You can see who the heathens were—the blacks. And of course the righteous people of the kingdom of

God were the whites. So they built this system, vindicating it theologically…the government was a limited democracy, in the sense that it was a democracy for whites only.

Unlike his father, Malcolm Hedding took up theology rather than mining. Once he was ordained as a pastor, he began to attack apartheid from a biblical Christian position. "I tried always to show my congregation why it was wrong and unacceptable, and why they should distance themselves from it. I tried to help them see that if they couldn't change the political system, they should at least treat people of color with absolute dignity and respect and love and courtesy."

Eventually Hedding and his family moved to Durban. By this time he had a national ministry and he was traveling widely in response to frequent invitations to preach throughout South Africa. Hedding began to attack apartheid in more public way. "And that's when things got hot," he told me. He went on to say,

Suddenly this thing came out of the closet, so to speak. I began to take the apartheid system apart theologically on a more public platform. The more I did this the more I got requests to speak, and before long I was actually holding seminars on this issue, even at hotels for business groups. But the more I began to press the boundaries, the more alarmed the Bureau of State Security got.

In 1986 an infiltrator turned up at Hedding's church from the Special Branch—the government's top security agency. The young man's assignment was to gather as much incriminating information as possible about Hedding's anti-apartheid stance. But during one of Hedding's sermons, the spy unexpectedly found himself convinced that the message of the Christian Gospel was true. In response, he expressed a newfound belief in Jesus. He also deeply regretted and repented his intention to report on Hedding to the authorities.

During a private meeting with Hedding the following Tuesday, the erstwhile spy told Hedding, "I want to confess that I'm actually a freelance journalist from the Bureau of State Security, and to let you know you are in big trouble. In fact, I suggest you get out of the country as fast as you can. If you don't, they will detain you without trial, and what will happen to your wife and your family? I have been a party to everything you have said about the system."

The short version of the story is that Malcolm Hedding packed up his family and fled to Israel, where friends had invited them to stay. They returned to South Africa once the government collapsed. But by the time he went back, Hedding was preaching about Biblical Zionism from the same Bible he had used to attack the apartheid system. Both subjects were, for him, theological issues. In his view, both the affirmation of apartheid and the attacks on Zionism were based on the misapplication of holy scriptures for unholy purposes.

In 2000, the Christian Embassy at Jerusalem's board of directors invited him back to Jerusalem. Today, he believes more than ever that his background in South Africa and his involvement with Israel have given him a deep understanding of the term "apartheid" and all it implies. He is visibly annoyed when he speaks of the issue.

> Calling Israel an "apartheid state" is absolute nonsense! The barrier fence and wall have nothing to do with apartheid and everything to do with Israel's self-defense. And they have been proven successful. There was no such barrier until the second *Intifada* where people were being murdered on the highways. And the rest of the country does not dehumanize its minority in the sense of apartheid. The issues are totally different.

> The so-called West Bank and Gaza are areas of dispute, which Israel acknowledges as such. And, as we know, Israel agreed under Barak to a solution, which was for us, astonishing— giving up most of East Jerusalem. There have been amazing

compromises made by the majority to facilitate the needs of the minority. The Palestinians have rejected them all.

According to Hedding, during the apartheid years, 170,000 people in South Africa held power over 40 million because of the undemocratic nature of the system. The majority black community was dehumanized and robbed of its dignity. In some cases they went through forced removals from their homes and neighborhoods simply because of their color.

It was a bitter irony that the August 2001 United Nations World Conference on Racism took place in Durban, South Africa. In the very heartland of some of the world's worst racism, and against the backdrop of the South African struggle against it, the conference trivialized the term "apartheid" by applying it to Israel. Nowadays, Jimmy Carter and Desmond Tutu have chosen a different backdrop. Hedding says, "They seize on the security barrier as a physical symbol of apartheid. If either of them has a picture taken in Israel, you can expect them to be posed in front of 'The Wall' because of its symbolism."

But he insists, "If you don't start from the theological foundation—which is what we did in South Africa—you can never address this thing honestly. You can't do it by pointing to symbols and things like the wall and the security check points and equating them with apartheid. The West makes the constant error in avoiding the theological nature of this conflict, instead trying to deal with it in a secular humanistic political context. They can never solve it because they won't own up to the truth that we are dealing with a conflict with Islam. I think they are being fundamentally dishonest."

I asked him what he would say to Bishop Tutu if given a chance.

"'What I would say is this," he replied: "'Desmond, of all people, you who unearthed the very foundations of the apartheid system and then knew exactly how to confront it, what are you doing today by resorting to this superficial analysis of the issue in Israel? Why are you ignoring totally the radical Islamic desire to totally dismantle the Jewish State? Why do you not have the honesty to get up and say it?'"

Carter's Controversial Book

Conversations with other friends in Israel that year expressed everything from dismay to disgust to disdain over Jimmy Carter and his book. In a café with Ruthie, in Petra's kitchen, in receptions with other Israelis I didn't know so well, there was a profound sense of injustice, concluded with, "So what else would you expect?" Said with a shrug, the flippant question actually reflects a Jewish expectation that they will, once again, be falsely accused—in this case, for building a self-protective wall.

Friends in Washington spoke of reports about money pouring into the Carter Center from sources that certainly mirrored his views. Besides Saudi princes, there were donors from Oman, the United Arab Emirates, Kuwait, Venezuela and OPEC.

At the time his book came out, Israelis weren't the only ones who were upset with Jimmy Carter. One of his colleagues at the Carter Center, Kenneth W. Stein, who had served as an aide and confidante for twenty-three years, and had accompanied Carter during several interviews with several Middle East leaders, resigned shortly after the book's release. He wrote in an email to friends and former students, which was later made public,

> President Carter's book on the Middle East, a title too inflammatory to even print, is not based on unvarnished analyses; it is replete with factual errors, copied materials not cited, superficialities, glaring omissions, and simply invented segments. Aside from the one-sided nature of the book, meant to provoke, there are recollections cited from meetings where I was the third person in the room, and my notes of those meetings show little similarity to points claimed in the book.

Being a former President does not give one a unique privilege to invent information or to unpack it with cuts, deftly slanted to provide a particular outlook.

Having little access to Arabic and Hebrew sources, I believe, clearly handicapped his understanding and analyses of how history has unfolded over the last decade. Falsehoods, if repeated often enough become meta-truths, and they then can become the erroneous baseline for shaping and reinforcing attitudes and for policy-making. The history and interpretation of the Arab-Israeli conflict is already drowning in half-truths, suppositions, and self-serving myths; more are not necessary.

By the time another year had passed, 14 members of a Carter Center advisory board had also resigned in protest of the book's contents and inflammatory title. The 14 explained their concerns in letters sent to fellow Board of Councilors members and to Carter. "We can no longer endorse your strident and uncompromising position. This is not the Carter Center or the Jimmy Carter we came to respect and support."

Yet, notwithstanding these protests, despite a broad array of terrible reviews, and in spite of widespread editorialized aversion to Jimmy Carter's bias against Israel, the word apartheid stuck. And it remains stuck today, a vilifying label slapped carelessly across Israel's international reputation. "Israel—The Apartheid State" headlines op-eds, defines protests, is scattered across blogs, punctuates obscene comments on websites and appears in news stories as if it were an undisputed fact. "Israeli Apartheid Week," complete with outrageous anti-Semitic speakers and demonstrations, is marked by Muslim Student Unions across university campuses around the world, especially in North America and Europe.

One unexpected voice has spoken out strongly against the apartheid allegations. Judge Richard Goldstone has hardly been seen as a friend of Israel, thanks to his report on Israeli's 2009

"Cast Lead" operation in Gaza, in which the Israel Defense Forces were accused of intentionally targeting civilians. Later, in a public retraction, Goldstone denied that his investigation had led to such a conclusion. Then in November 2011, Goldstone wrote an editorial in the *New York Times* about Israel and apartheid. His words were especially powerful because Goldstone is South African.

> In Israel, there is no apartheid. Nothing there comes close to the definition of apartheid under the 1998 Rome Statute: "Inhumane acts ... committed in the context of an institutionalized regime of systematic oppression and domination by one racial group over any other racial group or groups and committed with the intention of maintaining that regime." Israeli Arabs—20 percent of Israel's population—vote, have political parties and representatives in the Knesset and occupy positions of acclaim, including on its Supreme Court. Arab patients lie alongside Jewish patients in Israeli hospitals, receiving identical treatment…
>
> Jewish-Arab relations in Israel and the West Bank cannot be simplified to a narrative of Jewish discrimination. There is hostility and suspicion on both sides. Israel, unique among democracies, has been in a state of war with many of its neighbors who refuse to accept its existence. Even some Israeli Arabs, because they are citizens of Israel, have at times come under suspicion from other Arabs as a result of that longstanding enmity.

Still, as Nazi Joseph Goebbels famously proclaimed in so many words, *If you tell a lie big enough and keep repeating it, people will eventually come to believe it.* And every year a week of "Anti-Apartheid" events take place in countless colleges and universities around the Western world, where anti-Israel demonstrations continue to demonize the Jewish State in every imaginable way. They stridently accuse it, and its "evil Zionist" population, of innumerable varieties of hatreds—attitudes and behaviors that are virtually impossible to find in the land Israel of itself.

Shopping in Mixed Company

The Mamilla Mall is a recent and welcome addition to the Jerusalem cityscape. It is a modern, upscale collection of shops that attaches, by way of a broad staircase, to the Jaffa Gate and the Old City. Because weekends begin on Fridays in the Middle East, on Thursdays the open-air pedestrian walkways, shops and outdoor cafés are especially crowded with shoppers of all descriptions.

Late one spring morning I made my way to the Mamilla Mall. Weeks of clouds and rain had passed. A warm sun gleamed onto the pale-gold Jerusalem stone, providing a stunning backdrop to an unusually colorful and bustling scene.

I was about to have brunch with my friend Tova Leibovits; we were waiting to be seated on a terrace on which tables overlooking the Old City were in great demand. All at once the spot we had our eye on was snapped up by two chic young Arab women. Their heads were covered in designer scarves and their well-fitted jeans and accessories were upscale. They sat at a table next to an "ultra-Orthodox" Jewish family in their own distinctive attire. And next to them was a table full of middle-aged American tourists in cargo shorts, souvenir t-shirts, and a clutter of cameras, GPS gadgets and fanny-packs.

I glanced around and saw that no one was paying attention to the Muslim women or to the many Arab shoppers passing by on their way to the shops. Nor did anyone stare at the ultra-Orthodox Jews—men in black hats or black yarmulkes, women in long skirts, with wigs covering their hair. In Jerusalem, like nowhere else, you can figure out what people believe in by the way they dress. But no one around us seemed to notice or care what anyone else was wearing—or believing. For obvious reasons, Jimmy Carter's "Apartheid State," flashed into my mind.

It so happened that on that same night I was scheduled to have dinner with the Heddings—Malcolm and his wife Cheryl, their daughter Charmaine and her 10-year-old son Ethan. It had been a few years since my *Jerusalem Post* interview with Malcolm. I reminded him of it, and then described the scene at Mamilla and asked, "So could that have happened in South Africa during the apartheid years?"

"No way," he laughed. "Everything was separate. The blacks had separate toilets. Separate drinking fountains. Separate benches. In some places there was a curfew so they had to get out of sight and leave the town to the whites after sundown. It was like the American Deep South used to be."

"Could blacks eat in the same restaurant as whites?"

"Never! When we traveled with a black man who was part of our church, one of us had to go inside the restaurant and order take-out food so we could all eat together in the car. Otherwise he would have to eat alone."

On the way home, I suddenly remembered another vignette from Mamilla. I had rushed into the Mac cosmetic store to make a quick purchase before leaving. I was in a hurry and there was only one clerk—a pretty Jerusalem girl wearing rather dramatic makeup. She was assisting two fashion-forward Arab women in silk headscarves, stylish trousers and well-tailored jackets. The three were having an animated discussion—in English—about eye shadow and eyeliner colors. The only disagreement between them had to do with hues: Teal or olive green? Luminescent or matte? There was no way I was going to be waited on anytime soon. The clerk was trying out a new spring palette on one of them, testing the colors on her hands as she applied them. The three of them were chattering non-stop.

As I left, I encountered a group of African pilgrims whose iden-tical yellow caps told me they were from Nigeria. They burst into a Gospel song as they made their way to the Jaffa gate. People smiled and took their picture. An art display of Bible-story sculptures graced the plaza. Cell phones rang, horns honked on the nearby street, and people of every age and description laughed and talked and celebrated the glorious weather.

And so it was that March arrived in the charming and controversial city of Jerusalem, eternal capital of the land of Israel. Those of us who love the little Jewish State rejoiced in her goodness and beauty. Those who hate her were making preparations for the global 7th Annual Israel Anti-Apartheid Week.

No Jews in Palestine?

Seasons changed and Hanukkah lights returned once more, flickering in the windows of Jerusalem's houses and blazing in synagogues, small and large. There is a sacred quality to Hanukkah. Perhaps, for me, it's the absence of unwanted obligations; the overall lack of hustle and bustle. For Christians in America, there's much discussion about the tension between the spiritual significance of Christmas—the birth of Jesus as the long-awaited Messiah—and the demands of lavish gift-giving, expensive party preparations and, at times, over-the-top financial compulsions.

Like many Jewish holidays, Hanukkah celebrates a Jewish victory over a mighty foe determined to destroy Judaism and its believers. This similarity in holiday themes has resulted in the rather ironic summary of all such Jewish feasts: "They tried to kill us. They failed. Let's eat!" It is a time for candles, songs and food—including those beautiful, blessed donuts.

In 2010, Hanukkah began earlier than usual, at the beginning of December. Just a couple of weeks later, something else was illuminated besides the Jerusalem streets— something ugly and hateful. On December 25, Palestinian President Mahmoud Abbas declared emphatically to a group of reporters in Ramallah, "We have frankly said, and always will say: If there is an independent Palestinian state with Jerusalem as its capital, we won't agree to the presence of one Israeli in it."

For Israelis, so many with family links to the Holocaust, such statements recall the Third Reich's ultimate goal of *Judenrein*. Former Israeli Minister and Ambassador to the US Moshe Arens put it this way,

> The concept of removing all Jews from a certain region is surely repugnant to any person not prepared to deny somebody's rights on the grounds of his ethnic or religious origin. It brings back the worst memories of the tragedy that befell the Jewish people in World War II. When it is applied to a part of the Land of Israel it is also contrary to the very foundations of Zionism, a movement based on the right of Jews to settle and live in their land, a right that has received international recognition.

Statements by so-called moderate Palestinian leaders like Abbas defy logic: they accuse Israel of apartheid on one hand, and refuse to countenance a single Jew living in a Palestinian state on the other. More than 1.5 million Arabs live in Israel as Israeli citizens. As for the disputed territories, the constraints enforced by checkpoints and other limitations to movement are hardly racist—I am a blonde woman with an American passport and I have to wait in line too. These rules are entirely the result of security measures.

How will it end? What is the solution? Will there be another resounding victory for the people of Israel over their Arab foes? There have been a few in my lifetime, but the pressure has continued nonetheless, relentless and ever increasing. Considering the history of the Jewish people across the span of history, that is nothing new; the age-old hostility to Jews—whether as individuals or a nation—remains a terrible reality.

In every ancient holiday story, the people of Israel have triumphed through human valor but also with the help of God on their side. Maybe we should remember to address our appeals for justice towards Heaven's throne as well as pounding on the doors of earthly powers. The saying in Israel, "Work as if everything depended on you and pray as if everything depended on God" has merit. In which case, lighting sacred candles in the window for the peace of Jerusalem shouldn't be delayed until Hanukkah's happy return. No need to wait till Christmas, either.

CHAPTER SIX

UNSETTLING MISCONCEPTIONS

My friend Ruthie Blum describes herself as a right-wing Bohemian. While the rest of us women of a certain age may gleam quietly in the candlelight, she sparkles and shines. She loves unusual clothes, flashy earrings and the occasional cigarette. She's pretty, has a frequent and contagious laugh and loves gossip. She's an original personality if ever there was one.

Ruthie is also irrepressibly outspoken about Israel's place in the world. Her famous father, Norman Podhoretz, is sometimes described as the "grandfather of all neo-cons." He was Editor-in-Chief of the prestigious *Commentary* magazine for decades before retiring. Today John Podhoretz, Norman's son and Ruthie's brother, fills that same role at *Commentary*.

Norman, however, fell from political grace in Ruthie's eyes during the Gaza disengagement in 2005. At that time, 8000 Jewish "settlers" were forcibly removed from the Gaza Strip thanks to a unilateral decision made by the Ariel Sharon government (more about that in Chapter 8). Like many Israelis, both religious and simply patriotic, Ruthie was outraged by the disengagement, while her father was pragmatic about its strategic value. Today, although Norman's views have mellowed somewhat, still both of them agree to disagree when the subject is raised, which thankfully doesn't happen all that often.

Ruthie's living room reflected her Bohemian tastes. It was furnished in scarlet and gold pillows, Persian carpets, countless candles and wall-to-wall books. It was there that she and I listened together to President Barack Obama's famous "Cairo Speech" in early June 2009. We were both aghast at the tone of the speech, its poorly researched statements about Islamic history and its apologetic tone vis-à-vis American-Muslim relations. We were also taken aback by the President of the United States' outspoken criticism of Israel—America's most loyal Middle East ally—and his dictatorial tone on the subject of Israel settlements.

Once Obama finally fell silent, we finished our wine and hashed the speech over in dispirited tones. After a pause in the conversation Ruthie said, "I'm going to write my father an email and see what he thinks!"

I was renting Ruthie's downstairs studio apartment for the summer, while I waited for my own apartment to be renovated in Jerusalem. So the next morning, when I saw Ruthie, the first thing she said was, "Well, I heard back from my father."

"So what did he think? Did he think you and I were overreacting?"

She shook her head. "No. To be honest I'm surprised. I had written to him, 'Look, I know you're going to say I'm being too hard on Obama, but I think he went way too far in trying to placate the Muslims.'"

"So what did your father say?"

"He said, 'You're wrong, Ruthie. For once I don't think you've gone far enough!'" She laughed. "Now that's a first!" she added, then read to me the rest of his email:

"I don't think he was just trying to flatter and appease the Muslim world," he wrote. "I think President Obama's speech was a declaration of war against Israel."

The Settlement Debate

In the days preceding President Obama's Cairo speech, he and Secretary of State Hillary Clinton had placed the words "Israeli settlements" on the front pages of global newspapers. In the administration's rush to revive the Middle East peace process,

Obama and Clinton had demanded a freeze on settlements, including "natural growth." To the ears of many Israelis, "no natural growth" amounts to a ban on childbearing, mother-in-law suites and playrooms for the kids.

Clinton put it this way: "The Obama administration wants a complete halt in the growth of Jewish settlements in Palestinian territory, with no exceptions." Meanwhile Obama, in his Cairo speech—after explaining Israel's modern day existence only in terms of the Holocaust, and never once referring to the Jews' historical claim to their land, biblical, historical or otherwise—had his own hard line: "The United States does not accept the legitimacy of continued Israeli settlements. This construction violates previous agreements and undermines efforts to achieve peace. It is time for these settlements to stop."

Of course, arguments about settlements are nothing new. Even in California, I had heard the words "settlers" and "settlements" for years but had only a vague idea of what they actually meant. What, precisely, is a settlement? At the time of Obama's first declarations, the definition of this hot-button political term was more than a little confusing to me.

During my first year in Israel, I was invited by an American friend to visit her son and his family. He is a rabbi in Kfar Etzion—part of the Gush Etzion settlement bloc (population 60,000). This rabbi, his wife and five children live in an attractive home, situated in what a Californian like me would call a "gated community."

The Kfar Etzion community existed before the War of Independence in 1948. During that war, it was overrun by Arab forces and most of its population was massacred. The area remained under Arab rule, but the survivors of the massacre vowed to return. They did so following the Six Day War in 1967.

Today, along with its brave history, Kfar Etzion boasts a population of 400, two matching synagogues—one Sephardic and one Ashkenazi—and a deeply communal spirit. Granted, the heavily armed guard at the gate bears no similarity to the senior citizens wearing badges and smiles, happily waving at cars entering California gated communities. Meanwhile, an IDF base bristles with weaponry just across the valley. But my mental image of Wild West outlaws squatting on illegal land bore no resemblance to the child-friendly gardens and leafy streets I saw, and the peace-minded modern Orthodox residents I met.

Sometime in 2008, I got to know a family from Ariel—friends of friends—whose daughter, a promising jazz singer, frequently performs in Tel Aviv. These folks are anything but religious settlers. They are, in fact, self-described agnostics. They moved to Ariel decades ago when it was the only place where they could afford to buy a flat or raise a family. The father is a brooding Holocaust survivor who lost more than 40 family members in the concentration camps and made *aliya* from the Balkans as a young man. The mother is a pretty and cheerful sabra. They have three daughters, one in the IDF, and earn their living in the hi-tech industry.

Then came my very closest look at a settlement—I moved into one. At the time, Ruthie lived in Har Adar—a lovely and quiet suburb of Jerusalem, verdant with flowers and trees, blessed with spectacular views of Jerusalem and of surrounding Arab villages. Har Adar, although barely across the Green Line (The Green Line is the 1949 Armistice line following Israel's War of Independence), is also a settlement since it was built after the 1967 War on land that was secured during that conflict. I arrived for the summer just in time to hear Obama's demands that all settlement growth must cease. As fate would have it, I had just increased Har Adar's population by one.

Former Ambassador to the UN and President of the Jerusalem Center for Public Affairs Dore Gold has written extensively about settlement issues. In his 2009 essay "U.S. Policy on Israeli Settlements" he writes,

"Israeli settlements in the territories captured in the 1967 war date back more than 40 years," "They began as military and agricultural outposts that were located for the most part in strategically significant areas of the West Bank, which Israel planned to eventually claim. These settlements were also situated in areas from which Jews had been evicted during the 1948-49 war [for example Kfar Etzion]..." Gold continues,

> Many observers are surprised to learn that settlement activity was not defined as a violation of the 1993 Oslo Accords or their subsequent implementation agreements. During the secret negotiations leading up to the signing of Oslo, Yasser Arafat instructed his negotiators to seek a "settlement freeze," but Prime Minister Yitzhak Rabin and Foreign Minister Shimon Peres refused to agree to Arafat's demand. Nonetheless, Arafat agreed to the Oslo Accords despite the lack of a settlement freeze.

The Israeli government never officially annexed the areas captured in 1967. Nor were the Arab residents incorporated as citizens. As David Ha'Ivri has written in the Jerusalem Post, "Acting schizophrenically, Israel refrained from annexing the area captured from Jordan, while it invested major resources in developing and settling Jews in communities built throughout the region."

Settlements and Outposts

Over the years following 1967, other settlements were erected deeper in Judea and Samaria for various reasons, including ideological ones, many of them in an effort by religious Zionists to re-plant Jewish roots in such biblical places as Shiloh, Beit El and Efrata. It was not until the Jimmy Carter administration that the US State Department declared settlements to be in violation of international law. And, as a testament to its imprudence, Carter's policy was reversed by all of his successors, who deemed the settlements problematic but certainly not illegal.

How would you describe a settlement? I think of a village with uniformly white walls and red tile roofs, distinguishable from the surrounding towns by the absence of a mosque. But that's not the only description that applies. From rundown trailers to wisteria-covered villas, the size, character, appearance and reputation of the various cities, towns, regional councils and neighborhoods labeled "settlements" vary significantly. There is, however, one kind of settlement that really seems to embody the gun-toting, Wild West stereotype of "Israeli settlers" that inhabit the world's imagination. These are called "outposts," and they are populated by the most unruly of all the settlers—the Hilltop Youth.

Move, Run and Grab...

In 1998, on the eve of the Wye Plantation talks that were to divide up the West Bank, then-cabinet minister Ariel Sharon famously told the settlement movement that "everybody has to move, run and grab as many hilltops as they can to enlarge the settlements, because everything we take now will stay ours... Everything we don't grab will go to them,"—"them" being the Palestinian Arabs.

Inspired by this command from their old hero and by the religious vision of a Greater Israel—based on biblically defined borders—a band of religious nationalists began to occupy the barren, windy hilltops of Samaria.

The first such Samarian hilltop outpost was established by Avri Ran, a settler from Itamar, a settlement community that overlooks the ancient city of Shechem (today's Nablus). From Itamar, Ran sent his sons to plant outposts on the successive peaks of a ridge running eastward down towards the Jordan Valley. Today the Samaria Regional Council, which includes 60,000 residents, has spread to more than 30 small communities, including outposts.

Itamar, which serves as a sort of settlement hub, has paid dearly at times for its frontline position. Arab infiltrations into Itamar have resulted in more than a dozen deaths. In 2002, three students of the Hitzim yeshiva high school were shot dead. Just weeks later, a Palestinian terrorist attacked the Shabo family, killing the mother,

Rachel, and three of her children. A commander in the neighborhood watch program was also killed. Most recently, in 2011, one of the most brutal massacres in recent memory took place in Itamar. Five members of Udi Fogel's family—Udi, his wife and three of their children, including a 3-month old baby—were stabbed to death in their beds. The baby was beheaded (I'll describe this atrocity in more detail in the pages to come).

As for the Hilltop Youth, stories and arguments about them are abundant. Some commentators defend their patriotic courage and commitment to Judaism; others describe them as troublemaking anarchists with no respect for parents, rabbis or the State of Israel. Analysts expound that these kids have grown up under a failed Oslo peace process, a horrific wave of terrorism in the Second Intifada, and the August 2005 uprooting by Prime Minister Sharon of the very settlements in Gaza that he had helped to establish. As some explain it, among this third generation of settlers are "those who no longer listen to or trust anyone."

When I was invited by the *Jerusalem Post* to visit a few of them in their far-flung communities, I was eager to go. In my mind, when it comes to settlers, these sounded like the "real thing," unlike my secular suburbanite neighbors in Har Adar ("And they're also leftists—living in a settlement!" Ruthie reminds me when the subject of that neighborhood's peculiar demographics arises.)

I was first introduced to David Ha'ivri, liaison for the Samaria Regional Council from the far-right community of Kfar Tapuah, when we arrived in Itamar. He had agreed to take a small group of us to one of the more established hilltop outposts, Givot Olam (which means "Hills of the World" in Hebrew), several peaks over on that ridge east of Itamar. Ha'ivri described it as a thriving "ranch" that is not only the largest producer of organic eggs in Israel, but also provides goat milk for retail establishments throughout the country. Givot Olam also contains the largest ancient Jewish winepress and wine cellar ever found in the region, dating back 3,200 years—almost to the time of Joshua's conquest of the land.

A Visit to Givot Olam

Ha'ivri first guided us to the central feature of the outpost, a light-filled community center with a spotless kitchen, dining room and outside tables that provide a gathering place for the 50 young and industrious residents who build its structures and tend to its animals. Yes, there are guns around. And yes, we were quietly informed that we weren't particularly welcomed by all who were there, less because we were Christians than because we were journalists, and therefore assumed to be hostile. "They've been burned by reporters before," Ha'ivri explained.

Nonetheless, after a cup of coffee laced with goat's milk and sugar, we went out to see the place. I'll leave it to politicians and rabbis and scholars to argue the pros and cons of outposts such as Givot Olam and will simply describe what is there.

Our first stop was at a stone memorial dedicated to Joshua, the biblical hero. The mild-mannered young artist who designed it, Asaf Kidron, was deeply grieved by Sharon's disengagement from Gaza. Here, on one of the very hilltops Sharon had encouraged Israelis to settle, Kidron has fashioned a monument fashioned out of stones gathered from every place mentioned in the Bible where Joshua set foot. Kidron's handiwork includes a lengthy tribute to that earliest of Israelite leaders, who challenged his people to have courage and strength as they took possession of their God-given land.

It was impossible for me not to be moved by the young artisan's work and words. For a number of reasons, the passage in the Bible referring to the Israelites coming into the land and claiming their land has held important personal meaning for me. The calls for strength and courage had long spoken to my spirit in times of fear, doubt or dread. And the idea of stepping forward and possessing what God has promised is a spiritual principle of depth and power.

We stood in an ancient winepress carved in bedrock circa 1,200 BCE, while Ha'ivri told us about award-winning boutique wines now being produced in Samaria. We also descended a narrow stone staircase for a quick look inside a centuries-old wine cellar nearby.

From there we walked to small but beautiful synagogue, also decorated by Asaf Kidron. It was the first building constructed in Givot Olam after its gifted and controversial founder, Avri Ran, had pitched his tents on the hilltop. Since those earliest days, electricity and water and public transport have arrived. An "at-risk youth" program has been set in motion, while small children with colorful backpacks walk safely to and from school, eggs are harvested, goats are tended and the organic farming enterprise prospers.

Givot Olam's residents enjoy peace and security. But not without hard lessons having been learned, and not without an array of rifles arrayed in what looked to me, at first, like an umbrella holder. In 2005, Avri Ran said, "The Arabs are not afraid of me. They revere me. They are wary of me, yes. Have I set out regulations? Certainly. There is not one Arab in the Nablus region who dares to work contrary to my rules. Every Arab knows this. What does this say? This says that there is a Jew in town, a son of Abraham our father—that the ancient Jews have returned a little to the Land of Israel. And a Jew must be respected..."

It was Friday, and our hosts had to finish their duties before Shabbat, but on our way off the hilltop, we stopped briefly to see the goats in one of the ranch's immaculate barns. I walked into a surreally tranquil scene, with sun filtering through skylights, and singing birds flying in and out of the broad doorways. Ha'ivri pointed toward a loft above me as I stood inside the barn. "Do you see that piano?" he asked. "Someone plays the piano while the goats are being milked, to soothe them."

Minutes later, we headed for Har Adar. I left Givot Olam with the idea that I'd probably return someday. For one thing, maybe it was the California girl in me, but I was curious about the occasional local wine and goat-cheese tasting events that are held in there from time to time. But I also hoped to learn a little more about the people who live on the windswept hilltops: What do they hope for and what do they fear? How will they react to President

Obama's ongoing hard-line stance against settlement growth, and to the Israeli government's response? Just how serious are they about their vow that there will be no more uprooting of settlements or outposts "without a price?"

Their answers may be as unyielding as the ancient Samarian stones. Because if what I've read about these settlers is true, in recent years they have drawn a few hard lines of their own.

Ancient Tekoa

Since my memorable visit to Givot Olam, a couple of other neighborhoods have welcomed me—settlements, but each unlike the other. The community of Tekoa has deep biblical roots. It sits on a ridge overlooking the Dead Sea, in close proximity to the Herodion, site of Herod the Great's winter palace and his recently discovered tomb. Apart from its proximity to Herod—the same Herod who rebuilt the Jerusalem Temple and a number of other magnificent structures during his reign from 36 BC until 4 AD— Tekoa is mentioned in the Bible as the birthplace of the prophet Amos, who is described as "one of the shepherds of Tekoa," and its workers helped reconstruct the wall around Jerusalem, according to the book of Nehemiah. They must have been a proud people; according to the account, "The next section was repaired by the men of Tekoa, but their nobles would not put their shoulders to the work under their supervisors."

Both in biblical history and other records, Jews have lived in Tekoa for thousands of years. Yet it is looked on as a settlement, no different from an array of five trailers on some desolate hilltop in Samaria.

One Saturday, some Jerusalem friends invited me to tag along as they visited a couple they'd been close friends with for years. We headed out in the general direction Gush Etzion but took a different route before long and found ourselves winding around on a very steep dirt road that was supposedly heading toward their home. It dead ended on a rocky slope and it took a while to figure out what to do with the car, but before long we were trekking across a field, down another steep hill and onto a deserted street. We were in Tekoa.

It was very quiet, in terms of human sounds—cars, radios or voices. There was, however, a strong wind with a voice of its own, and its movement that day seemed relentless. But soon we found ourselves inside a graceful home—a portrait of simplicity if not minimalism. Every furnishing and decorative touch was carefully conceived with the eye of an artist. And Ricky, the woman of the house—who not only served as architect, landscape designer and interior designer but also home owner—was as artistically and beautifully put together as her home. With short-cropped silver hair and a lovely smile, she exuded the same quiet refinement as her home.

She took us to see another house she was just completing. The views from everywhere were breathtaking. The mountains of Moab were purple on the horizon, and I thought I saw a glimmer of the Dead Sea in the distance. The landmark closest to Tekoa is the Herodion. But the most memorable point of the day was the serene beauty of the place—and of the people who live there.

Tekoa itself boasts both secular and religious residents and reports that they live together in harmony. Our hosts seemed to me like the best of both worlds. They were observant but quietly so. The family's *Havdala* ceremony was a lovely example of this. This small ritual occurs at the end of Shabbat, and is meant to separate the sacred day of rest from the six ordinary days of the week. It takes place on Saturday evening, traditionally after the first three stars have appeared in the sky.

The couple's daughter joined us for the brief ritual, which I found both beautiful and moving. Our host, a warm and soft-spoken man who works in the high-tech industry, lit a blue and white double-wicked candle. He filled an antique-looking cup to overflowing with sweet wine, placed it on a saucer and lifted it up.

Kos yeshuot esa uve-shem Adonai Ekra.
Hinay El yeshuati; evtach ve-lo efchad.
Ki azi ve-zimrat Ya Adonai, va-yehi li lishua.

I lift this cup of salvation and proclaim in the name of Adonai. Behold! Adonai is my salvation; I will trust in Him and will know no fear. Adonai is my strength and my song; He is the source of my deliverance.

He said a blessing over the wine.

Baruch atah Adonai, Eloheinu,
melech ha'olam borei p'ri hagafen, Amen.

Blessed are you, Lord, our God,
sovereign of the universe, who creates the fruit of the vine.
Amen.

A little box of spices—I think it contained cinnamon and cloves—was also blessed.

Baruch atah Adonai, Eloheinu, melech ha'olam borei minei v'samim.

Blessed are you, Lord, our God, sovereign of the universe, who creates varieties of spices.

The box was passed around so each of us could enjoy the smell of it. The sweet fragrance of the spices was meant to comfort us because we were losing the sweetness of the spirit of Shabbat.

A blessing was said over the candle's small fire, and we all held our hands toward it. This flame marks a clear distinction between Shabbat—when no one is supposed to "kindle a fire"—and the six days of the workweek.

Baruch atah Adonai, Eloheinu, melech ha'olam borei m'orei ha'eish

Blessed are you, Lord, our God, sovereign of the universe,
who creates the light of the fire.

Finally, one last prayer was offered,

Baruch atah Adonai, Eloheinu, melech ha'olam
hamavdil bein kodesh l'chol
bein or l'hoshech bein Yis'ra'eil la'amim
bein yom hash'vi'i l'sheishet y'mei hama'aseh
Baruch atah Adonai, hamav'dil bein kodesh l'chol. Amen

Blessed are you, Lord, our God, sovereign of the universe
Who separates between sacred and ordinary,
between light and darkness,
between Israel and the nations,
between the seventh day and the six days of labor.
Blessed are You, Lord, who separates between sacred and
ordinary. (Amen)

With that, the wine was passed around, and each of us took a sip. The candle was extinguished in a few drops of the wine. And with warm embraces and many smiles, a new day and a new week had begun in Tekoa, and all around Israel.

After I got home, I thought about the millennia Tekoa had been in existence. In a study Bible, I looked up the biblical reference. It truly is a place of prophets and kings. Yet today, it is just another "settlement." Disputed territory. It reminded me of a defiant statement I'd read by Yisrael Medad, an American-born Israeli commentator. Mr. Medad has lived in Shiloh since 1981. He is head of information resources at the Menachem Begin Heritage Center in Jerusalem. In 2009, he wrote in the *Los Angeles Times*,

No one, including a president of the United States of America, can presume to tell me, a Jew, that I cannot live in the area of my national homeland. That's one of the main reasons my wife and I chose in 1981 to move to Shiloh, a so-called settlement less than 30 miles north of Jerusalem.

After Shiloh was founded in 1978, then-President Carter demanded of Prime Minister Menachem Begin that the village of eight families be removed. Carter, from his first meeting with Begin, pressed him to "freeze" the activity of Jews rebuilding a presence in their historic home. As his former information aide, Shmuel Katz, related, Begin said: "You, Mr. President, have in the United States a number of places with names like Bethlehem, Shiloh and Hebron, and you haven't the right to tell prospective residents in those places that they are forbidden to live there. Just like you, I have no such right in my country. Every Jew is entitled to reside wherever he pleases."

A Little Night Music

Daphne Netanyahu phoned me one afternoon and asked if I wanted to join her and her husband Iddo at a concert later that evening. Daphne and Iddo, a brilliant and sophisticated Jerusalem couple, have been wonderful friends to me and have shared far more than their generous hospitality. They have also introduced me to aspects of Israeli history and heritage that I could never have learned from anyone else.

Daphne apologized for the short notice, but for me it only made the opportunity more appealing—I'd been working for hours and really needed to take a break.

"Should I dress up?" I asked, not sure about the venue.

"I'm wearing a skirt," she told me. I agreed to do the same.

They picked me up a couple of hours later and we began to drive. I had no idea where we were going—but it clearly was not the Jerusalem Theater, which is less than five minutes from my apartment.

It seemed to me we were traveling a considerable distance—the lights of Jerusalem were by then behind us and the large settlement bloc of Ma'aleh Adumim glowed brightly on our right.

We soon passed a guarded gate, drove into a small community called Anatot, and found our way to the last house on the last street before a dead-end barricade. We seemed to be looking across the Judean desert, but it was hard to see much—it was a windy night and dust filled the air. Iddo explained that we were near the birthplace of the prophet Jeremiah, "but the actual site is now an Arab village called Anata. This place is relatively new—it was built after 1967."

We made our way through the wind to the front door, and were soon made welcome by a genial host, Daniel Fradkin. "For years he was principal of the second violin section of the Jerusalem symphony orchestra. He's now a teacher in the Jerusalem Academy of Music," Daphne had explained earlier.

The average-sized living room was dominated by a well-worn grand piano; paintings and books graced the walls, and an assortment of chairs and sofas were arranged around the walls. The setting was as informal as could be. There were probably about 25 people there; most seemed to be old friends. Everyone was chattering away in Hebrew, which, thanks to my atrocious language skills, made it possible for me to simply observe. The guests were dressed unselfconsciously; many of them were middle aged. There was a young boy of around seven seated in the audience, the only child there.

Our host disappeared for a few minutes and then reemerged, bearing a violin and bow. With him was a younger man who quickly and almost shyly seated himself at the piano. I noticed that he was wearing a cross around his neck. Mr. Fradkin said something by way of introduction—still in Hebrew. A hush fell across the room.

All at once we were caught up in an elegant performance of a Beethoven composition for violin and piano. It was a world-class presentation; something for which tickets in Vienna or Moscow or London would have cost a small fortune. I was captivated, carried to another world by the music and the impeccable virtuosity of the musicians. Only the desert wind blowing through the open windows reminded me where I was from time to time: in another far-flung Israeli "settlement," where art was offered to a few good friends for the sheer joy of it.

After the Beethoven and a few other selections from Shubert, Chopin and Schumann—some performed solo by the pianist—we gathered in another room where a local winemaker offered the best of his wares: a hearty merlot. There I learned that the pianist, Yury Martynov, was visiting from Moscow, and his son had come along with him. Martynov told me that he had never been to Israel before and couldn't wait to make a pilgrimage to the Christian sites in Galilee the following day.

Daniel Fradkin, who had begun his study of the violin at six years old, had emigrated from the former USSR to Israel in 1973. Ever since, he has been a fixture in the Jerusalem music scene, performing on a violin he inherited from his father as well as a *viola d'amore*, a baroque violin. On that particular evening, delighted with the prospect of being accompanied by a particularly gifted pianist, Fradkin had simply chosen to share the pleasure with his friends.

As we drove away, we slowed down for a checkpoint and passed a turnoff to the village of Anata where Jeremiah—that great prophet of so many woes—had entered this troubled world. There wasn't another car on the road, not a soul in sight. Before long, we re-entered the glittering lights of Jerusalem. I thought about the music that so often drifts from homes all around the city and doubtless throughout the country, both day and night. It is a language of its own, and it seems to ascend from the very heart and soul of the Israeli people. Out of nowhere part of a poem I'd written years before came back to me.

...Learn not to speak,
But with flutes and horns and violins
Reveal yourself in subtle counterpoints and poignant chords.
Even though you never share with anyone
What your silent heart keeps hidden,
When, and if, you find that someone weeps with you,
Hearing and knowing your song,
You will have said enough.

CHAPTER SEVEN

ANCIENT RIVALRIES

K atherine met me at the King David Hotel one afternoon in 2011. She is an exquisitely pretty, twenty-
something South African woman, with a Christian
zeal for Israel that is both touching and apolitical.
We were to have "tea," which for me, at that particular spot,
usually means a cappuccino and a mini-cookie. Before I could
finish perusing the menu and be tempted by anything else she
burst out, "You won't believe what happened to me last evening!
I feel like I just escaped with my life!" Her eyes were wide and there
was not a hint of irony on her face.

At the time, Katherine lived in a tiny apartment—a garage
turned into a studio—in Abu Tor, which is a mixed Arab and Jewish neighborhood south of the Old City, off Hebron Road, not far
from the chic Baka area. The border between Israel and Jordan ran
through Abu Tor between 1948—when Israel became a state—
and the 1967 war, when Israel reunited all of Jerusalem. It is one of
few neighborhoods where Jews and Arabs live together, although
generally in separate areas.

"I was walking home from the Old City, and I somehow got
lost and found myself in the Arab section. All of a sudden a gang of
kids started throwing rocks at me, screaming at me…"

"Why would they do that?"

"I think they must have thought I was Jewish—I had on a hat
and a long skirt."

"You must have been terrified."

"Yeah, I ran as fast as I could. I could hear the rocks hitting the ground behind me. Then one of them ran out in front of me and tried to block me." I noticed that her eyes were teary and her hands were a little shaky as she lifted her tea to her lips.

"What did you do?"

"I just prayed and ran and prayed and ran! Finally a shopkeeper heard the noise and rushed into the street. He started shouting at the kids, gesturing at them. He was really angry. Thank God he chased them off."

We didn't talk about what might have happened to Katherine if the shopkeeper hadn't intervened. I think we both knew she would have been physically assaulted. Even as it was, the rage of those young Arab boys had left a mark on Katherine's soul.

Children of Abraham

In the years I've been in Israel, I've seen reports from watchdog groups that monitor the Palestinian media and publish YouTube recordings of horrendous broadcasts, teaching small children that killing Jews and dying as martyrs should be the goal of their lives. They typically include images of toddlers in suicide belts, and mothers teaching their children songs about dying as *shahids*.

Along similar lines, a perusal of Friday mosque sermon texts—translated from Arabic and available online—reveals a similar message for adults: "Death to Israel" "Kill the Crusaders and Zionists! "With Allah's help we will drive the Jews into the sea!" The messages are relentless, and are repeatedly featured on various Arab television outlets, including Palestinian Authority broadcasts, in print media, and of course on the Internet. Perhaps most unforgettable are the images of cheering men and women in the streets of the Arab world, passing out candies and shouting slogans in celebration of the terrorist attack of 9/11 and other such "successes."

I have also read a few hateful anti-Arab comments following published news stories—usually on news sites, in blogs and on Facebook. I've seen angry expressions flicker across people's faces when the subject of Arab deprivations and complaints is raised. But in nearly six years, I've yet to hear any Israeli say, "I hate Arabs—I want them all out of this country or dead!" In fact, I've yet to meet anyone who genuinely dislikes Arab people in general. But what I've heard and seen again and again is Israelis' *mistrust* of Arabs. It seems to me that it is a mistrust deeply rooted in fear, disappointment and loss, based on personal history and not on racism.

The stories of anti-Israel violence are many, and are too often gruesome. Israeli retaliations to such incidents, military and targeted, are more likely to make the international news. But everyone who lives in Israel knows that another bomb, or shooting, or knifing, or stoning, or vehicle massacre or suicide assault could happen at any moment. It's just a fact of life. Katherine was fortunately spared. But incidents like hers raise questions about why—why the hatred? Is it all simply politically inspired? Is it the fruit of envy or despair? Is it rooted in religious differences?

The short answer is probably "all of the above." Certainly the volumes of writing on the subject of terrorism and counter-terrorism could fill entire libraries. Clearly politics and cultural dissatisfaction contribute to the problem. But religion is also a root. And that piece of the puzzle definitely dates back a long way—so far back that a lot of people don't think much about it any more. From the Judeo-Christian perspective, the hostility involves a history lesson about the Jewish Patriarch Abraham—a story that stretches across the countless centuries to the book of Genesis.

According to the Bible, God had promised his faithful friend Abraham a son, and through that son a nation of people as numerous as the sands of the sea. But Abraham was an old man, and Sarah, Abraham's beautiful, beloved wife was barren, seemingly unable to conceive the son of promise. In frustration (and according to an ancient custom) Sarah offered her maid Hagar to Abraham, in hopes that she could bear the child on Sarah's behalf. Hagar conceived immediately, and just as quickly the two women turned angrily against each other. Hagar fled Sarah's wrath, and as she hid near a spring, she encountered a messenger of the Lord, who spoke to her about the child she would bear.

> And the angel of the LORD said unto [Hagar], Behold, thou art with child and shalt bear a son, and shalt call his name Ishmael; because the LORD hath heard thy affliction. And he will be a wild man; his hand will be against every man, and every man's hand against him; and he shall dwell in the presence of all his brethren....(Genesis 16:11-12)

As the story continues, Sarah miraculously conceives and also bears a son—Isaac. Half-brother to Ishmael, Isaac survives his near-sacrifice by his father Abraham on Mt. Moriah. God's promise to Abraham begins to be fulfilled as Isaac's sons, daughters and grandchildren multiply. In subsequent generations, especially after the Exodus from Egypt, the children of promise populated the land of promise.

Relations with Ishmael's offspring were not always happy.

Things went from bad to worse after Islam was founded in Arabia in the 7th Century, and greater animosity arose. Some members of Ishmael's family—now known as Arabs and subsequently as Muslims—found particular passages of their holy book the Quran that seemed to instruct Muslims to hate and even kill Jews.

Arab Uprisings and Intifadas

Fast-forward to more recent times, to the 19th century. There has always been a Jewish population in the Holy Land, or "Palestine" as the Romans re-named it. But in the 1880s, immigrations of Jews into what was then Ottoman-ruled Palestine increased. Many of those early Jewish pioneers were fleeing anti-Jewish pogroms in Russia and elsewhere. They arranged to purchase property from Arab landowners—often at exorbitant prices, which they gladly paid. They hired Arab workers to help cultivate the land, traveled to Istanbul to get building permits, and befriended their Arab neighbors. In many cases, strong friendships were formed that lasted from one generation to another. Other Arabs, however, attacked and robbed their homes and farms. The Jews had to learn, sometimes the hard way, not to show weakness or fear, but to strongly defend themselves.

In *The Goodly Heritage*, Avraham Yaari describes an incident from circa 1880. It not only illustrates life in the *Yishuv*—Yishuv was the name of the Jewish community of Palestine prior to the existence of the State of Israel—but it ends with a lesson about "peace through superior firepower," a principle that is often emphasized by those with a keen understanding of the Arab-Israeli conflict.

> In the early days of Rosh Pina [the first settlement in the north] a clash...occurred with a tribe of Bedouin, who insisted on watering their cattle without permission at the trough put up by the settlers. Water was a scarce commodity; but the Bedouin were deaf to all remonstrance. In the end, they were driven off. Incensed by such cavalier treatment on the part of the despised Jews, they attempted to retrieve their tarnished reputation by attacking the settlement in force. But they encountered determined resistance; and when a well-aimed stone unseated the sheikh, who was leading them on horseback, they retired in confusion and gave no further trouble. Indeed, amicable relations were established from that time on, and an arrangement was come to whereby the settlers were allowed to make use of the extensive grazing-grounds of the Bedouin while the latter were permitted to water their cattle at Rosh Pina.

After World War I, the Ottoman Empire's 400-year rule over Palestine ended and authority was passed on to the British. Meanwhile, the Balfour Declaration had promised the Jews a national homeland. The Zionist movement, whose mission was to create that Jewish homeland in Israel, was becoming more outspoken.

In mid-August 1929, following a Jewish demonstration near the Temple Mount, which involved flags and patriotic songs including Hatikvah, Arabs were incited by false reports of Jewish attacks on the Al-Aqsa Mosque in Jerusalem (these same false reports about attacks on Al-Aqsa are still used today in the Arab media). The incitement has long been attributed to the infamous anti-Semitic Grand Mufti of Jerusalem, Hajj al-Husseini, who later collaborated with Hitler in plans to exterminate the Jews in the Middle East.

The violence stirred up by those false rumors led to the first modern "pogrom" in Israel, during which 67 Jewish residents of Hebron were murdered. Hebron is a city in the southern Judean heart of the West Bank. Its importance—and conflict—lies in the fact that it is believed by Jews, Christians and Muslims to be the burial site of the great Patriarchs—Abraham, Isaac and Jacob—and their wives. For this reason, Jews have settled in the city for millennia, except between 1948 and 1967, during which time they were prohibited.

Aharon Reuven Bernzweig, an elderly Jewish visitor to Hebron in 1929, wrote, "We had forebodings that something terrible was about to happen—but what, exactly, we did not know. I was fearful and kept questioning the local people, who had lived there for generations. They assured me that in Hebron there could never be a pogrom, because as many times as there had been trouble elsewhere in Eretz Israel, Hebron had remained quiet. The local population had always lived very peacefully with the Arabs" (Jerusalem Post, 8/26/2011). Bernzweig was among the 400 Jews who were hidden and protected by families of Hebron's Arabs.

In 1936-1939, the "Great Arab Revolt" gripped Israel; Arab attacks on Jews and Jewish communities were renewed. But a principal object of the attacks was the British presence, and as a result, the British and Jews were aligned against the rioting Arabs. The British ultimately succeeded in ending the rebellion. During those years, Jewish immigration—legal and illegal—increased as anti-Semitism in Europe rose.

Then came World War II and terrible reports about European Jews being slaughtered. These were unverified at first, but were soon substantiated by horrific discoveries of Hitler's attempted extermination of the Jewish people, the Holocaust. In 1948, the nation of Israel was founded. The declaration of Israel's statehood was followed by an immediate military attack on the fledgling state by numerous Arab nations. The Jews won that battle. And they won again in 1967 and 1973 and in innumerable lesser battles. But the war has never really ended. In the 1980s and 2000s, it took the form of uprisings—*Intifadas*. Arab politicians—including PA President Abu Mazen—admit that the Second Intifada, from 2000 until 2004, which cost thousands of lives, both Jewish and Arab, was a mistake. But even today the threats continue.

Journalist Sever Plocker wrote in 2008,

> The second Intifada contradicted and disproved two basic assumptions, axioms almost, which were commonly accepted at its outset and end. The first one: Economic prosperity brings peace. The second one: Terrorism cannot be defeated by force. Both these arguments were and still are deeply rooted in our collective perception and instigate the leading narrative when it comes to the Israeli-Palestinian conflict. Both axioms are politically correct and provide an orderly doctrine for analysis and interpretation.
>
> Bidding these arguments farewell means abandoning viewpoints we have become accustomed to and heading into the unknown. Therefore, so many prefer to forget that there was ever an Intifada here and ignore its lessons. However, that which is repressed will resurface—it always does.

The Bombing at Mahane Yehuda

My friend Dr. Petra Heldt, whom I introduced earlier, was critically injured in a 1997 Hamas terrorist attack at the Mahane Yehuda market—a large open-air marketplace near the center of Jerusalem. Petra was severely burned on her face, hands, arms and neck; her injuries took more than three years to heal. For the first two years, she suffered excruciating pain and could do nothing for herself. Her husband, Dr. Malcolm Lowe, also a scholar, nursed her back to health.

One day Petra and I drove to the market where her attack took place. We made our way through the lively aisles, which were teeming with shoppers and shopkeepers shouting out prices. A cornucopia of fruits, breads, wines, vegetables, cheese, meats, fish and every other imaginable delicacy filled the atmosphere with color and fragrance. Customers towing carts, mothers with babies and toddlers, and a scattering of wide-eyed tourists elbowed their way toward securing the various items on their grocery lists. It was both chaotic and cheerful.

But then we walked to another section of the market, where Petra quietly said, "It was here…" We were standing in front of a vegetable stand, with a fishmonger just to the left. "I was buying some tomatoes, " she continued, "when I found myself over there." She pointed to a wall behind us, several yards away. "Almost immediately I heard the second blast, and I started to run toward the street." She pointed to the left.

Petra did not realize as she began to run that she was still afire from the explosion. In her state of shock she was entirely focused on getting to a taxi. She hailed a cab—he stopped and a woman climbed in with her. "Take her to a hospital!" the woman told the horrified driver, who could see that Petra's injuries were still smoldering.

It occurred to Petra that she had left her backpack behind. She wanted to go back for it but quickly realized that she would have to leave it for "later." The small clinic where they first stopped quickly called an ambulance, and she was taken to Hadassah Hospital at

Ein Kerem, where she would endure seemingly endless treatments, skin grafts and acute pain in the world-famous and world-class burn ward there.

Today, Petra's scarred hands and forearms bear witness to her injuries; her facial scars require a closer look. She had the best medical care imaginable. I asked her about the surprise, the horrifying shock she experienced. "Did it change your attitude toward the Arab community?" I asked her.

"Not at all," she said. "I know a great deal about Islam—I have studied it carefully. And this kind of attack was not anything new. It has happened, in various ways, for centuries to Jews and Christians and other non-Muslims who are seen as *dhimmis*, or second class citizens, under Muslim rule."

"But you weren't under Muslim rule. You were in Israel."

"It doesn't matter. In their eyes, Israel—all of Israel, not just the West Bank—is occupied Muslim land. They are fighting to get it back. And in their minds, every person in Israel is a target in their jihad. No, it didn't change my mind at all."

Khaled abu Toameh: An Alternative View

Katherine and Petra, like multiplied thousands of Israelis, have had experiences that have formed, in part, their uneasy view of Arabs. Still they do their best, as the saying goes, to "build bridges of understanding." But who are the Palestinian Arabs? And what do they think? Over the years, I've talked to some thoughtful Arab people—mostly from Muslim backgrounds—who have helped me better understand Arab perceptions.

Khaled abu Toameh is a distinguished journalist and documentary producer who writes for the *Jerusalem Post* and Gatestone Institute. His documentaries have appeared on the BBC and in the US, Australia and Scandinavia; he lectures at universities worldwide and enjoys an international following. He is an Israeli-Arab—and a Muslim—who has spent a lifetime watching the ebb and flow of troubles between Palestinians and Jews.

I spoke to him at Luciana, a cheerful Italian-style café in the German Colony where we met one fall morning. My first question had been on my mind since recently reading about the Hebron massacre in 1929. It is seldom reported that, despite the 67 murdered Jews, their compassionate Arab neighbors—at risk of their own lives—protected some 400 Jews and kept them from harm. Could that, I asked Khaled abu Toameh, happen again today?

"It's hard to predict," he answered, "but I don't think this would be repeated today because the Jewish population has changed. People have a grudge about the Jewish settlers living in downtown Hebron. And I would say that the settlers in many ways have brought it on themselves by provoking their neighbors. By not teaching their children to have good relations with their neighbors, by allowing their children to spit on women, to kick vendors, and merchants."

So here was the controversial subject of settlements again, and of settlers. But Khaled wasn't finished. "The way I see it, the overwhelming majority of the settlers are law-abiding people and good citizens, but there's this hardcore fanatic group that is very vocal and very violent and it's even causing damage to the settlers themselves—defaming them by giving them a bad name. I meet many settlers who are law-abiding citizens. But in downtown Hebron there is a problem with that type of population. You can't live among 200,000 Arabs and spit in their face every morning."

He confirmed what I'd heard before—that times really have changed in Israel in recent years. Interestingly, he blames it, at least in part, on the so-called Peace Process, and specifically the Oslo accords. Khaled told me,

I remember the good old days, before the "peace process" began—days when this was just one open country. Anyone from a refugee camp in Gaza could wake up in the morning and drive to any part of Israel and work there or live there. But ever since the peace process started, we've had barriers and restrictions and walls and fences.

I remember the good old days, when Jews used to drive into refugee camps and villages and do their shopping, and buy their groceries and spare parts for their cars, and see their dentists and eat in nice restaurants—hummus and fish. For awhile this came back, just before the 2nd Intifada, because the situation was calm and Jews felt safe going to the Palestinian areas. But the 2nd Intifada destroyed everything. And I don't think Jews will ever go back, at least not in the foreseeable future, after some of them have been lynched and murdered mercilessly.

I asked him about my own perception—that Israelis don't hate Arabs, but that they harbor deep mistrust for them. He nodded in agreement,

Yeah, most Jews today don't trust the Arabs. They don't even trust us, the Israeli-Arabs. And you know what? I can even understand why they don't trust us. Because the way many Jews see it is, "What more do these Arabs want from us? We brought the PLO here, we armed the PLO, we helped with their economy, and in the end we got an Intifada."

And the way many Jews see it, the more concessions you make to the Arabs, the weaker you are seen. And your concessions may even bring violence later because they are interpreted as a sign of weakness. Also, there was involvement by many Israeli Arabs in the intifadas. And there was fiery rhetoric, by even the moderate Arabs. All of these have caused the Jews to lose faith in the Arabs. There is no trust today. The gap is very wide.

I had heard this concessions-breed-violence theory before. I asked, "So is it true? Do you agree that Israeli concessions are understood by Palestinians to be a sign of weakness?" He answered affirmatively.

> Sadly, some Arabs and Muslims do see Israel's concessions as a sign of weakness. Look what happened in Gaza. The people in Gaza give Hamas credit for driving the Jews out. When the Jews left, it sent the message that suicide bombings and rockets caused Israel to run away. That happened before in South Lebanon, too. Israel woke up one morning and ran away. And people said, "This is wonderful! Hezbollah has been firing and killing so the Jews ran away." And it's very sad. Israel's concessions bring violence. When they make concessions it increases the appetite of the radicals. They say, "This is great! If we just continue, in a few more years the Jews will end up in the sea."

We spoke briefly of the Arab Spring, which Toameh prefers, with a slight smile, to call the "Arab Chaos." In that context I asked him what he fears most about the future, "My fear is of Islamist rule and more radicalization," he answered. "The Islamists are much more experienced. They know how to attract the masses. And there is a return to religion in the Arab and Muslim world. For people who are disillusioned with the dictatorships, 'Islam is the solution.'"

An Unwelcome Assignment in Bethlehem

Another Jerusalem friend who helped introduce me to a Palestinian perspective is Neheda Barakat. A vivacious, witty and attractive young woman, she too is an international journalist who came to work in the West Bank as the producer of a weekly public affairs broadcast. The show was intended to focus on problems and challenges faced by the Palestinian people that were *not* related to the conflict with Israel. Neheda—Ned, as she prefers to be called—was born in Tripoli, Lebanon.

Ned's family moved from country to country, and she grew up in a home that was filled with conversation about news and current affairs. "My father was a great consumer of both print and broadcast media and that I guess rubbed off on me and was probably the driver behind my chosen career."

Able to appreciate them as colleagues, Ned was impressed with the dedication of the journalists she met in Bethlehem and elsewhere in the West Bank, who were eager to report their stories and to do so robustly and with integrity. "The passion for their craft was no different from those in the same profession worldwide."

She became better acquainted with them in an early workshop she led, where the journalists enthusiastically began to discuss possible topics for a "self-examining" approach to Palestine. They openly spoke about corruption, Mafiosi tactics, injustices and other hindrances. But as the discussion continued, Ned suddenly felt overwhelmed with concerns for their safety. It was clear that there was a genuine risk involved in truth-telling, and everyone knew it. She assured one reporter who had looked somewhat despondent about the dangers, "No one is asking you to be a hero. No story is worth your life."

One afternoon a young assistant, about 18 years old, brought Ned a cup of coffee. She invited him to sit down and have his coffee with her. "Our conversation covered a lot of ground," Ned recalls. "He told me that he had left school because after the Intifada his father no longer had work."

He suddenly got up and closed her office door.

Then, in a whisper, he told me how prosperous his father
had been prior to the Intifada, working for the Israelis. He
explained how good life was, "but Hamas spoilt it all. We had a
house and we were about to buy another one, we were at school
and even had a car." He sat for a moment dejectedly, then got
up and opened the door and sat down again. He took another
sip of coffee and said, "So...what's it like living in Australia?"

Israel was the last place Ned had ever wanted to work. "I had a Lebanese background—although I hadn't spent much time there. But it was primarily my profession that forged my opinion of Israel. I felt resentment towards Israel. I felt it was both monstrous and mysterious, and I did not have the courage to go there because I did not want to subject myself to nor witness the Israelis' treatment of the 'other Semites.' More importantly, I didn't believe that I had the emotional and intellectual maturity to cover the story of Israel and Palestine.

"Fast-forward to 2008, and my attitude changed, although not in an instant." She writes that apart from a couple of female IDF soldiers at a checkpoint, who were rude and abrasive, most Israelis welcomed her. In fact, for those who spent a little time with her, she realized that she had become "a subject of fascination: here was a Lebanese/Australian journalist, living on Heleni Hamalkah Street, and working in the West Bank with the Palestinians. In fact, one wonderful host put on a Shabbat dinner in my honor."

Ned describes her perspective on the controversial "Security Fence:"

"The Wall," which I described as "shock and awe," achieves a purpose of safety. That safety I understood by making myself go to the site of the last suicide bombing, which was at a café in Jerusalem's German Colony [The Café Hillel on Emek Refaim St. was bombed in September 2003; seven were killed and more than 50 injured].

One morning on a weekend I took myself to that café, not just for breakfast but to get a grasp of what would have possibly been the scene. I went through the door and past the security guard, I placed myself in a corner on an outside table with a vantage point of the venue. The scene could've been anywhere in the world, a scene that I'm familiar with, a scene that I belong to: mums, dads, husband, wives, children, grandparents, girlfriends, strangers, all full of life and vigor, being human. Talking. Laughing. Quiet. Reading newspapers. Eating their breakfast under rays of sunshine.

I scanned the scene, for a moment forgetting why I was there. Then my eyes focused on the guard at the door …I tried to imagine a scene of carnage…and all those patrons that I "picture snapped" into my mind. And I understood the "Shock and Awe" Wall. I understood.

Ned went on to say, however, that she also understood the Palestinian view. "You definitely want to be on the Israeli side of the wall, because the view from the other side isn't so comforting. The Wall, for the Palestinians, is a reminder of 'the conquest.' It wraps the Palestinians into their own poverty and internecine strife—and not just politically." Her conclusion:

I learnt that the Israelis are not the monsters I thought they were. I learnt much about myself and my profession in context of this conflict: that every story there is seen through the prism of the conflict. But no longer from this journalist.

An Arab for Israel

Another friend, Nonie Darwish, an Egyptian by birth, has a remarkable personal history. Our first conversation was an interview in Jerusalem, in which I asked her about her life, about Arabs, Jews and Israel and her unique and sobering perspective.

Nonie Darwish was born in Cairo, and in the early 1950s moved with her family to Egypt-occupied Gaza, where her father, Lt.-Gen. Mustafa Hafez, was appointed by President Gamal Abdel Nasser to command Egyptian army intelligence. Hafez founded Palestinian *fedayeen* units to launch terrorist raids across Israel's southern border. Between 1951 and 1956, the fedayeen killed some 400 Israelis.

We sat in a café not far from the Jerusalem Convention Center, where she was a speaker at a conference. Nonie attended elementary school in Gaza, and I asked her about her childhood memories. "What was your school like?" I wondered. Nonie explained that it was very unlike the schools in America, where she now resides.

"In elementary school, even as little children, we were taught about hatred, vengeance and retaliation." She said that the idea of peace was a negative one. "Peace was never an option, but a sign of defeat and weakness. Teachers filled our hearts with fear of Jews; that made hatred come easy and terrorism seem acceptable, even honorable. Looking back, I never heard a peace song in Arabic. All we heard were songs glorifying jihad, martyrdom and winning wars."

Tragically for the family, General Hafez died when Nonie was eight years old. In July 1956, the Israelis killed him. In fact, his death was the Israel Defense Forces' first targeted assassination. In the Egyptian community, Nonie's father was immediately recognized as a *shahid*— a martyr for jihad. But although he was—and still is –remembered for his heroism, for the surviving family living was not so easy. "My mother had to face life alone with five children in a culture that respects only families headed by a man. In the 1950s few women drove, and she was called names for buying a car to take us to school."

Eventually the family returned to Egypt. It was there, in Cairo, that Nonie's mind began to change. She started questioning things she heard and saw around her. One of her best friends from school was a Christian. She was visiting the girl's home during the Friday prayers at a nearby mosque. Because the sermons were broadcast far and wide on loudspeakers, she and her friend could not help but hear the verbal attacks on Christians and Jews from the mosque's loudspeakers. Nonie recalls hearing, "May God destroy the infidels and the Jews, the enemies of God" And she remembers her own reaction, "Believe it or not, if you grow up with cursing prayers, they can sound and feel normal. But my Christian friend looked scared, and I was ashamed. That was when I first realized something was wrong with the way my religion was taught and practiced."

Nonie eventually graduated from the American University in Cairo and later worked as a journalist. She's now an author of two best-selling books, most recently *Cruel and Usual Punishment,* in which she recounts her perspective and experiences regarding Islam's all-encompassing *shari'a law.* She has been to Israel several times. Considering the fact that her father was killed by the IDF, the differences she points out between Israel and the rest of the Middle East are quite remarkable. Nonie Darwish says,

Israel really brings hope to the region. Israel is the only country in the Middle East that allows religious freedom. Even though it is the tiniest country in the region, it is not afraid to allow Muslims to have mosques to pray in; it is not afraid to allow Christians all these freedoms. It is really a credit to Judaism that it doesn't have the possessiveness Islam has.

You know, it's amazing, with all the land the Muslims have, and all the wealth from oil, and all the armies, that no Arab country is secure in its existence. Why else would 1.2 billion Muslims feel threatened by five or six million Jews? It says a lot....

My greatest fear for Israel is that it will lose the will to fight. Its founders are dying off, and now the same liberalism that is making the West weak is there too. I'm afraid Israel will give away too much, and the country will become too small to defend. Because the more you give, the more the Arabs want; it's part of the Arab culture. My Arab people are beautiful people, and I pray to God that they will find forgiveness in their hearts.

Thanks to Neheda Barakat, I got an opportunity to meet more of Nonie's "beautiful people" one night while Ned was still in Jerusalem. We decided to drive to Ramallah and meet up with, as Ned put it, "some *real* Palestinians." So we drove through the checkpoint—no delay going into the city—and soon had our first encounter. Unfortunately, it wasn't with an Arab. We were driving on a three-lane road, which was divided by intermittent cement blocks. I was pointing out an enormous number of empty plastic bags blowing in the wind and piling up along the sides of the road, when Ned yelled something like "What The…?"

A donkey, pulling a cart with two passengers, had somehow crossed the other three lanes of oncoming traffic and, with a distressed expression on his solemn face, was heading directly into our path. Ned zigged. And zagged. She told me later what was going through her mind: "I had been to the Gulf War, the LA Riots—hung out with the south central LA gangs, Soweto, meddled with the Yakuza, and had been in the West Bank for some five months. And the only way I was going to go down was by a bullet or a bomb. *Not* a donkey!"

Thankfully, we managed to avoid the head-on collision. We picked up one of her co-workers, Basel, at his animation studio and headed for dinner. We decided on an Italian restaurant that specialized in pizza, and quickly ordered a bottle of wine—the only red wine on the menu. Ned remembers it as undrinkable. I thought it was surprisingly good, all things considered. Mostly importantly, it erased the incoming donkey from our minds.

As we ate and talked to Basel about his plans, one of his friends—an actor, wearing a Che Guevara t-shirt and a beret—sauntered by, said hello, and sat down with us. He seemed like an earnest young guy, and he invited us up to his apartment where a gathering of friends had begun.

We followed him up the stairway, and I noticed that there were faded images of the Virgin Mary taped to the walls at each landing. Making our way up to the top floor, we entered a warm, sparsely furnished apartment where five or six people were cooking and hanging out. A large Cuban flag hung from a loft. A bottle of Johnny Walker Black was sitting on a counter, with a couple of empty glasses remaining alongside.

The conversation went from a photography exhibition that was being held the next day in Jerusalem, to what life was like in the Palestinian refugee camps outside of Israel (not good), to what each of our new friends wanted politically. "Che" wanted "a leftist government," another young man was most concerned about the refugees' "right of return." One of them told me that he knew Obama was on their side—he'd been a friend of friends even before he was a senator, and he hoped, as President, that Obama would continue to support them. Basel said he hoped Jerusalem would never be divided. Mostly, though, he wanted to go to film school at UCLA and earn his degree. Which, I've since learned, he did.

I remember thinking that our little party must have resembled similar gatherings at Berkeley in the 70s—a free-spirited collection of twenty-something artists and activists with all kinds of identity-based opinions and, as they liked to put it, "leftist" ideals. They certainly weren't Hamas supporters. Or crazed terrorists. Their discussion was about life in Palestine. They resented the Israeli occupation. The hated the checkpoints and the security fence. But they also disliked the NGOs that exploit refugee children for fundraising purposes. And nobody thought the PA was anything but corrupt. As Ned wrote to me later, the conversation was mostly, "about humanity. Adversity. Despair. Power. Conquest. Contradictions. Conflictions. Color. Happiness. Sadness. And hope."

Chana Zweiter's Kalaidoscope

And then there is Chana Zweiter, a religious Jewish educator who founded Kaleidoscope, a program bringing Arab and Jewish students together to promote understanding. I met her through a friend in California and have enjoyed hearing about her courageous work. One afternoon, I took the train to meet her in the town of Lod (near Tel Aviv's Ben Gurion Airport). I watched her program in action as Jewish and Arab teenagers learned some words from each other's languages, talked among themselves about their daily lives, and participated in a ball game together. They seemed at ease with each other; Chana explained later that their parents—who have to approve their children's involvement in Kaleidoscope—have a much harder time with the interaction than the students.

Not long ago, Chana met with a group of teachers from Baka El Garbiya, a village in central Israel. Working alongside her Arab colleague, Ehab, she asked the participants, "Why did you decide to take part in this workshop?" They knew that it was to be a prelude to larger workshops, which would include Jewish teachers as well.

Most of them said something like, "Because I think it's important for Jews and Palestinians to come together. And if I don't work at it, I can't expect my students to."

But one teacher, Mustafa, didn't agree. "I don't know what your agenda is," he answered with a chill in his voice. "You should know, though, that I have very strong feelings about this conflict, and you won't be able to change them. So what *is* your agenda?"

"I appreciate your openness," Chana began tactfully, "and that you felt comfortable enough to be so honest with me." She went on to say, "I don't pretend that I can change your feelings in a few hours. But my agenda is clear—that during this workshop and the ones to follow, you will all ask yourselves questions without knowing the answers. And I hope you'll become comfortable with not having all the answers." Here she paused briefly, then concluded with a smile. "I hope that you'll feel confused."

At the end of the three-hour session, when Ehab and Chana asked the teachers what they took away from the workshop, Mustafa answered, "I'm *so* confused." And he laughed.

The conflict can be confusing. And complicated. And even incomprehensible. I can think of no better example of the ambiguities than another story from Neheda Barakat. During her tenure in Bethlehem, Ned was frustrated that some of her Palestinian journalists habitually began their workdays late in the morning despite "call sheets" that required a 9 AM start. There were myriad reasons for this, and some of the excuses were absurd. But one explanation was astonishing. She writes,

> One day one of our tape editors was missing and no one could raise him on the phone. It was a crucial production day—in fact it was a pre-record day—and everyone was required for the 9 am start. At about mid-day he surfaced and he knew he'd better have a good reason. He did.
>
> He told me that at about 2 am there was a raid on his home by the Israeli Army, and his house was searched top to bottom. He added that he didn't know what they were looking for. "So what happened?" I asked.
>
> "Well, at the end of their search I made them some tea and we sat down had tea and chatted until about 4 am. It took me a while to get back to sleep." He shrugged, "and then I forgot to set my alarm."

CHAPTER EIGHT

GAZA DISASTERS

Before I left for Israel, I lived in a beach house, just two blocks from a long stretch of sand in Dana Point, California known to local surfers as The Strands. It is a tranquil place for a morning walk, and for months I made my way down the long cement stairway to the water before indulging myself with my morning coffee. I liked walking at the edge of the surf, thinking about whatever came to mind and discreetly people watching.

There were a few familiar faces who reappeared on The Strands from time to time, but these were outnumbered by designer-clad guests from the Ritz-Carlton hotel that reigned over surf and sand from the crown of an adjacent bluff. One morning I was surprised to see two male joggers—thirty-something—wearing identical orange t-shirts. It wasn't the color that surprised me, however. It was the Hebrew letters on the shirts. I immediately realized that they were making a statement about something half a world away. And that something was called by a rather un-descriptive name: The Gaza Disengagement.

Why those two protesting joggers were on "my" beach wasn't clear. Maybe they were guests at the hotel, or Dana Point residents who had recently visited Israel. I was even less clear about the subject of their protest. I only knew that the legendary old Zionist warrior Ariel Sharon, now Prime Minister of Israel, had reversed his earlier views and now, surprisingly, he wanted to remove (forcibly if necessary) some 8,000 Jews from the Gaza Strip, and that Israel's population was deeply divided over the idea.

What little discussion I'd had with friends in Washington DC had involved matters of strategy—it cost too much for the IDF to defend 8000 settlers, and they needed to be "disengaged" from their Gaza Strip homes and relocated within Israel proper. It was about money and about defense and about unilaterally exchanging land for peace.

I knew it was controversial, because according to the Israeli media, the IDF was on notice that it might have to physically remove families from their homes, businesses, synagogues, schools and communities if the settlers refused to leave. And it appeared that some of the settlers were not going to go without a fight. The color orange had come to represent the protestors' disagreement with the government. And, here the protest was, spilling all the way around the world in the form of orange t-shirts bearing the slogan "A Jew doesn't expel a Jew." Despite their stern message, they added a splash of color to a grey California morning.

Benjamin Netanyahu, who was at the time the Minister of Finance in the Sharon government, resigned in protest of the disengagement. Considering what was to take place in the years to follow, his 2005 words on the subject resonate rather prophetically:

> I don't know when terrorism will erupt in full force—my
> hope is that it won't ever. But I am convinced today that the
> disengagement will eventually aggravate terrorism instead
> of reducing it. The security establishment also expects an
> increase in terrorism. The withdrawal endangers Israel's
> security, divides its people and set the standards of the
> withdrawal to the '67 borders.

The Disengagement took place in August 2005. The settlers' homes were bulldozed and schools and synagogues were torn down or relocated inside Israel. A number of greenhouses, which had served as a source of revenue for the Jews, were left for the Palestinians. Nevertheless the Palestinians looted the greenhouses and then destroyed them.

In January 2006, Ariel Sharon had a massive stroke. He was witness to the initial agony of disengagement, but was never fully aware of the prolonged sorrows that came to pass because of his project. Nor was he cognizant of subsequent events in Gaza, or the related Palestinian political upheaval.

The Aftermath of Disengagement

If ever there was divisive subject in Israel, it remains the Disengagement. It has come between friends and family members, and not just between the usual "Leftists" and "Rightists." At least two female friends have told me they would never date a man who supported Disengagement. Angry discussions still explode over the present circumstances of the expelled settlers—whether they have received the promised compensation, whether they are trying to find work or live off the government in spite, and whether they will ever again be able to recapture the quality of life they once enjoyed in their seaside communities.

Following this heartbreaking episode in recent Israeli history, another took place barely six months later. In exercising free and democratic elections in the Palestinian territories, the Arabs went to the polls on January 25, 2006. Rather than supporting Fatah, the faction responsible for the Palestinian Authority (PA), they massively opposed the PA's corrupt misuse of billions of dollars. Instead, they elected a Hamas majority into the Palestinian Parliament. In that sobering exercise in democracy, Hamas won 76 of the 132 seats to Fatah's 43. And in Gaza, which had long suffered factional violence between the Palestinian Authority and Hamas, the world watched during the first six months of 2007, as a bloody battle ended with the installation of Hamas—identified by most nations as a terrorist organization—as the ruling junta in Gaza.

Along with the gruesome violence that unfolded as Hamas assaulted, arrested, tortured and killed Fatah members in Gaza, they also began to enforce a localized form of shari'a law, banning alcohol, women without head coverings, nightclubs, and the public mixing of unmarried men and women. Christian churches were attacked, and the small Christian community—mostly Eastern Orthodox and Roman Catholic—saw increasing threats. Many of them fled; a Bible store manager was murdered.

But the biggest source of frustration—and eventually rage—in the years following the Disengagement and the Hamas coup were thousands of rockets fired into Israel's civilian communities from Gaza. *The New York Times'* June 2006 headline, typically understating the severity of Israel's terrorism issues, put it this way: "How Clumsy, Inaccurate Gaza Rockets Could Start a War." The story went on to say,

> However crude, the Qassam rocket, fired by Palestinian militants from Gaza into Israel, has nonetheless won its spot as symbol of the moment in the long conflict here. ...Most immediately, the number of rockets fired by Palestinians from Gaza, and whether they happen to hit anyone, will be crucial in determining whether the Israeli-Palestinian conflict explodes again into high-intensity warfare.

In fact, more than 10,000 of those "clumsy" rockets have now struck Israel since the Disengagement. And still counting. And yes, in 2008-9, they did start a war.

As Hanukah 2008 neared, there was a tension in the Jerusalem air. The drum roll of anger and aggravation over Hamas' relentless rocket attacks was intensifying. Pundits, politicians and ordinary citizens alike were complaining about the Israeli government's refusal to "march into Gaza and clean house." Daily reports of rockets were headline news in Israel.

In the international media, however, Israel's "disproportionate" retaliatory strikes were the big story, and sometimes the rockets weren't mentioned at all. When they were, they were often framed as pathetically weak and primitive responses to the high-tech

Israeli aerial attacks. By comparison, the rockets were homemade and virtually harmless.

By that time, most of us had heard that the IDF was on alert. Taxi drivers reported that the reserves were on call for active duty. Friends mentioned that their sons and daughters in the army were being moved around, although it wasn't clear why. Curiosity and uncertainty prevailed. The whole country was strung as tightly as a harp string.

Then all at once, for me, the whole drama was interrupted by something wonderful, something entirely different.

Family Reunion in Jerusalem

For nearly a decade, generous friends of our family had been hosting Christmas and New Years celebrations in various international cities. These events were beautiful, unique and always included my sons and daughter-in-law and me on the guest list. What this meant was that around December 21, 2008 my family and I were reunited for the holidays—in Jerusalem.

Admittedly, the absence of Christmas hype and promotion has not grieved me during the years I've lived in Israel. By the time I actually saw my family each year, the months-long bombardment of carols, Santas and gift suggestions had nearly run its course, and I was mentally prepared for two weeks of celebration. All the better, in 2008, to be able to share "my" world with them in the very place where all the Christmas celebrating began in the first place.

As I've mentioned before, particular Christian "holy sites" in the Holy Land are more meaningful to me than others. Some people are moved by one locale, and some by an entirely different scene. I suspect that those of us from Protestant backgrounds may not be as emotionally stirred as Catholics and Orthodox believers by the sight of cross-bearing pilgrims, chanting and weeping along the Via Dolorosa. Or by the Church of the Nativity's stone-carpeted grotto in Bethlehem, where hanging lanterns are suspended over the traditional site of Jesus' birth. Or the architectural and ecumenical chaos of the Church of the Holy Sepulcher where Jesus is believed—even by numerous Protestant scholars—to have been both crucified and resurrected.

One area in Jerusalem that is surely part of the Gospel story is the Mount of Olives, located directly east of the Old City and rising above it. It is also of great significance to Orthodox Jews, who seek to be buried in its cemetery—across from the Golden Gate to the Old City. Because of an ancient tradition, they hope to be the first ones raised from the dead when their Messiah appears, for it is there that the resurrection of the dead will begin. They also believe that it is the Golden Gate through which the Messiah will enter Jerusalem.

I was interested to learn that in 1541, Ottoman Sultan Suleiman the Magnificent sealed off the gate, allegedly to prevent the Messiah's entrance. The Muslims also built a cemetery in front of the gate, based on the belief that the precursor to the Messiah, according to Jewish tradition, the prophet Elijah, would not be able to pass through, because walking through the graves would ritually defile him. One thing is sure—the ground surrounding the Mt. of Olives is a sea of graves: Muslim, Christian and Jewish.

At the base of the Mt. of Olives are the ancient olive trees of Gethsemane, some of them said to be 2,000 years old. Here Jesus poured out his heart in prayer in the hours between the last supper with his disciples and his trial and crucifixion. From Gethsemane, looking across the Kidron Valley at night, perhaps among those very trees, Jesus could have easily seen the lit torches of the Roman guard approaching to arrest him. And it was here that the wayward disciple Judas betrayed him.

Meanwhile, inside the Old City, the story continues. Beneath the "traditional sites" of Jesus' passion and resurrection lie deep scholarly debates and divisions. Archeological digs fuel these arguments; sometimes they affirm early traditions and sometimes they do not.

It is easy to be cynical amidst all the hawkers selling religious paraphernalia, tales about the carefully preserved splinters of the "True Cross," and an endless parade of Christian priests in every sort of attire, solemnly censing their jealously guarded sections of the Church of the Holy Sepulcher. But there is, at the same time, something real in the air, something powerful and hauntingly unfinished.

The Holy Mountain in Jerusalem has drawn faithful pilgrims for more than 5,000 years. It remains a place of the One Great Hope—that the completion of all things will dawn here, fulfilling ancient promises: "And the glory of the LORD shall be revealed, and all flesh shall see it together: for the mouth of the LORD hath spoken it..."

Tour guides like to remind us that it's not the GPS that matters when it comes to spiritual journeys, but the deeper meaning of the events that unfold. And of course that is true. In fact, one of my less-than-orthodox friends once chided me, saying that our quest should not be for the "Historical Jesus" but for the "Cosmic Christ." Whatever that actually means, there's no question that the air of Jerusalem is redolent with the faith of our fathers, and at times it all but shimmers with traces of miracles.

Journey to Galilee

Nonetheless, the scenery surrounding the Sea of Galilee is more conducive to my own pilgrim's quest than the congested streets and alleys of Jerusalem's Old City. And so it was with great joy that I was able to travel with family and friends to Tiberias, Capernaum and the surrounding countryside during that exceptionally blessed 2008 holiday season. For us, as we talked and laughed and remembered other holidays gone by, Gaza seemed as far away as California, and no more threatening. "Peace on Earth, goodwill to men" was a reality—for the time being.

Because there are not so many tourists in Galilee during the chilly winter season, it was possible to wander along the pebbly

beach and so easy to believe that a 1st Century rabbi and his followers had walked there too. The depth of the lake and shape of
the coastline may have changed somewhat, but the shrines and
chapels that have been constructed there are unpretentious, and
their settings allow for reflection. On a nearby hillside, the "Mount
of the Beatitudes" gently slopes down toward the quietly lapping
water. There, a cluster of curious, anxious peasants must have been
filled with wonder and hope, hearing the encouraging words of the
Sermon on the Mount spoken for the first time.

> *...do not worry about your life, what you will eat or drink; or
> about your body, what you will wear. Is not life more than food,
> and the body more than clothes? Look at the birds of the air; they
> do not sow or reap or store away in barns, and yet your heavenly
> Father feeds them. Are you not much more valuable than they?
> Can any one of you by worrying add a single hour to your life?*
>
> *And why do you worry about clothes? See how the flowers of
> the field grow. They do not labor or spin. Yet I tell you that not
> even Solomon in all his splendor was dressed like one of these. If
> that is how God clothes the grass of the field, which is here today
> and tomorrow is thrown into the fire, will he not much more
> clothe you—you of little faith? So do not worry, saying, 'What
> shall we eat?' or 'What shall we drink?' or 'What shall we wear?'
> For the pagans run after all these things, and your heavenly
> Father knows that you need them. But seek first his kingdom
> and his righteousness, and all these things will be given to you as
> well. Therefore do not worry about tomorrow, for tomorrow will
> worry about itself. Each day has enough trouble of its own.*

In Capernaum—actually Kfar Nahum, the village of
Nahum—the ruins of a 4th century synagogue remain. Among its
old pillars, in one corner and down several steps, are the remains of
a 1st century synagogue. This sacred space is just a short walk from
another ruin, which is enclosed within a Roman Catholic church.

The church is built atop an ancient home, a dwelling that is believed to have been Simon Peter's house—a 1st Century shrine to St. Peter is said to have been found there. The synagogue may be the one where Jesus taught in Mark 1, in which we read, "forthwith, when they were come out of the synagogue, they entered into the house of Simon and Andrew, with James and John." Peter's mother was sick with a fever, but " he came and took her by the hand, and lifted her up; and immediately the fever left her…" The synagogue is just steps away from St. Peter's home.

From the interior of the church, we looked out through viewing windows across the ruins of Capernaum's village, where the walls of houses and other structures can still be clearly seen. Our guide, Ari Ram, explained the importance of Capernaum to the spread of the Christian message. It lay at a crossroads, where traders, caravans, and armies moved in all directions during the three decades of Jesus' earthly life. Whatever they saw and heard as they passed through the Galilee countryside—reports of healings and hope and the Kingdom of Heaven—was carried far and wide by eyewitnesses.

After some wonderful dinners graced with exceptional local wines, we traveled to the Golan Heights, past Mount Hermon and on to the far north, to a hillside overlooking the Lebanon border. It was quiet there, cold and foggy. We could clearly see Hezbollah's strongholds just across the way, and we met some of the young, friendly but well armed IDF women who were stationed there. Being tourists, we took snapshots, smiling and joking about our hazardous backdrop and the looming threat of Hezbollah missiles hidden in the basements behind us.

It was thought-provoking to be in such a place with my children. They were glad to have bragging rights when the stories were later retold for the benefit of their California friends. But for me, the thought of families fleeing those hills for their lives also began to play in my mind as we drove south in the bus. Our family has had its injuries, financial hurdles and other struggles. But we've always been "safe and sound." In sun-drenched and easy-going Southern California, dangers of bombs, bullets and bloodshed have never crossed our minds.

A few days after our visit to the North, my daughter-in-law Elizabeth's parents—Mike and Karin Runyen—arrived in Jerusalem from California. Once again we took in some of the Jerusalem historic sites. By then, as we trekked through the Old City, the cauldron of anger about Gaza rockets was close to boiling over. On December 27, the Israeli Air Force initiated a series of "surgical strikes" targeting Hamas leadership and rocket launching facilities. It was a relentless, lethal and successful operation. To say that the rest of the world disapproved would be to understate the hysterics that erupted. Demonstrations in the Palestinian communities were noisy and at times violent.

Elizabeth's parents had never been in the Middle East before. They were well informed about international affairs but had no reason to question the wiles of Jerusalem taxi drivers. The day before they left, they hired a driver to take them to Bethlehem to see the Church of the Nativity, Manger Square and the surrounding town. Bethlehem is only about 20 minutes drive from the center of Jerusalem, but light years away from its western lifestyle. I was unable to go with them, and Colin and Elizabeth decided to take the day off and rest.

Only Arab drivers with special permits are able to travel in and out of Bethlehem and other Palestinian cities—Jews are no longer allowed to enter. The young man the Runyens hired was either irresponsible or intentionally mischievous. He dropped them off into what at first appeared to be a crowd of sightseers. However, they were soon surrounded by an angry throng and were, for a few minutes, involuntarily caught in a slogan-shouting tide of protestors waving Palestinian flags. They could clearly see snipers atop buildings with automatic weapons. Bullhorns shouted out encouragement to the already overexcited mob. They were in the midst of a hostile anti-Israel demonstration, one of many that were sweeping across the West Bank during the Gaza War.

The Runyens were "intimidated and frightened by the sheer number of the protestors," and rushed into the Church of the Nativity. Once they had settled their nerves and looked around for a few minutes, they emerged and, thankfully, their driver reappeared to pick them up. But instead of leaving the city through the main road and checkpoint—the way he'd entered—he decided to take an "alternate route." As they drove past an Israeli surveillance tower, they saw angry Arab teenagers throwing rocks at the Jewish soldiers. In response, the Israelis released blue-grey clouds of some sort—they guessed that it was tear gas. Finally, their driver managed to get them back on the road to Jerusalem.

Meanwhile, Colin, Elizabeth and I were wondering what had happened to them. They were more than an hour late returning to Jerusalem. When they finally showed up, they were a bit shaken. So was I. For me, their little adventure once and for all replaced the tranquility of Galilee with a more updated and sinister reality. *If it's bad here*, I wondered, *what's going on in the South?*

It didn't take long to get caught up with the news, which I had blissfully ignored during our holiday festivities and tours.

On the day my children arrived, December 21, 50 rockets and mortars had hit southern Israel. Israel attacked two rocket launchers in response.

On December 22, three rockets struck Israel; five more on the 23rd.

On Christmas Eve, more than 69 Qassams struck, along with dozens of mortar shells. Homes and factories were damaged, as well as a children's playground.

On December 26, a dozen more rockets and mortars struck Israel's civilian communities.

On December 27, the Israeli air assault began, initiating what would later be called Operation Cast Lead.

On January 3, 2009, ground attacks were launched. All the while, dozens of rockets continued to fall.

The international media was in an uproar about Israel's retaliatory attacks. As usual, the thousands of rocket strikes that had triggered Israel's responses were, in some cases, hardly mentioned. If
they were, they were trivialized. A report from *The Times* (London)
on January 8 was typical of the European media: "...the morale
of the population in southern Israel has been shaken by Hamas's
sporadic hits with mini-rockets inflicting only minor damage and
relatively few casualties..."

In fact, more than half a million people were in striking range
of the rockets—which were, by the way, destructive and deadly.
Israel's ferocious response to them was declared a war crime by
the world media and an assortment of human rights groups. The
subsequent and infamous "Goldstone Report," authored by South
African Jewish Judge Richard Goldstone and his team of research-
ers, accused the IDF of intentionally targeting civilians. Goldstone
later recanted some of his accusations, but his turnaround came too
late to silence the international clamor, which was deafening. The
lies and exaggerations about Israel's conduct in Operation Cast
Lead continue to this day. Even documentary evidence of Hamas
using women and children as human shields, and shooting rockets
and mortars from civilian homes, schools and even hospitals has
failed to stop the uproar.

A Visit to the Rocket Zone

Once my family was safely California-bound, I found an opportunity to visit the areas surrounding Gaza. On a chilly January morning, three of us made our way from Jerusalem to Israel's southern
region where so many people were struggling to live normal lives
within range of Hamas's rockets. As we approached our destination, I noticed a towering column of black smoke on the horizon,
billowing from northern Gaza, where the battle was raging.

We passed the community of Sderot, and soon arrived at
Kibbutz Gevim, situated just a few miles from both Sderot and
Gaza. The women I accompanied on this day trip were there to

assist in a temporary evacuation of the kibbutz's senior citizens. The two Christian organizations my friends represented had partnered to provide these elders with a few leisurely days in the seaside resort town of Eilat, a welcome respite from sirens and explosions.

I talked with several genial but visibly anxious men and women as they waited for their chartered bus to arrive. Many of them had lived at Kibbutz Gevim for more than half a century; a few were founders of the kibbutz. They had no intention of leaving permanently but were eagerly looking forward to getting a good night's sleep in Eilat, with no "red alerts" and no rush to the safe room in their houses or to a nearby bomb shelter.

"Do you think this war will make your life better?" I asked one weary old man named Mordecai. "Yes, I think so," he nodded. "And not just my life. It will also be better for the people in Gaza once Hamas is broken," he pointed towards the pillar of smoke on the horizon. "They're having a hard time, too."

A woman named Edna seemed particularly jumpy, her hands in constant movement. "Aren't you afraid to come here?" she asked me with a troubled frown. "My own family won't even come to visit! I have to meet them in Tel Aviv." The sound of a large explosion startled us all, punctuating her comment. She added acidly, "Anybody who says they aren't afraid to live here is lying."

During my visit to the kibbutz, several residents mentioned medications that made it possible for them to function—prescriptions for anti-depressants and anti-anxiety drugs are very much in demand, and for good reason. I learned that a few months before, a small boy from Kibbutz Gevim had been injured by a Qassam strike; in fact not a single child could be seen in the carefully-tended kibbutz playground, and I was told that most of the children are bed-wetters thanks to their high levels of constant stress. One woman described her house, which had taken a direct hit and needed extensive repairs. Other rockets had ignited fires and damaged structures. Everyone spoke of the nerve-wracking noise that never seemed to end: sirens, explosions, helicopters and warplanes.

The ordinary men and women who live in proximity of rockets—a perimeter that has enlarged considerably since 2009, thanks to more sophisticated Iranian rockets smuggled into Gaza that have longer range and more precise targeting than the Qassams—couldn't be clearer about their dearest hopes: they want nothing more than to live out their lives in peace. Unfortunately, they face an extraordinarily hostile enemy. Hamas's actions reflect the spirit of their 1988 Charter, which calls for the death of Jews and the eradication of Israel.

Our little gathering at Kibbutz Gevim wasn't especially religious. It amounted to an ad hoc coalition of concerned Christians hoping to make life a little easier for a group of war-weary Jews. Everything centered on life-affirming gestures and life-sustaining actions, both deeply rooted in both Christianity and Judaism.

Even as we said our goodbyes, another deafening explosion shattered the morning stillness.

Bomb Shelters for Children

On February 28, 2009, just a month after Israel declared a unilateral ceasefire following Operation Cast Lead, a Grad rocket struck Ort Amit Technical High School in Ashkelon—a heavily populated coastal city north of Gaza. Carrying a huge payload, it shredded the interior of the school's central courtyard, spewing shrapnel in all directions. Thankfully, the attack of the unusually large unguided rocket took place on a Shabbat, and because there were no students attending class, there were no injuries. Rebuilding the ravaged structure took weeks, however, and the strike did not bode well for Ashkelon in several ways.

First, and most obviously, the Grad assault indicated Hamas' defiance of the ceasefire, which, in fact, has been broken by rocket or mortar attacks from Gaza hundreds of times since then. Second, the size and trajectory of the Grad that struck Ashkelon demonstrated that longer range and deadlier Iranian rockets, far surpassing early made-in-Gaza Qassams, are now stockpiled in Hamas's arsenal.

And third, this new threat underscored the vulnerability to rocket fire in the city of Ashkelon, and particularly the lack of bomb shelters for school children in the greater Ashkelon area. During Cast Lead, 200 rockets struck the city, and 50 directly hit houses or schools. Ashkelon's power station is also a target, even though it provides energy to 65% of Gaza's electrical grid.

In January 2010, marking the one year anniversary of the Cast Lead ceasefire, two humanitarian organizations joined together in efforts to resolve the dangerous safety gap for Ashkelon's civilian community. The International Christian Embassy Jerusalem (ICEJ) along with Operation Lifeshield (OLS)—a non-profit provider of ground shelters in areas of Israel that have been hardest hit by Hezbollah and Hamas rockets—installed and dedicated two small shelters. One was placed at a children's center in Moshav Mavqiim—located just a mile from Gaza. Another was installed at a kindergarten in Moshav Talme Yafe.

What is it like to raise children in a place where the very real threat of explosives is part of a family's daily reality? I reflected on my visit to the north with my sons and daughter-in-law. Making sure kids are safe is a parent's first priority. But we've had it easy. We over-protective soccer moms and dads of Southern California face very different challenges from the brave Israeli parents who furnish their bomb shelters with coloring books and crayons and favorite snacks.

At that kindergarten near Ashkelon, I stared as a bomb shelter—solid cement—was lowered by a crane and situated next to the nursery school. Little boys and girls, colorfully dressed and wreathed in delighted smiles, giggled with excitement as they watched what looked like a giant Lego being settled on the ground. They were less than five years old and had little-to-no idea what that thick-walled concrete block was for. They only understood that it had been brought there just for them, and for that reason, it was a very special day. Doubtless their teachers were relieved to have a place of shelter when the "red alert" siren sounded. Now they could run just a few steps and be relatively safe.

How did those teachers explain the bomb shelter's purpose to such innocent little children? I'm not sure. When I asked one of them, she simply smiled, "They know we want them to be safe..."

According to IDF Spokesman Capt. Kory Bardash, since Operation Cast Lead, Hamas has rearmed Gaza and now possesses an array of thousands of improved, sophisticated Iranian-made rockets with large payloads. One defense against this threat is Operation Iron Dome, a rapid response missile defense, which has been highly effective at neutralizing rocket bombardments. Successful testing of the system was first announced by the IDF on January 8, 2010. In response, *The Times* reported, "Gaza militants met the announcement with a barrage of at least ten mortar shells, causing no damage but underlining the continued threat to Israel's southern communities." Since then, it has proved itself effective under several prolonged rocket attacks.

At the time, I spoke to Uzi Rubin, a prominent analyst of Middle East missile procedures, who shrugged off some recent arguments against Iron Dome's effectiveness raised by Ha'aretz journalist Reuven Pedatzur, an outspoken critic of Israel's defense systems. Pedatzur cited statistics to defend his argument.

Rubin retorted, "Information regarding Iron Dome's capabilities is classified. How long it takes to activate a response; how close the proximity to Gaza—this is all highly classified. No journalist has access to the information necessary to create such statements. If journalists know, Hamas knows. And that's not going to happen."

He also insisted that bomb shelters are essential. "I do not like the name 'Iron Dome'—it is a bad choice. No system can provide an 'Iron Dome;' there is no 100% protection. No matter what the defense system, some rockets will get through. Nothing works perfectly and that's why shelters are necessary. You don't stand outside looking up at the sky during a rocket attack."

In 2011, Iron Dome was activated. Uzi Rubin's justification of its design was validated with something like an 85% success rate in intercepting incoming rockets. His insistence that there also needed to be bomb shelters also remains true. The ones I watched being installed that day were soon put to good use. As this is written, rockets are still being launched from Gaza. And as they approach Israel, "red alert" alarms sound. Shopkeepers, artisans, farmers, café customers, soldiers, pedestrians, schools and families scurry for shelter.

A young mother, Esti Lehman, described her experiences in a 2011 blog post,

> A summer night, the window is open and grasshoppers are making music for us on a gentle breeze. This evening I went to bed early, after another hot summer day with the children. Thoughts pass through my head when suddenly the loudspeaker outside goes on, and a woman's soothing voice announces, "Color Red, Color Red." A loose translation: a mortar shell or Qassam will hit in another 15 seconds...
>
> I switch to autopilot. Shake my husband, "Run and get them." The two of us shoot up, almost pushing each other as we race, breathless, to the other side of the house—to the children's room.
>
> In that second I am always struck dumb—and for a fraction of a second, I am united with all those Jewish mothers who came before me, and who experienced with me this dreadful moment—"Who should I take?" The last thought a mother wants to think flashes through my head, "Which of them should I take first?"

More than ten thousand times that story has been repeated in Israel's communities. Ten thousand rockets launched. And millions of mad dashes for safety.

In the meantime, although Israel is in the center of the crosshairs, the rest of the world has also seen more than enough columns of black smoke towering above our cities, heard enough

body counts, and witnessed enough of terrorism's tragic con-
sequences. Considering the statements of groups like Hamas,
Hezbollah and Al-Qaeda and others of their ilk I can't help but
wonder—are we taking seriously enough the hateful religious
ideology that inflames radical Islamists? In the pages that follow
we'll look more closely at that belief system and how it deals with
Jews and Christians.

CHAPTER NINE

BLIND SPOT

It was New Years Eve 2008, and my son Dylan and I had gathered with close friends for our annual Christmas and New Years festivities. In past years we'd celebrated in Rome, Sydney and Vienna. Now in the waning days of 2007, we found ourselves in Mumbai, India and thanks to our hosts' generosity, our gala was to be held at the city's beautiful Taj Mahal Palace Hotel.

We checked into our exquisitely appointed rooms a couple of days before the party. After having spent the last week-and-a-half in Bangalore, Delhi, Agra and elsewhere, we were particularly impressed with the old-world elegance of Mumbai. We took photographs of the impressive boulevards, colorful gardens and regal buildings. But the Taj Hotel was especially lovely, over-looking the harbor, its fairy-tale architecture serving as a beloved landmark both to tourists and the local population. We, too, fell in love with it.

On December 31, after drinks and snapshots, we settled down to dinner. We were sparkling in holiday finery and eagerly anticipating the beginning of a new year in an entirely unfamiliar setting. The photographs of the evening are colorful, capturing the carefree mood we all shared on rather spectacular evening.

Two friends with whom I've written other books—Paul Marshall and Roberta Green Ahmanson—and I were discussing our most recent offering (at the time it was soon-to-be-released), *Blind Spot: When Journalists Don't Get Religion.* We had worked as editors and contributors for this Oxford University Press publication, which focused on the fact that some journalists, especially those who are not religiously observant themselves, frequently overlook, misunderstand or under-report the importance of religion to current events.

Of course it never crossed our minds that in less than a year, we would be seeing the very setting of our conversation and celebration destroyed by Islamist terrorists. Or that the reporting of Mumbai's siege would so aptly illustrate the thesis of our book.

Terrorism in Mumbai

Not quite a year later, late at night in my Jerusalem apartment, I was checking the headlines on-line. All at once I found myself frantically trying to make sense of a growing number of news bulletins, video clips, live feeds and photographs coming in from Mumbai. It seemed that a murderous assault on the city had been launched, and one of the two five-star hotels attacked was "our" beautiful Taj Mahal Palace. Of course the grisly scenes of people gunned down in cold blood were the real tragedy. But for me, it was also jarring to see places inside the hotel where I had walked, shared lunches and dinners with friends, laughed with my son and welcomed in the New Year. It was now smeared with blood and littered with broken bodies. It was impossible to stop watching, and sleep was out of the question.

I was vaguely aware that the perpetrators were being carefully identified as "militants," their presumed motives as "economic," their targets as "Western" and their description—more than once—as "so young, dressed in casual clothes..."

Even though it was clearly a terrorist attack, most reports avoided the words "Muslim" and "Islamic." It was, in fact, a while before the noun "terrorism" was employed.

On some Web sites there was occasional speculation about possible Al-Qaeda connections. Yet even in that context, any religious aspects of the attacks remained unmentioned.

Then reports began to emerge that Mumbai's Chabad House had been attacked by "militants." Chabad is a Hebrew acronym for "Wisdom, Understanding, and Knowledge," and serves as the popular name for a Hasidic Jewish sect known as the Lubavitchers. The Mumbai Chabad House, like many around the world, operates to serve the local Jewish community and to extend hospitality to Jewish tourists and visitors. They offer not only prayer but also the frequently hard-to-find provision of Kosher food.

Media accounts first reported that the local head of Mumbai's Chabad, Rabbi Gavriel Holtzberg, his wife Rivka and others were being held hostage. Mombai's population is nearly 13 million. Its dwindling Jewish population is estimated to be around 4,000. But along with two world-famous hotels—including the Taj Mahal—the city's splendid and historic Chhatrapati Shivaji Terminus train station, the Cama Hospital for women and children and a local police station, was it just bad luck that the humble little Lubavitcher Jewish center was also targeted?

Eventually reporters acknowledged that this wasn't simply an incident of continuing Pakistani vs. Indian hostilities—although those hostilities are very real. After the Chabad House invasion, after a group calling itself the "Deccan Mujahideen" took credit for the battering of Mumbai, the Muslim theme began to be repeated more frequently. A smattering of commentators and bloggers even recalled Osama bin Laden's inflammatory statements, especially since 9/11, and his repeated calls for international jihad.

Of those statements Paul Marshall wrote in *Blind Spot*, "These religious themes have continued. On April 23, 2006, while castigating the United Nations, bin Laden denounced 'pagan Buddhists,' presumably the Chinese. He claimed that the 'world's crusaders alongside pagan Buddhists hold the five permanent seats in the UN Security Council.' Bin Laden also stressed India's role and referred to a 'Crusader-Zionist-Hindu war against the Muslims...'"

Mumbai's Hindu population certainly bore the brunt of the attacks. Thanks, no doubt, to Bin Laden's rhetoric, Hindus were clearly targeted. And whether the Mumbai attacks were the specific handiwork of Al-Qaeda or not, the global religious war took on new proportions. *Time Magazine* quoted French terrorism specialist Roland Jacquard: "This didn't involve suicide bombers and booby-trapped cars that we commonly see in Islamist terror attacks—ones which usually end with the explosion-deaths of the kamikazes carrying them out. This is essentially a small army sent into the heart of society with orders to kill and keep killing as long as possible." For three days, the city was under siege, and more than a few described Mumbai not just as a site of selective terrorist attacks but as a war zone.

Tragically, it was the murders of Rabbi Gabriel and Rivka Holtzberg and their fellow hostages that made the nature of the conflict clear to the world.

The Holtzbergs were not strangers to difficulty. They had endured the ongoing heartache of seeing two infant sons, Menachem and Dov Ber, stricken with Tay-Sachs disease, a deadly genetic disorder. Their third son, Moshe, was thankfully healthy; in November 2008, he was two years old, living with his parents in the Chabad House, where the Hozbergs offered generous hospitality to Jewish visitors from all over the world. Rivka was pregnant with their fourth child at the time of the massacre. The bodies of Rivka and six others were covered with prayer shawls when they were found, which seemed to indicate that Rabbi Holtzberg had somehow reverently honored the others before being murdered himself.

Moshe's Indian nanny Sandra, a Christian, found the toddler bloodied and crying next to his dead parents. The Holtzbergs' bodies were taken to Israel to be buried, and Moshe and Sandra joined the families at the funeral there. In a heart-rending video clip, Moshe was heard crying *"Ima, Ima!"*—"mother" in Hebrew—during the service; Israeli immigration authorities made it possible for Sandra Samuel to remain with the child and his grandparents in

Israel. The young woman was quoted as saying, " "No one knows how much Moshe saw, or how much he knows. His back is bruised where terrorists hit him. Now I want to see that this baby who has been given into my care, he grows big, brave like his father. By God's grace I hope I am there to see it."

As investigations into the Mumbai massacre were completed, it became very clear that the Holtzbergs were not killed for being in the wrong place at the wrong time. They weren't caught in the crossfire between Muslims and "Western targets." They weren't players in any Pakistani-Indian conflict. The Holtzbergs were not murdered for anything other than being Jews—radio transmissions between the terrorists and their leaders were emphatic about targeting the Chabad House. The Holtzberg's son is an orphan because his parents were Jews. The Holtzbergs were casualties in a religious war that has cost millions of lives in Sudan, and thousands in Nigeria, Bali, Indonesia, Madrid, New York, London and, of course, in Israel.

Terror: Made in Pakistan

Clarity about the Mumbai atrocities did not materialize overnight, and no one but the local authorities is fully aware of all the gruesome details to this day. But one thing was clear: the attacks had originated in Pakistan. It didn't take long for investigators to learn that the raging anti-Semitism that had cost Rabbi Gabriel and Rivka Holtzberg and six of their guests their lives had its roots in Pakistan, a nation that is particularly notorious for its abuses of religious minorities. Pakistan no longer has a visible Jewish community to abuse—the last openly Jewish Pakistani, Rachel Joseph, died in 2006.

We are often reminded that Judaism, Christianity and Islam comprise the world's "three great monotheistic religions." Of course, distinctive beliefs set the three faiths apart from one another. And while they all share a belief that there is but one God, within each great religion are divergent interpretations, comprising myriad denominational debates: Reformed, Conservative and Orthodox movements in Judaism; the Shia/Sunni/Sufi divide in Islam; the Catholic/Protestant/Eastern Orthodox schisms in Christianity; and all the other innumerable readings of holy texts that fall somewhere in between.

The most radical contemporary interpretations of Islam are unique, however—and mercilessly so—in one sense. Radical Islamists declare and demonstrate that, in their view, human life is of less value than the Islamic religion itself. Human beings—and their God-given breath of life—are found wanting in comparison to the sanctity of Islam's holy book, the Quran. And the revered reputation of its prophet Mohammed. And calls to jihad—holy war—from radical leaders against non-Muslims.

At the time of the Chabad "Nariman House" attack, reports later confirmed, the terrorists were assured by their handlers in Pakistan that the lives of Jews were worth 50 times those of non-Muslims. *The Times* reported, in an article titled, "Mumbai Attacks: And Then They Came for the Jews," "The organisers had sought [Nariman House] out with care. Most Mumbaikars knew of the Taj Mahal hotel. Few were aware of the small Jewish center tucked away on a backstreet. ..."

The intentional targeting, and the savage and torturous treatment of the hostages, particularly of Rabbi Holtzberg and his wife, exposes that the hatred of some Pakistanis for Jews remains undiminished more than 60 years after the founding of the two states—Israel and Pakistan.

The hatred of Jews in Muslim countries comes as no surprise. What is less well known is that Muslim hatred of Jews is linked to hatred of Christians. This is captured—particularly in the Middle East—in the familiar slogan "First the Saturday people, then the Sunday people." Variations on this theme are chanted in marches and emblazoned in graffiti. Pakistan's "Saturday people," the Jews, are virtually gone. Now it is the Christians, the "Sunday people," who are in constant danger. As we'll soon see, Pakistan serves as an example because of its combination of anti-Semitic sensibilities and its ongoing abuses of Christians, and it bears a striking resemblance to a number of Middle Eastern countries with similar patterns of violence and abuse.

Today, almost miraculously, a handful of Pakistani political leaders continue to stand courageously against radical Islamists. In doing so, they surely invite dangers of their own. In 2011, Shahbaz Bhatti—the Federal Minister for Minorities Affairs and the only Christian in the Pakistani Cabinet—was murdered because he had outspokenly opposed Pakistan's draconian blasphemy laws. Pakistan's then-Ambassador to the U.S., Husain Haqqani, took the unusual step of holding a memorial service to eulogize Shahbaz Bhatti, who was murdered for, in his killer's words, "Blaspheming the Prophet Mohammad."

Haqqani's powerful statements at the memorial service reflect the hopes, prayers and vision of likeminded countrymen and women toward reforming their homeland's deadly religious laws. Ambassador Haqqani concluded his remarks by saying,

Those who would murder… Shahbaz Bhatti deface my religion, my Prophet, my Quran and my Allah. Yet, there is an overpowering, uncomfortable and unconscionable silence from the great majority of Pakistanis who respect the law, respect the Holy Book, and respect other religions.

This silence endangers the future of my nation, and to the extent the silence empowers extremists, it endangers the future of peace and the future of the civilized world.

We are all familiar with the haunting words of Pastor Martin Niemoller, written about pre-war Nazi Germany:

"First they came for the communists, and I didn't speak out because I wasn't a communist.

Then they came for the trade unionists, and I didn't speak out because I wasn't a trade unionist.

Then they came for the Jews, and I didn't speak out because

I wasn't a Jew.
Then they came for me and there was no one left to speak for me."
We cannot close our eyes, turn our backs and be silent about injustice
and discrimination.
When a Shahbaz Bhatti is murdered, and we remain silent, we have
died with him...

Nearly a Million Jews Expelled from their Homes

Pakistan, although not an Arab country, holds in common with several Arab nations the fact that it has either killed, expelled or subjected to continuous persecution its Jewish citizens. The Arab countries, however, remain the most notorious for this abuse. Consider a 2010 statement by Prof. Shmuel Trigano in his article, "The Expulsion of the Jews from Muslim Countries, 1920-1970: A History of Ongoing Cruelty and Discrimination,"

> Between 1920 and 1970, 900,000 Jews were expelled from Arab and other Muslim countries: from Morocco to Iran, from Turkey to Yemen, including places where they had lived for twenty centuries. The 1940s were a turning point in this tragedy; of those expelled, 600,000 settled in the new state of Israel, and 300,000 in France and Canada. Today, they and their descendants form the majority of the French Jewish community and a large part of Israel's population.
>
> How does one explain this exodus? It is the *blind spot* of contemporary political consciousness and an object of denial. There is not even an expression to name this major event. "The Forgotten Exodus" is the most commonly used term. But it actually masks the nature and impact of this historical event. "Forgotten" by whom, other than ideologues? ...For those who underwent the expulsion have not forgotten it at all. Moreover, it is also an important historical fact (Emphasis added).

Trigano is, of course, correct. It is a historical fact. And it is also a blind spot. It is a blind spot that has distorted the whole understanding of the state of Israel, as well as the issue of Palestinian refugees.

Much of the peril the Jews faced in Arab lands had to do with the ambitions of Hajj al-Husseini, the Grand Mufti of Jerusalem. As we saw in Chapter 7, his collaboration with Adolf Hitler to bring about the "Final Solution to the Jewish Problem" in the Middle East contributed greatly to the rising tide of anti-Jewish hatred. He successfully politicized latent, ancient impulses among Arabs. Even in the Maghreb, where Jews had been treated comparatively more humanely than elsewhere in the Muslim world, eventually more than 360,000 Jewish men, women and children were forced out of their homes and livelihoods in Libya, Tunisia, Algeria and Morocco.

I first learned about these Jewish Refugees from Arab lands almost by accident. I was attending the 2009 Herzliya Conference—an annual event sponsored by the Institute for Policy and Strategy at the Interdisciplinary Center (IDC), in Herzliya, Israel. Often the workshops address something of interest to me or are important to my work. But that year, there was a gap in the schedule and I wasn't sure what do to. I more or less wandered into a panel discussion about something I'd never heard of, called "The Forgotten Refugees." There was a documentary by that name, produced by The David Project, that was to be screened later, but the commentators were talking about the history behind the documentary.

Panelist after panelist left me increasingly puzzled. The settlement of European Jewish refugees in Israel is, of course, a well-known story. But that was not the subject here. This was about Jews from the Muslim world. Most spoke of their own families fleeing for their lives, leaving behind property, homes and the wealth and tradition of generations. Some talked matter-of-factly; others spoke with great emotion and even tears. They mentioned one country after another. They told story after story, each one more painful than the last.

Then the Q and A began. People in the audience spontane-
ously stood up and spoke of their grandparents, of their parents, of
themselves being driven out of their homelands—places Jews had
lived, in several cases, for millennia. Many of those who spoke had
barely escaped with their lives. Otherwise, they had lost everything.
As they spoke, they wept. And as they wept, the audience cheered
and applauded, seeming to be more than well aware of the essential
storyline.

So why hadn't I heard about this "Forgotten Exodus" before?
I'd been in Israel for a few years by then. I'd read half a dozen
lengthy histories of Israel or histories of the Jewish people, yet they
had barely mentioned such a monstrous event. Why had nearly
a million refugees fallen off the radar screen? I was particularly
shocked to find that there were at least as many—and probably
many more—Jewish refugees from Arab or non-Arab Muslim lands
than there had been Arab refugees from or within Israel's borders.

From a friend, Rachel Machtiger, I received a report from
scholar Maurice M. Roumani, which included the statement,

> In contrast to the high profile maintained by the Palestinian
> refugees, Jewish refugees in Israel began a costly rehabilita-
> tion program and played down their refugee status as much
> as possible. Their story was little known until 1976, when a
> new organization named WOJAC [World Organization of
> Jews from Arab Countries] undertook to make their voice
> heard so that no Middle East refugee settlement could take
> place without their claims being part of the equation. These
> claims are based on both historical and legal rights from
> centuries of continuous living in the Mediterranean region
> under Muslim rule.

First the Jews, Then the Christians

The exit of Jews from these countries wasn't the end of the abuse, as
we'll see in chapters yet to come. After the Jews' expulsion, subse-

quent attacks on Christians began in many of those same nations. Today anti-Christian violence rages, and the Christian populations in Muslim lands are rapidly diminishing. Only as I began to discover this recurring pattern of violence did I first learn about the graffiti, and the repeated chant "First the Saturday People, then the Sunday People."

So it was, for several reasons, that I started looking for further information. And what I learned continues both to amaze and alarm me.

From 1948 to 1970, between 850,000 and a million Jews fled or were expelled from Arab lands. Many of these forgotten refugees were members of ancient Jewish communities that predated both Islam and Christianity. More than a few were wealthy, powerful and successful. Nearly all of them left their homes with little more than the shirts on their backs, leaving behind houses, bank accounts, investments, personal treasures and their means of livelihood. They resettled, mostly in Israel. From then until now, they have received no reparations, no inventory of their lost possessions, no resolutions by the United Nations, and virtually no consideration in negotiations for Middle East peace.

A look at the numbers of Jews who once lived in Arab lands and their populations today provides a rather stunning perspective. The numbers of Jews presently living in those countries is, by necessity, approximate.

Iraq: In 1948, 135,000 Jews. There are said to be less than 10 left today.

Yemen and Aden: In 1948, 63,000 Jews. Today, there are less than 250.

Syria and Lebanon: In 1948, 30,000 Jews. Now there are about 25 Jews left in Syria and around the same number in Lebanon—if that many.

Egypt: In 1948, 100,000 Jews. Now there are less than 100.

Libya: In 1948, 38,000. No Jews are believed to remain in Libya today.

Algeria: In 1948, 140,000. Less than 100 remain.

Morocco: In 1948, 265,000 Jews. Today there are estimated between 3-4,000 remaining.

Tunisia: In 1948, 105,000 Jews. Today, about 1500 Jews live there.

Today, now that the Jews are out of the picture (except in raging diatribes against Israel), anti-Christian violence rages unchecked in most Muslim majority states, and their Christian populations are also rapidly diminishing. Recent terrorist attacks against Christians in these countries have spotlighted the Christians' hopeless circumstances, characterized by threats of terror and bloodshed, and culminating in a silent exodus from their ancient homelands. Beatings, extortions, church burnings, rapes, mob violence and murders by Muslim radicals continue not only in the Middle East but beyond, resulting in death and injury to hundreds of Christian believers each year.

If I am not for others, what am I?

Unfortunately, even some influential Christians have the story dead wrong. The Vatican's Special Assembly for the Middle East of the Synod of Bishops, which took place in Vatican City in October 2010, did not direct its blame at the real culprits. Despite evidence to the contrary—and to the consternation of Israelis, the greater Jewish community and many Christian groups and organizations—the Synod's bishops chose to focus their attention on the "Israeli occupation" of the Palestinian territories rather than naming the actual perpetrators of ongoing violence against Christians: radical Islamic terrorists.

Jesuit priest Raymond J. de Souza—who clearly doesn't toe the Vatican's line—commented, "Radical Islam is the elephant in the sacristy at the synod. Arab Christians are reluctant to speak critically of their fellow Arabs, and there is intense pressure in the Islamic world to put the blame on Israel, Jews and the Christian

West. Christians in that milieu fear being considered traitors should they too loudly insist upon their rights."

Further underscoring the weakness of the Vatican's declaration is the fact that attacks by Muslims on Christians extend well beyond the Middle East. As we've seen, Christians continue to pay the highest price for their faith in Pakistan, where hundreds of Christians have been murdered in recent years. And besides Pakistan, in 2010, Christians were killed for their faith by Muslim terrorists in Nigeria, Kenya, Ethiopia, Afghanistan, Somalia, Philippines and Bangladesh. The threats against Christians in these countries continue to multiply. The Al-Qaeda affiliated terrorist group, Al-Shabab in Somalia, for example, has threatened to kill every Christian in the country. The number of Christians fleeing Muslim lands is impossible to calculate. Many, if not most, such refugees leave in secret to protect their families and co-believers.

The Vatican's focus on Israel, rather than on radical Islam, as the root cause of abuses against Christians, is both disingenuous and destructive. Both Judaism and Christianity are unwelcome in many Muslim lands for reasons of Islamist ideology—the declaration of *jihad*, or holy war, against infidels. Without a clear and honest analysis that addresses radical Islam, there can be no effective policy enabling besieged Christians to live at peace in their homelands. With the Jews gone from many Muslim countries, Christians are now in the jihadis' crosshairs.

Sadly, very few reports of these incidents reach the West, except in cases of massacres or political significance. Yet because of the tragic history of the Jewish people, and despite the abuses Jewish people have endured at the hands of "Christian" mobs, Jews are often the first to react when they hear about anti-Christian violence. It has often been prominent Jews, rather than Christians, who have first sounded the alarm about anti-Christian persecution, and especially that taking place in the Muslim world.

In 1997, I co-authored with Paul Marshall *Their Blood Cries Out*, a book on the global persecution of Christians. Michael Horowitz wrote in the foreword:

> The mounting persecution of Christians eerily parallels the persecution of Jews, my people, during much of Europe's history. … The silence and indifference of Western elites to the beatings, looting, torture, jailing, enslavement, murder and even crucifixion of increasingly vulnerable Christian communities further engages my every bone and instinct as a Jew. My grandparents and those who lived with them in the ghettos of Poland would well understand the meaning and the certain effects, of such patronizing hostility. The ignorance and silence displayed by Western Christian communities toward the suffering of fellow believers completes the litany of parallels to earlier sordid chapters of the world history...

The world has begun to take note. In late October 2011, the European Parliament adopted a resolution accusing both Egypt and Syria of persecuting Christians. Regarding Egypt, the resolution stated,

> Since March 2011, tens of thousands of Coptic Christians have reportedly left Egypt. On 9 October, at least 25 were killed and more than 300 wounded in Cairo during a peaceful march organised by Copts. Parliament strongly condemns the killing of protestors in Egypt, and stresses the importance of an independent and transparent investigation. Authorities should ensure that Copts do not fall victim to violent attacks and can live in peace and freely express their beliefs throughout the country. MEPs call for protection of churches, to put an end to their destruction and to continuous aggression by Islamic extremists.

As for Syria, the European Parliament's resolution went on to say,

> MEPs are also deeply concerned about the situation of Christians in Syria. … thousands of Iraqi Christians went to Syria to escape targeted violence in Iraq. Nevertheless, the Christian population in Syria may have dropped from 10% to 8% of the total. Parliament condemns actions inciting inter-confessional conflict, urges Syrian authorities to provide reliable and efficient protection for the Christian in the country.

The more I have pondered the largely untold story of the "Forgotten Refugees"—and today's similar circumstances faced by Christians in the same Arab lands they fled—the more intrigued I've become. I kept asking people in Israel what they knew about the Jewish refugee story. One of the organizers of the Herzliya Conference panel discussion I attended was of great help to me in locating men and women who had actually been refugees themselves.

During the summer of 2009, while I stayed in Ruthie Blum's Har Adar apartment, I began to track these people down. One of them, Linda Menuhin, "Anne Frank of Baghdad"—whose story appears in the following pages—lives in the same community as Ruthie, on the same street. In fact, I was able to walk to that first interview. Linda was cooking Iraqi food when I arrived at her home and the smell was irresistible. I sat at the kitchen table and watched her as she prepared *kubé* (meat stuffed dumplings) for a family feast while she told me about her escape from Iraq and the terrible loss of her father, whose body has never been found.

Other former refugees were further afield. But I was astonished by the number of times I was told, "Oh yes, my parents came here from Tunisia," or "My grandfather came from Iraq in the 50s," or "Both my parents were Yemenite—I was born in a tent village…" Once the subject came up, everybody knew somebody, and often that someone was in his or her immediate or extended family.

One interesting point is that, unlike the Palestinians who fled or were driven out of their homes, a majority of the Jews who fled Arab lands seem not to have perceived themselves as refugees. It is true that some continue to fight for material restitution or at least for recognition of their catastrophic losses. Organizations have been formed to represent them. The World Organization of Jews from Arab Countries, has estimated that Jewish property confiscated or abandoned in Arab countries would be valued at $300 billion today. WOJAC also has estimated that the Jewish real estate left behind in Arab lands would amount to four for five times the size of the State of Israel.

Some want to continue to fight for what their families lost. Others have a different perspective. As Linda Masri Hakim wrote in *Iraq's Last Jews,*

> We probably had one of the most valuable houses in Baghdad at the time, but we never tried to get restitution for our house and other property. My husband filled in property restitution forms for his family's property, but I have never bothered because I know it's a waste of time. No one will fulfill the Jews' claims. We are just a minority that most Iraqis still hate. I'll tell you something about the Iraqi Jews—in fact probably about Jews in general. We never look back. We always look forward. I'm not going to go back and claim a house, which used to be mine 40 or 50 years ago. I really couldn't care less. I live for the future. The European Jews were the same way after the Holocaust. If you look back, you never go forward.

In the chapters that follow, I will introduce you to some of the colorful and outspoken people I met after I discovered for myself this under-reported passage in history. I was able to sit with most of them face to face and learn about their remarkable experiences firsthand—a generation forced to flee for their lives and leave the only world they'd ever known.

Their experiences, and those of countless others who suffer still today, bring me back to Hussein Haqqani's eulogy for Shabbaz Bhatti. The Ambassador's words resonate for many of us—Jewish, Christian or whatever we choose to call ourselves—as we watch history repeating itself once again. We feel grieved. We feel angry. And we feel powerless. Yet we are driven to do whatever we can to change the frightening turn of events in today's world. Haqqani concluded,

I recall the words of the great Rabbi Hillel, who said two thousand years ago,
"If I am not for myself, who will be for me?
If I am not for others, what am I?
If not now, when?"

If we are silent, we allow evil to win.
If we are not with others, what are we?
It is unacceptable.
It is unIslamic.
And If I may use a term that has been abused, it is blasphemy.

CHAPTER TEN

JEWISH NAKBA

Moving from Morocco to Israel at the age of 13 was like moving from one planet to another. Israel was not only a different country, it was a different culture and these were completely different Jews and it was a completely different Judaism. It was September 1972 and within a year and a half of my arrival there was a war, the Yom Kippur war, and my little brother died; all this happened before the end of 1973. These traumas are the source of my writing, and perhaps the reason I started to write.—Mois Benarroch, Israeli Poet

Benarroch is well known, and he has written extensively about his troubles, but he was hardly the only uprooted Jewish child of Morocco who found himself on a frightening journey, moving away from everything he'd ever known. There were hundreds of thousands of others. Today most of them, along with their sons and daughters, are active participants in the daily life of Israel, having successfully begun their lives over again in, as Benarroch says, a different world. But it was never easy.

A Childhood Interrupted

Imagine, for example, a frightened six-year-old girl trying to catch her balance in the stifling and cramped lower deck of a violently tossing ship. She is not alone on the turbulent sea—her parents and a sibling are nearby. But fear is in the air, along with the sight and smell of terrible sickness. The child understands little about her circumstances. She is aware that she is going to a place called Israel, where three of her brothers now live. She realizes that she is saying good-bye forever to her Morocco home. But that's all she knows about her journey.

Meanwhile her present misery, and that of her beloved family, eclipses all else. The girl's name is Dina Gabay. The year is 1955. Dina, her parents—Avraham and Rachel—and their family are fleeing ever-increasing dangers in their town of Sefrou, near Fez.

Only in later years did Dina come to appreciate the constant pressure her parents had endured before their departure from Morocco. There were small things—insults and ceaseless intimidation. For example, her father, who owned a large and successful butcher shop, was at the mercy of local thieves, who sometimes simply walked into his business and demanded that he give them whatever they wanted—at no cost. "Not once and not twice," Dina explains, "but whenever they wanted something. These were our good Muslim neighbors, you know?"

Avraham Gabay knew better than to argue. "If you said something they didn't like, you were in danger," Dina recalls. "Most of the time everybody got along. But when you are in a lower place in society, you don't dare to stand up for yourself." There were bigger threats too, including mysterious disappearances. First her father's best friend vanished. Then one of Dina's cousins, who was known in the community as a remarkably beautiful 14-year-old girl, also disappeared, never to be seen again.

In the Moroccan Jewish community, such things weren't exactly unusual. And they had happened more and more frequently after 1948, when Israel declared itself an independent state. At that moment, the centuries-long, low-grade oppression Jews experienced in their role as dhimmis under Muslim rule ignited into ugly confrontations, humiliation and random attacks. These episodes occasionally exploded into full-blown pogroms in which hundreds were killed or wounded.

It is sometimes forgotten that North Africa was gripped by the iron first of Nazism in the early 1940s, either through

German occupation (Tunisia), Italy's Fascist regime (Libya), or under France's Vichy regime (Algeria and Morocco), all of which served the Third Reich's anti-Jewish purposes. Robert Satloff, in his book *Among the Righteous: Lost Stories from the Holocaust's Long Reach into Arab Lands,* describes one particular political pronouncement that in some ways resembles the ghettoization of Europe's Jewish communities:

> In Morocco…Jews bore the brunt of a special decree that was imposed nowhere else in North Africa: All Jews who lived in the new, modern neighborhoods of large cities had to give up their homes and relocate back to the narrow alleys and crowded lanes of the traditional Jewish quarter (*mellah*). To add insult to injury, the date by which all Jews had to fulfill the requirements of this decree fell on Yom Kippur, 1941, the holiest day on the Jewish calendar. By that day, one-fifth of Casablanca's 50,000 Jews, along with comparably sized groups in the imperial cities of Rabat-Salé and Fez had to find new lodging. One result, noted an historian, was to hasten the spread of disease in the already cramped quarters of the old Jewish Quarter.

Satloff also details the brutal operation of more than 100 forced labor camps in which thousands of Jews and others suffered, and more than a few did not survive. Besides those sent to the labor camps, "many thousands more lost homes, farms, jobs, professions, savings and years of education. Still more lived in a state of perpetual fear and daily privation, victims of a ration system that gave them the least and gave it to them last."

The Allied armies landed in North Africa in 1943, and in the wake of this a few anti-Jewish pogroms took place in Morocco. Then, after Israel's declaration of independence, in 1948, brutal rioting cost 44 Jews their lives, and injured many others.

Much of the peril the Jews faced in the Middle East from the 1930s on had to do with the notorious ambitions of Hajj al-Husseini, and his collaboration with Adolf Hitler to put extermination camps in place across the Middle East. Those plans were finally laid to rest when the allies, under the command of General Dwight D. Eisenhower, defeated the Axis armies. But they left an important legacy for the Jewish population of North Africa.

During the 1950s, the threat to Morocco's Jews reemerged.

An article in *Commentary* magazine published in September 1954 described their distressing circumstances. This was the atmosphere during the early years of Dina Gabay Levin's life. "In disputes with Muslims, or on civil commercial and criminal issues among themselves, Jews are almost entirely subject to Islamic courts... even under the best of circumstances [the courts] regard Jewish litigants as unclean, inferior beings."

While the Gabay family felt increasing pressure from the surrounding Muslim community, Morocco itself was in political upheaval over French colonialism. As has often happened in anticolonial independence movements, Jews were stigmatized as enemies of surging nationalist factions. In Morocco, as elsewhere, they paid the price.

In 1954 and 1955, Morocco's Jews were attacked by pronationalist forces in Casablanca, Rabat, Mazagan and Petitjean, with numerous deaths and injuries. Throughout the country, property was seized and arsonists attacked Jewish schools. In the five years following Israel's independence, around 30,000 Jews made *aliyah*—which means "making ascent" or moving upward in both a physical and spiritual sense by imigrating to Israel; the numbers dramatically increased in subsequent years.

Historian Heskel M. Haddad explains,

The major cause of the Jewish exodus from Morocco was the two pogroms that occurred in 1948 and 1953. Within a few years, several thousand Moroccan Jews immigrated to Israel. But mass immigration of Jews from Morocco occurred in 1954 when it became clear that France intended to grant Morocco full independence. Tens of thousands of Jews left Morocco, thereby betraying the typical anxiety of Jews in an independent Arab country.

Jewish emigration was forbidden in 1956 after Moroccan independence from France, which led to Zionist underground activities, secret departures and desperate flights—like that of the Gabay family. Israel's Mossad organized clandestine operations, allowing a continuous stream of emigrants, working with a dissident movement of local Moroccans, who courageously smuggled thousands of Jews out of the country.

"We left all of our property," Dina remembers, "our house and my father's business. We couldn't take anything with us. We left in the night and rushed to the ship. All kinds of people were fleeing. In fact some of those that went to Israel had been wealthy. My uncle, for example, was very rich. He was a carpenter and had a large factory. He had also built a school for Jewish children, which he owned. When he decided to go, he left everything behind—his home, his factory and the school."

As in many 20th Century Jewish communities that fled hostility in Muslim majority nations, many of the Jews who left Morocco had been leaders in their societies; they were wealthy, successful and comfortable in their way of life. Doctors, lawyers, merchants and bankers were among the frightened masses that sailed away from their homelands.

The day of the Jews' departures has often been described as their personal *Nakba* —the Arabic word for catastrophe.

Nakba Day is now an annual Palestinian "holiday" inaugurated by Yasser Arafat in 1998. Its purpose is not to commemorate the "catastrophe" of Israel's 1967 conquest of territories that are now regarded as occupied. Rather it is meant to commemorate the catastrophe of 1948, the establishment of Israel as an independent state.

In particular, it is used to bring to the fore the issue of Arabs who abandoned their homes in what later came to be the State of Israel. This was an unfortunate consequence of the 1948 war. But as almost all contemporary historians of that period now affirm, it was largely the result of Arab policies and not Israeli ones. Nor were these Arabs the only refugees. As we have seen, hundreds of thousands of Jews were driven out of Arab and Muslim lands, and their plight was instigated by the actions of Arab and Muslim leadership.

In the Jews' shattering departures from their homes—many families had lived in North Africa since the 15th century and some even before—most of the Jews of the Maghreb lost everything but the clothes they wore. In a stunning riches-to-rags reversal, they found themselves among the poorest of the poor.

Catastrophic New Beginnings

After the terrible voyage—she can't remember how long it took, only that it seemed interminable—Dina Gabay and her family were taken from the ship to a squalid tent city—one of many *ma'abarot*, where tens of thousands of refugees from the Maghreb were kept in almost unlivable conditions upon their arrival in Israel. The young nation, not yet 10 years old, was ill prepared for such an influx of displaced people. The Gabay family felt utter desolation. "Every night we just wanted to run away, but there was nowhere to run."

A Jewish Agency report describes the ma'abarot of the time:

The structure of the camps was essentially similar: Families lived in small shacks of cloth, tin or wood, no larger than 10 square meters to 15 sq.m. each. Other shacks housed the basic services: kindergarten, school, infirmary, small grocery, employment office, synagogue, etc. The living quarters were not connected to either water or electric systems. Running water was available from central faucets, but it had to be boiled before drinking. The public showers and lavatories were generally inadequate and often in disrepair. A paucity of teachers and educational resources severely hindered the attempts to provide the camp children with suitable education. Work, even relief work, was not always available.

And yet, despite the multiple troubles they would confront in starting over, Morocco's Jews continued to leave their homeland—for reasons of financial disaster, for dreams of a better future in a Jewish country, and because of intense Muslim hatred. In 1965, Moroccan writer Said Ghallab described the attitude of his fellow Muslims toward their Jewish neighbors:

> The worst insult that a Moroccan could possibly offer was to treat someone as a Jew.... My childhood friends have remained anti-Jewish. They hide their virulent anti-Semitism by contending that the State of Israel was the creature of Western imperialism.... A whole Hitlerite myth is being cultivated among the populace. The massacres of the Jews by Hitler are exalted ecstatically. It is even credited that Hitler is not dead, but alive and well, and his arrival is awaited to deliver the Arabs from Israel.

Despite their trauma, many Moroccans distinguished themselves in their new Israeli society. Author Yehuda Grinker wrote of them, "These Jews constitute the best and most suitable human element for settlement in Israel's absorption centers. There were many positive aspects which I found among them: First and foremost, they all know [their agricultural] tasks, and their transfer to agricultural work in Israel will not involve physical and mental difficulties. They are satisfied with few [material needs], which will enable them to confront their early economic problems."

After three months in the absorption center, the Gabays were reunited with Dina's three brothers, who had made their way to Israel at 13, 15 and 17. By then, the boys were in their late 20s and had served in the Haganah during the War of Independence. Once the family was back together, they went to live together in Rishon LeZion.

As a child, she could hardly have imagined such a turn of events, but like others among her homeland's émigrés, Dina married, had a family and proved herself more than suitable to life in Israel. In fact, she grew up to become deputy mayor of the Israeli city Rishon LeZion, a role in which she served until 2007. Today she remains a spokeswoman for the city and for the Moroccan Jews in Israel.

For over half a century, the flight of nearly 900,000 Jewish refugees from Arab lands has led to controversy both inside Israel and internationally. As we've seen, more Jews were forced to flee from Muslim persecution than the approximately 762,000 Palestinian Arabs who left their homes in the newly declared State of Israel. The full story has rarely been told. For reasons too complex for brief analysis, Israel did not, as one writer tactfully said, "put the catastrophe that overtook the Arab Jews on its international public relations and national agenda..."

Changes began to surface in February 2010. After years of effort, and by a majority of votes, a bill to seek compensation for Jews from Arab countries was passed in the Knesset. Zvi Gabay (no relation to Dina Gabay Levin), a reporter for *Yisrael Hayom*, wrote, "For the first time since the establishment of the state, the rights of the Jews from Arab countries are receiving legal recognition in Israel. Up until now, Israeli administrations have chosen to ignore the issue, even as the topic of the Arab refugees and their rights have been front and center on the public dialogue in Israel and the world, under the code name the 'right of return.' The time has come to rectify the situation."

According to the bill, a "Jewish refugee" is defined as an Israeli citizen who left one of the Arab states, or Iran, following religious persecution. The landmark declaration—long awaited by those who lobbied for its passage—specifies that the question of compensation must be included by the government in all future peace negotiations.

Dina Levin, like so many others, finds this turn of events very gratifying. She says, "The new declaration is a very important historical step for the people of Israel, especially for the Jewish communities from Muslim nations. I hope this bill will be put into action and will not stay only as a declaration. That way, finally there will be justice for the tremendous number of Jews who left their property behind in the Muslim nations when they immigrated to Israel."

Despite the struggles Morocco's Jews experienced in the 20th Century, Morocco was, even then, the most hospitable of all Arab countries to its Jewish population. During World War II, Sultan Mohammad V—who remains a hero in the memory of many Moroccan Jews—managed to hammer out concessions as he wrestled with France's Vichy government over the anti-Jewish statutes it introduced in 1940. He was even more helpful to Jews behind the scenes. When a nationwide census of Jewish-owned property was called for, the Jews understandably feared that this was a precursor to widespread confiscation of their homes, lands, livelihoods and everything they called their own. Robert Satloff writes,

> Secretly, the sultan arranged for a group of prominent Jews to sneak into the palace, hidden in a covered wagon so he could meet them away from the prying eyes of the French. According to one of those present, he promised the Jews that he would protect them and assured them that the census was not the first stop in a plan to seize their goods and property. [After the Anglo-American invasion of Morocco, the sultan arranged for the destruction of the census documents.]

...Thanks to such acts of solicitude toward his Jewish
subjects, Moroccan Jewish lore celebrates Sultan Mohammad
V as a savior, one of the finest, fairest, and most tolerant rulers
Jews had ever known. His reputation has taken on mythic
proportions, with Moroccan Jews even inventing tales of his
heroism.

Over the years, despite the anti-Jewish attitude of its citizenry,
Morocco's government has quietly and unusually retained relations
with Israel. In 1976, it hosted meetings with Israeli Prime Minister Yitzhak Rabin; the following year it did the same for Foreign
Minister Moshe Dayan. More recently, it has quietly sought to
encourage discussions for a peaceful settlement between Israeli and
Palestinian leadership.

However, as is the case in the rest of today's Muslim-majority
countries, there is a rising tide of extremism simmering dangerously beneath the surface. In 2003, 12 suicide bombers struck
Casablanca, killing 45 (including the bombers) and injuring
scores. In the spring of 2007, a flurry of suicide bombings rocked
Casablanca again; only the bombers were killed, but several people
were injured.

In early 2011, Moroccan authorities arrested 27 people, including a member of Al-Qaeda's branch in North Africa, for planning
terrorist attacks in the kingdom. The suspects were under the
authority of "a Moroccan national who is a member of Al-Qaeda
in the Islamic Maghreb and who wanted to create a rear base in the
country for terror attacks," an Interior Ministry statement said...
cited by Moroccan news agency MAP. No names were released,
but those who were arrested "planned to commit terrorist acts with
explosives-laden belts and car bombings."

During the "Arab Spring" demonstrations that gripped the
Arab world in 2011, more than 40,000 young Moroccans took to
the street. King Mohammad VI promised to make broad and unprecedented changes to the nation's constitution, and more or less

quieted the protests. But the revolutionary undercurrents remain. And the majority vote in a 2011 election went to an Islamist party.

Morocco's former Ambassador to the U.S., H.E. Aziz Mekouar, told the *Washington Post* in early 2011 that unlike any other Muslim country, Morocco supports freedom of worship. Ambassador Mekouar said, "In Morocco freedom of religion is totally guaranteed by the constitution. We think anything, anything, any religious violence is unacceptable." He notes that there are "tens of thousands of Christians and a very important Jewish community in Morocco."

Crackdown on Christians

The Ambassador's remarks were made following media inquiries about a spate of expulsions of Christians from Morocco in 2010, when a number of long-time Christian institutions were also closed. Although Christians only account for about 1 percent of a population of 32.7 million, there are reports that conversions to Christianity among Muslims are noticeably mounting, a reality that has not pleased local Muslims, or worse, their increasingly radicalized leadership. Accusations of proselytizing—illegal in Morocco as in other Muslim countries—were the explanation for the unusual crackdown on Christians. It is likely that rumors of increasing conversions to Christianity from Islam put added pressure on the government.

Some converts to Christianity have spoken up, albeit using pseudonyms. "Abdelhalim" explained to a Christian reporter, "'For many of us, Islam is perceived as a social straitjacket and not as a real faith, and Christianity as a religion of tolerance and love,' said the businessman, who converted at the age of 19 and was later followed by his family. Yet in the eyes of the state they remain Muslim. 'Officially, my son and I are Muslim,' Abdelhalim said. "'We hold Christian marriages and bless the young couple but this is not recognized by the state. They must go before the Muslim clergy and marry according to Shari'a [Islamic law]. If they don't do this, they can be charged with adultery.'"

"Youssef," another convert, added, "'I have been summoned to the police station dozens of times.'" He nonetheless affirmed that Morocco is considered more tolerant than other Muslim countries, thanks to King Mohammed VI.

Nonetheless, a July 2010 story was headlined, "The King is Unamused by Christians who Proselytise," in which *Fez* reported, "Evangelical Christians in the poor world are rarely accused of undermining public order. All the more surprising, then, that in recent months around a hundred have been deported from Morocco for just that. The Christians, mostly from the United States and Europe, have been accused of trying to convert Muslims to Christianity, a crime punishable by imprisonment under Moroccan law, which protects the freedom to practice one's faith but forbids any attempt to convert others."

Compass Direct, a Christian news service, reported that same year,

> Since March, the Moroccan government has expelled more than 100 foreign Christians for alleged "proselytizing." Authorities failed to give Christians deportation orders or enough time to settle their affairs before they left. Observers have called this a calculated effort to purge the historically moderate Muslim country, known for its progressive policies, of all Christian elements—both foreign and national. Amid a national media campaign to vilify Christians in Morocco, more than 7,000 Muslim clerics signed a statement denouncing all Christian activities and calling foreign Christians' aid work "religious terrorism."

The unusual 2010 crackdown on Christians in Morocco has fueled speculation that the Moroccan government is being progressively strong-armed by radical Islamists and has chosen to deport Christians rather than deal with potential violence against them. That theory is supported by other incidents that have been revealed since then.

According to one story, Islamists were posting photo collages and identities of Christian converts, which included facts about their church involvement, their personal addresses, and accusations about their behavior. They were identified as "hyena evangelists" or "wolves in lamb's skins," who were trying to "shake the faith of Muslims."

Another recent case was exposed by the American Center for Law and Justice (ACLJ). A young man who had converted from Islam to Christianity was attacked after attending a secret house church meeting. As he left, "He was approached by four men.... The men surrounded him and said they knew that he had left Islam and dishonored his family and Islam by becoming a *kafir* (infidel). The men stabbed 'Z' multiple times and left him for dead. One of Z's neighbors saw him lying on the ground, bleeding. He took Z to the hospital where he underwent two surgeries. He gained consciousness after three days and thanked God for saving his life..."

The "Saturday people, Sunday people" scenario is not as prevalent in Morocco as in other Arab states because Morocco has, so far, generally proven itself to be an exception to typical Arab outbursts of virulently anti-Jewish, anti-Christian persecution. It is different because the leadership of the country—the King and his advisors—is less ideological about religious minorities than most others. There may be curses against Jews or Christians spoken in mosques, or insults against Israel, Judaism or Zionists expressed freely among friends, but private statements are not given authority, and related activities or are not empowered by the government. Rather, such incidents are suppressed. That doesn't mean, however, that there are no opposing forces.

In August 2010, *Israel National News* reported two anti-Jewish incidents in Morocco. One took place in Mogador, also called Essaouira, where a building owned by Israeli businessman Noam Nir was the focus of an anti-Semitic protest. Another demonstration was held against Andre Azoulay, a Jewish advisor to King Mohammad VI, on the Eve of the Pesach holiday, 2010. In the article, Nir expressed his concern about increasing anti-Semitism in Morocco, and pointed out that he is not comfortable wearing a kippah (a skullcap) in public there.

Al-Qaeda and Lone Wolf Terrorism

Such reports, alongside those about crackdowns and deportations of Christians beginning in 2010, raise questions about the security of Morocco's minorities. Have radical influences begun to gain power despite Morocco's moderate leaders? Has the Arab Spring opened the door to Islamist influences in Morocco that were not emboldened there before? One group, *Al Adl Wa Al Ihssane*, is well known and seems to share a great deal of common ground with the Muslim Brotherhood.

Although everyone agrees that Al-Qaeda and other Islamist radical groups have evil intentions for every North African country, it is also true that many of the terrorists arrested in Morocco have been plotting "lone wolf" acts that are inspired by Al-Qaeda's propaganda, but not planned in cooperation with the organization itself. According to the Associated Press, between 2003 and 2008, the Moroccan government reported that 83 independent terrorist cells had been broken up. Four cells were dismantled in 2010. AP writer Paul Schemm explains,

> The discussion rooms of militant websites provide a glimpse at the seething rage found across much of the Muslim world as would-be mujahedeen trade tips on how to strike blows against the "Crusaders and Zionists," especially if they are unable to make it to the battlefields of Iraq and Afghanistan on their own.

All things considered, "Zionists and Crusaders" have been treated more respectfully by Morocco than by most other Muslim nations. We can only hope that the monarchy there—whatever Mohammad VI's weaknesses or idiosyncrasies—is able to withstand the rising tides of radical Islamism. Otherwise, those forces may tear apart what appears to be one of the few genuinely moderate Muslim countries in today's troubled world.

A Taste of Morocco in Jerusalem

Far removed from the treacherous winds of the Arab Spring, there is a beautiful haven of warm Moroccan hospitality in the heart of Jerusalem. Darna is a stunning restaurant, where every aspect of the décor—carvings, tiles, lamps, screens, dishes, cushions and even the candles—has been imported entirely from Morocco. The owner, Ilan Sibony, grew up in Casablanca. And despite the fact that he and his family have relocated themselves in Israel, he still has a deep love for the aesthetic beauty and incomparable hospitality of Moroccan life.

I met Mr. Sibony recently at Darna, where we sat beside jewel-toned stained glass windows inset in pink-hued walls. Across the way, antiqued carved wood framed a doorway that opened into yet another dining room, this one amber-hued. Colorful lamps are suspended from the ceiling; brass curlicue screens grace keyhole-shaped interior windows.

I asked Ilan Sibony about his life in Morocco, before he moved away in 1969, at 21 years old. He is a tactful man and careful with words.

I cannot say that life was difficult, but it was better to be a Jew in Israel than to be a Jew in Morocco. Yes, we could manage. But there is something about being a Jew there, where you feel that you are not as free as everyone else. You cannot criticize. And if you were found to be a Zionist you could go to jail. Zionism was condemned. The Zionist organization was not open—it was underground.

You could not find a book about Israel in Morocco; you could not find a disc of Israeli songs. Jews kept quiet. They could pray—in fact the only Hebrew you could find was in the prayer book. And when you came into Morocco, you had to be very careful about what was in your suitcase. You couldn't even bring a CD of Israeli songs from France. So there was a point where I decided to come to Israel. I met some people...they spoke to me about coming to Israel...

Ilan left Morocco with his father and brother—his mother had died before their departure. He settled into a kibbutz, where he spent seven years. After serving in the IDF as a paratrooper, he went to the Bezalel Academy of Arts and Design to study architecture. But soon practical demands took over. "My father was dead by then, and I had to work, so I opened a restaurant serving Mediterranean food. It started with five tables, then grew to twelve, then 15, then many more."

Meanwhile, there were changes in the rapport between Morocco and Israel. In 1993, Morocco's King Hassan II and Israeli Prime Minister Yitzhak Rabin held talks, which they described as "a step toward diplomatic relations." One of the positive results of these new efforts was the installation of phone lines between Israel and Morocco.

New rules or not, Morocco's Jews were still accustomed to being careful—even on the telephone. Ilan Sibony describes an awkward first phone call to his uncle.

Once I learned that I could telephone Morocco, I called my uncle in Casablanca and said, "Hello! It's Ilan! I'm calling you from Jerusalem!"

"Shhhh!!" My uncle said.

"But it's okay now for me to call from..."

"Shhh!" my uncle said even more loudly.

"It's okay for me to call you..."

"SHHH!"

"....from *Paris*..."

"Oh, you're in *Paris!*...okay, then...

Once he had soothed his worried uncle's nerves, Ilan learned during the phone call that his cousin's Bar Mitzvah was soon to take place in Casablanca, so he decided to return to his homeland and surprise everyone by attending the event. He did so and was overwhelmed with the experience. "I saw Morocco again, I tasted Morocco again, and it was just wonderful, just marvelous. When I came back to Jerusalem, I was full of enthusiasm, talking to everyone about Morocco. And while I was talking to the man who owned the Chinese restaurant that was here in this building, he told me that he was interested in finding a partner to take over the business."

Sibony still enjoys remembering the serendipitous moment when his beautiful restaurant was conceived. "There's a saying in Morocco that translates to something like, 'If you don't know something, how can you do it?' The Chinese restaurant owner said to me, 'So you want to open a Moroccan restaurant here?'

"The thought had never crossed my mind until that moment. But I said, 'Why not?'"

By then Sibony had completed his architectural training. After his recent trip to Morocco he held vivid images in his mind of the country's elegant and exotic ambiance and he knew exactly how to make the new restaurant look the way he wanted it to. He designed and remodeled the Chinese restaurant—which had by then seen better days. Then he began to import decor from Morocco. The windows were shipped from Rabat, as were the dishes, candles and cushions. He even brought craftsmen to Jerusalem to do the construction work, including expert tile layers to create the complex floor mosaic by hand. Because of recent improvement of relations with Israel, the Moroccan Ministry of tourism was very helpful and cooperative throughout the process. Ilan Sibony took a course in Moroccan cooking and then hired Moroccan chefs. He prepared menus, and with great excitement, opened the doors to Jerusalem.

Darna just celebrated its 16th Birthday, and it remains an up-scale dinner destination for Jerusalemites and tourists alike. The surroundings are romantic and exotic—worlds away from the nearby Russian Compound and Jaffa Road. The food is, as one might expect, delicious.

Before leaving, I asked Ilan what he foresees in Morocco's future. His expression became shadowed with concern. "I don't think so well of the so-called Arab Spring. It will end in winter." He paused to reflect for a moment. "The Moroccans," concluded, "are good people, very soft, and very hospitable. But the problem is that Al-Qaeda is more and more strong in Morocco. And the people are so nice, and they want to please. So they are making Al-Qaeda feel at home."

That made me wonder about the Jews who remain in Morocco. "Are they doing well?" I asked.

"They are doing okay. They know how to get along. But for Jews, Israel has always been the destination, the dream, the place to go." A smile flickered across his face. "Every Passover we pray, 'Next year in Jerusalem.' We've said that for 2,000 years. And as I told you at the beginning, it is better for a Jew to be in Israel."

CHAPTER ELEVEN

ANNE FRANK OF BAGHDAD

It is true that I have fulfilled my dream and arrived in Israel, but it seems that someone else has had to pay a high price for my liberty. My father, who refused to run away from Iraq and hoped to be granted a passport to leave the country legally, was kidnapped in September 1972 on the eve of Yom Kippur.

It was a real shock. We couldn't believe our ears. How could Father disappear. We understood later on that he was killed among many other Jews. Fate laid its cruel merciless hand on our loving father. We cannot catch even a glimpse of his shadow. He is lying deep in the earth and we cannot reach him there.

What a painful end!

As for my mother and sister, they managed to flee the country eight months after my departure. They managed to adapt themselves to the new country—Israel. We overcame the shock, but the shadow of my father is still living in our minds.

—Linda Abu-Aziz Menuhin, 1973

As we've seen, "Nakba Day" commemorates losses suffered by Arabs who fled their homes during the War of Independence. But they weren't the only ones with shattered lives.

"In recent years, many Jews from Iraq have started to talk about what happened to them. But I was so hurt and so locked into myself that I didn't think I could deal with it," says Linda Menuhin, who in 1970 fled the anti-Jewish violence in Baghdad. "More recently I've felt that I needed to heal this very bad bruise, so

I am in the process of opening up. Now I say that having to leave my home in Iraq was *my* catastrophe, my *nakba*."

In fact, hardly a day passes when the subject of the millions of Palestinian refugees seeking a "right of return" to their lost properties—or compensation for them—isn't discussed in relation to Middle East peace negotiations. Between 500,000 and 750,000 Arabs left their homes during the War of Independence in 1948; 60-plus years later, these refugees and their offspring are said to number more than four million, living both in refugee camps in the West Bank and in other Arab countries. The story of their losses and their controversial politicization is a familiar subject for journalists, activists, politicians, and Middle East observers.

Meanwhile, a different refugee story, represented by Linda Menuhin and more than a hundred thousand other Iraqi Jews, is far less familiar. Particularly overlooked is the ancient history of Iraq's Jews. Biblical scholars—Jewish and Christian alike—are well acquainted with the authoritative "Babylonian Talmud," which, besides the Bible, is a primary textual source of doctrine and dogma for most forms of Judaism. Although the Jerusalem Talmud was compiled earlier, when the word "Talmud" is used, it usually refers to the Babylonian Talmud. And it came from what is now Iraq.

The Babylonian Captivity

In 586 BCE, the Kingdom of Judah was defeated and conquered by King Nebuchadnezzar. Many of the kingdom's citizens were taken into captivity to Babylonia. This happened twice more in that same century. Some of the exiles returned to Israel when Persian King Cyrus gave them permission to go back; but others had begun new lives in Babylonia—now Iraq—and they chose to remain. After the destruction of the Temple and the expulsion of the Jews from Jerusalem in 70 AD, many more Jews fled to Babylon, where there was still a thriving Judaic community. In subsequent centuries, the region became the center for Jewish scholarship and remained so for centuries.

One of the most poignant of all ancient Jewish poems—Psalm 137—comes to us from the Babylonian Captivity. It is a cry of longing for a lost homeland. It is also an eloquent and timeless expression of the Zionist vision.

> *By the rivers of Babylon,*
> *There we sat down and wept,*
> *When we remembered Zion.*
> *Upon the willows in the midst of it*
> *We hung our harps.*
> *For there our captors demanded of us songs,*
> *And our tormentors mirth, saying,*
> *"Sing us one of the songs of Zion."*
> *How can we sing the LORD'S song*
> *In a foreign land?*
> *If I forget you, O Jerusalem,*
> *May my right hand forget her skill.*
> *May my tongue cling to the roof of my mouth*
> *If I do not remember you,*
> *If I do not exalt Jerusalem*
> *Above my chief joy....*

There was a Jewish presence in Iraq from the 6th Century BCE until the 21st century. Many of us have watched its final demise. But Linda Menuhin wasn't yet born when the 20th Century's virulent anti-Semitic violence first struck Iraq in 1941. It began with a pogrom, called the *Farhud*, one of many instigated by Nazi-collaborator Haj Amin el-Husseini, Hitler's Middle Eastern partner in crime.

Iraq's Last Jews

During the years while Hitler and his minions were still gaining strength, Husseini inspired a pogrom against Iraq's Jews. The British, who had just defeated the pro-Axis junta of Rashid Ali, did nothing to stop the bloodshed. During the Farhud, 180 Jews were murdered and nearly 250 wounded. From then until 1948, the persecution of Iraq's Jews ebbed and flowed. But once the state of Israel was established, tens of thousands of Iraqi Jews lost their property, their citizenship and their assets, and they ran for their lives. Iraq's Jewish population numbered around 135,000 in 1948, with more than 77,000 Jews living in Baghdad alone. They numbered between a quarter and a third of Baghdad's population. Today, it is questionable how many, if any, remain alive.

A compilation of historical profiles, *Iraq's Last Jews: Stories of Daily Life, Upheaval and Escape from Modern Babylon* recounts the lives of some of those who had to flee Iraq. Rabbi Sassoon Khedouri was the last spiritual leader of Iraq's Jewish community of Iraq, and served as its President for 37 years. His grandson, Zuhair Sassoon, offers glimpses of his family's struggles following Israel's victorious War of Independence.

> The turbulent political events throughout the years marred so many aspects of our lives. My bar mitzvah was a terrible event. It was 1951 and the atmosphere was chaotic because most of the Jews were leaving and the anti-Jewish sentiment was strong. We did the bar mitzvah on our rooftop, afraid of making a visible event in the house. It was a small and quiet ceremony with my grandfather, my parents, and a couple of Christian friends. Worse than that was the *brit milah* of my son, Ari. [Brit milah is the ritual of circumcision performed on the eighth day after the birth of a son.] It was August 1969. We did it in a small room, with only my grandfather, my father-in-law, my mother, my mother-in-law, my wife, and I in attendance. We didn't invite anybody because my father was in prison and Jews were being imprisoned and killed. The mood was somber.

Ronit Dangour, a Jewish woman who began her life in Baghdad, remembers the precise turning point when her world fell apart. It was, she recalls,

> …Monday, June 5, 1967 at 10 pm. At that moment, a Muslim woman who was a neighbor and very friendly with my mother, Victoria, called and told her, "There is a war." We hadn't known: we had exams and were busy, and we weren't listening to the radio. She told my mother, "For every Muslim that is killed in Palestine, we will kill ten Jews in Baghdad." She had turned on a dime. It was hard to believe that that same morning, mother made her *sambusak* (Iraqi dumplings) and brought it over and the woman had said, "Thank you. It's delicious." I tried to call my grandfather but there was no line. The phone was disconnected.

Linda Menuhin remembers all too well the terrifying months following Israel's military victory against several Arab nations. "After the Six Day War, I really began to feel afraid," she explains.

> The trouble began with a protest around the British Institute in Waziriya. I had to leave my classroom by a back door before the end of a test that would have qualified me to study in a British university, GCE. I could hear the radio very loud, shouting how the Arabs had won the war and how many Israeli warplanes they had destroyed. We could feel the heat, on the radio, in the market. We knew it wasn't true because at night we used to listen to Kol Yisrael, which was broadcast from Israel in Arabic.
>
> But then Jews all around us started being arrested. One of our very close friends was living with his old father. They came to pick him up from his house, "just for questioning," or so they said. They brought his body back in a sack.

Within two months, Baghdad's Jews were living in terror, keeping themselves out of sight. Their sports and social clubs were closed, their phones cut off and their assets frozen. Horrifying stories of abduction and murder circulated. Linda's family was evicted from their home.

Anne Frank from Baghdad

In desperation, Linda sent a letter to an aunt in America, telling of the Jews' terrible conditions in Baghdad. She wrote it in French, hoping Iraq's government censors wouldn't intercept it. The aunt sent the letter on to Israel. It was published in *Ma'ariv newspaper,* beneath the headline "Anne Frank from Baghdad." In 1969, the crisis came to a grisly climax when nine innocent Jews were publicly hanged in Baghdad, accused of spying for Israel.

Four years later, Linda wrote her youthful impressions of the scene,

> ...it was really a blow, a shock to see the Liberation Square on TV crowded with people dancing and singing as if they were celebrating a feast or a wedding. Our nine victims were... suspended in the air, on improvised scaffolds... their heads were twisted and drooping and their bodies dangled from the gallows. The attitude of the crowd proved to be savage, barbarous and ferocious. They cursed the dead, spat and pelted stones on them. It was the most humiliating, distressing, unforgettable sight I had seen in my life. My cheeks were flooded with tears. Our agony was beyond description.

Eventually, against her parents' wishes, Linda managed to escape from Iraq with her brother. The two made their way to Tehran, guided by mercenaries, and finally on to Israel. Linda's father, a well-known Baghdad attorney, was taken into custody by Iraqi authorities not long thereafter, never to be seen again. Linda continues to seek out people who knew him, who might tell her the details of his final days.

The rest of her family is in Israel, scarred by their past but thankful for their new lives. They, along with hundreds of thousands of others, comprise the "Forgotten Refugees" who fled Muslim lands in the mid-20th century. Each of these owns a family history of terror, desperation and profound loss.

In *Iraq's Last Jews*, Alda Zelouf recalls,

> We could not go anywhere or do anything without being followed. The security officer was still following me and asking questions about me, months after dad's release. We were always afraid that undercover police were behind the windows listening to what we were saying. And the police started imprisoning and killing girls. In one of the most horrible incidents of my time, the Kashkush family was killed in their home in April, 1973, the day before their planned journey from the country. They even had their passports and tickets and their bags were packed. One of the daughters in the family, by chance, attended her classes at the university that day and when she returned there was blood all over the house and her family was gone. Their bodies had been taken away—no one ever saw them again.

Even with recent Knesset legislation in place, will the story of these refugees eventually find its proper place in discussions regarding the Middle East peace process? In a 2005 report for the Jewish Center for Public Affairs, Dr. Avi Beker summed up the matter well:

> Historically, there was an exchange of populations in the Middle East and the number of displaced Jews exceeds the number of Palestinian Arab refugees. Most of the Jews were expelled as a result of an open policy of anti-Semitic incitement and even ethnic cleansing.

However, unlike the Arab refugees, the Jews who fled are a forgotten case because of a combination of international cynicism and domestic Israeli suppression of the subject. An open debate about the exodus of the Jews is critical for countering the Palestinian demand for the "right of return" to properties inside Israel and objective scrutiny of the historical record of the Arab-Israeli conflict.

Iraq's Christians at Risk

The cruelties experienced by Iraq's "Saturday people" diminished after the 1970s, as did the size of the Jewish population; it is now close to zero. In the meantime, other forces have since swept across the world, including two Gulf Wars, and more recently the emergence of a new Iraq—one that has experienced many years of explosive violence since Saddam Hussein's demise. Although he was a notoriously cruel dictator, for his own purposes he managed to keep religious persecution under control. Once he was removed from power following the US invasion of Iraq, Shia vs. Sunni violence accelerated alarmingly. And it wasn't long before the "Sunday people" began to pay with their lives in the chaotic aftermath of "Operation Iraqi Freedom."

The National Catholic Register reported in November 2011 that since the American-led invasion of Iraq in 2003, "Violence has claimed the lives of 905 Iraqi Christians, including one bishop, five priests and a number of sub-deacons. Despite the U.S. presence in the country, 54 churches have been bombed, mainly Chaldean. Prior to the invasion, Christians in Iraq numbered 800,000 to 1 million. Now just 400,000 to a half million remain."

In January 2011, Nina Shea, my friend and colleague at Hudson Institute's Center for Religious Freedom and long-time member of the United States Commission on International Religious Freedom (USCIRF), testified before the Tom Lantos Human Rights Commission of the U.S. House of Representatives,

This brutal, unrelenting campaign of religious cleansing began in August 2004, when five churches were bombed in Baghdad and Mosul. On a single day in July 2009, seven churches were bombed in a coordinated attack in Baghdad. Christian clergy and other leaders have been targeted, including Paulos Rahho, the Archbishop of Mosul, who was kidnapped and killed in early 2008. Last May, a bus convoy of Christian students traveling to their university in Mosul was violently assaulted. During these terrible years, Christians from every walk of life have been raped, tortured, kidnapped, beheaded, and evicted from their homes.

Many deaths were single incidents; shootings of young Christian women and men in their neighborhoods; a nun, brutally murdered by a mob; a judge, assassinated, a priest, kidnapped, tortured and finally killed; an Assyrian policeman tied up and shot by a Muslim mob. Some Christians died in bombings; some died in massacres, which are much like the pogroms that have swept across Jewish communities across many centuries. From 2004 until 2010, according the Assyrian International News Agency (AINA) at least 70 Iraqi churches were bombed, while numerous shootings took place as worshippers left services. AINA reported in late 2011, "The overwhelming majority of the attacks against Assyrians in Iraq have been by Jihadists (with a small percentage related to the cottage industry of kidnapping for ransom). In an atmosphere of rising Muslim fundamentalism across the Middle East, Assyrians and other Christians have been targeted by Muslims."

In January 2008, a set of choreographed bombings exploded within a few minutes of each other at four churches and three convents in Baghdad and Mosul. Thankfully, only six people were injured. A Chaldean priest called on the government to recognize that the bombings were part of a plan to drive Christians out of Iraq. "We have been living in Iraq before Islam, but those strangers who came to the city are causing the kidnappings and bombings and trying to sow sedition in the hearts of Iraqis."

In early March that same year, the Archbishop of Mosul, Paulos Faraj Rahho, was reported to be missing. It was soon revealed that he had been kidnapped and a ransom was demanded to spare his life. A huge amount of money was required, but the cleric was later found, beheaded, on March 13.

In May 2010, nearly 160 Christians were injured—some seriously—when three buses carrying Christian students from local villages to the University of Mosul were bombed. A local man was killed by a blast as he tried to help the injured. The buses were supposedly protected by the Iraqi government.

Christian converts from Islam face particularly distressing threats—it is widely reported that they are forced to live double lives rather than inform their Muslim families and friends of their embrace of Christianity. Extortion, expulsions from school, loss of jobs, attacks by mobs, and danger of rape, honor killings and murder are incessant. As we've seen, within traditional Islamic law, it is a capital crime to convert from Islam to another faith. Meanwhile, Muslim radicals view all Christians, like Jews and those of other faiths, as infidels who must either convert to Islam or face the "Sword of Islam."

On October 31, 2010—remembered today as "Black Sunday"—eight terrorists stormed into the Assyrian Catholic Church of Our Lady of Salvation in Baghdad just as Fr. Wassim Sabih finished the Mass. As the intruders started shooting, the priest fell to the floor, begging for the lives of his parishioners. His assailants silenced him with their guns. They held the rest of the congregation hostage, bizarrely demanding the release of two women in Egypt, supposedly held captive by Egyptian Coptic Christians. A team of Iraqi security forces tried to intervene, but in response the killers threw grenades into the crowd and detonated explosive vests. The total death count was 57, including two priests.

Horrifying Photographs

Like most people, I heard about this massacre on news reports; over many hours the numbers continued to increase as further details emerged. But the story remained somewhat the same: the killers had broken into the church during worship. Their pastors had offered to give their lives in exchange for their flock. Some parishioners ran and hid in adjacent rooms; they used their cell-phones to call for help, but it came too late. The reports I saw described explosions and shootings; bombs and bullets. Tragic deaths, but on some level it sounded like the murders were sudden and quick. Were they?

Just about a month later, I got an email from a friend who had served in America's Special Forces for many years. His last tour of duty was in Iraq, and he had befriended a Christian Iraqi soldier during that time. It so happened that this soldier was very close to the Our Lady of Salvation Church—close enough that he was able to go in immediately after the massacre, before anyone decided what should be photographed and what shouldn't. He sent the photos to his American friend, who forwarded them to me. The Iraqi Christian wrote in English on the text section of the email, *Please do not open this file before kids due to its bloody contents and pray for the victims and their families may Jesus protect us all.*

If there is a word for what I discovered in those photos—which I still have in my computer because it seems almost sacrilegious to delete them—I suppose the word is gruesome. When the mutilations took place I don't have enough forensic know-how to judge. And whether the beheadings were just done for sport on the dead bodies or as means of execution I can't say. But killing their victims quickly apparently wasn't enough for the terrorists.

It was horrifying to see babies in puddles of their own blood. Their mothers were next to them, dressed up for a pleasant evening of worship and fellowship. There were old men, middle-aged women, pretty young girls and little children. And there were the priests. Some of the bodies were intact, some were mutilated. But all the dead left behind tremors of heartache among their families, friends, and fellow believers. As days and weeks passed, the shock-waves reached the far corners of the world.

I never saw those photographs on any media sites; I tried sending them to people, but almost no one responded. Two Jewish friends tried to circulate them; only one succeeded. My friend Jillian Becker Gordon, a highly respected writer on counterterrorism, has a website called The Atheist Conservative. She posted several. Otherwise they never, to my knowledge, appeared.

That saddened me for many reasons, but one of those reasons disturbs me even now. Christian denominations don't always open their arms to one other. This is sometimes true of Evangelicals, who may not quite believe that Christians from the ancient world really share the same faith as theirs. They see the robes and incense and icons and somehow assume that Assyrian and Coptic and Russian Orthodox and Armenian and various other old churches—of course, for some including Roman Catholic—aren't really Christians. But it is also true of some of the "Old Church" faithful, who think Evangelicals are a weird American sect that isn't really part of the historic Christian world.

What struck me in looking at those photographs was the familiarity of the people who had been murdered. They wore jeans and sweaters and athletic shoes. The little kids were dressed up in cute Sunday-best outfits. Several of the girls had put some effort into creating stylish hairdos. Some of the men wore cool leather jackets. These women, men and children were so very much like the rest of us. They were loyal Christians, worshipping in the way they knew best. They were everyday, ordinary people who had gone to church. 58 of them never went home.

In *Foreign Policy,* Jamsheed Choksy lamented, "... the massacre in Baghdad is only the most spectacular example of mounting discrimination and persecution of the native Christian communities of Iraq and Iran, which are now in the middle of a massive exodus unprecedented in modern times as they confront a rising tide of Islamic militancy and religious chauvinism sweeping the region."

The following day, Al-Qaeda in Mesopotamia issued a bulletin: "All Christian centers, organizations and institutions, leaders and followers, are legitimate targets."

That was far from the end of the violence—although it remains one of the most notorious and well publicized atrocities. Scattered attacks on churches and Christian individuals have continued to terrorize Iraq's Christian communities.

In Mosul, on May 23, 2012, motorcycle-riding killers struck a Catholic priest's family, breaking into the residence through a back entrance. They murdered Fr. Mazin Eshoo's father and his two brothers, and raped his mother and his sister. Fr. Mazin himself had been kidnapped and released two years before.

What is it like to survive such traumatic and unforgettable scenes? Many say it is difficult to sleep or to feel remotely safe and secure for years after these incidents. In fact, it has been reported that one woman lived through the Black Sunday massacre only to be shot to death while sleeping in her bed a few weeks later. "Survivors' guilt" is pervasive, along with post-traumatic stress symptoms. And considering the number of attacks and deaths that have befallen Iraq's Christians, a feeling of constant dread—a reaction that the surviving Jews of Iraq so vividly remember—never really goes away.

With this in mind, it is not surprising that Christians in Muslim countries are quietly leaving their ancient homelands in increasingly larger numbers—a migration of people of such a magnitude that it is impossible to determine how many have gone. They leave in secret and do not speak of their plans even after they've reached a safe haven, for fear of putting their relatives, friends and believing communities at risk. They often leave with the shirts on their back, abandoning their property and livelihoods. Their flight is all too similar to that of the Jews, half a century before. And it is beyond irony that those Jewish refugees—many of whom settled in Israel—are now labeled "Zionist occupiers" and are allegedly responsible for the persecution of Christians in the Middle East. They are blamed rather than the real perpetrators: radicalized Muslims.

"Why should we be surprised?"

One Friday night I decided to walk to the Western Wall—I hadn't been there for a while and I have always enjoyed the sight of hundreds of Jews gathered there to begin the Sabbath. Already, the ultra-orthodox—the *haredim*—were rushing along the streets in their black garb to join a growing stream of worshippers—some more orthodox than others—heading toward the Kotel. But it was still early—Shabbat hadn't yet begun—and I was hungry. So I stopped at an atmospheric Arab-style restaurant called Nafoura that sits just inside the Jerusalem walls, near the Jaffa gate. Someone had mentioned to me that Syrian Christians owned it, and as I waited to be served, I idly wondered if the people who worked there had any connection with the Assyrian Christians in Iraq.

A fountain splashed peacefully in front of me as I ripped off a piece of pita bread and considered whether it would be appropriate to ask someone who worked there about the situation in Iraq. Too many questions aren't always welcomed by those whose friends and families are at risk, and I've learned that those who belong to the ancient churches in the Old City are particularly cautious about talking to outsiders. Besides, it wasn't clear to me at the time whether the Syrian Orthodox Church was the same as the Assyrian Orthodox Church. Still, I had no ill intent—maybe that would be evident.

Nafoura was almost empty—I was there at an odd time, after lunch and before the dinner hour—so my server wasn't busy. His name was George, and he was a very young looking man with intensely dark eyes. He couldn't have been more than twenty-five years old. After some small talk about the menu I said, "Do you mind if I ask you something?"

"Not at all," he said. Still, I thought he looked at me a little uncertainly.

"Do you know anything about the Christians in Iraq?"

George nodded politely but looked away.

"I know they are going through some very difficult times. I'm a Christian, too," I added.

He studied my face for a second or two. "Yes, I know about them," he said carefully. "Many of them have left Iraq."

"I heard they were going to Syria and Jordan. Is that what you've heard too?"

George shrugged, "I don't think Jordan is letting them in now—they say the border is closed. I'm not sure...but I don't think they can stay in Iraq anymore because it's too dangerous."

"Yeah, I've heard terrible stories about the dangers there. I read that an Archbishop was beheaded, and now all these other killings..."

"Yes, that's true. I've heard the same," George nodded. Maybe he wasn't providing me with volumes of information, but he no longer seemed nervous.

"So are you surprised to hear about these things?" I asked.

His answer brought tears to my eyes.

"Why should we be surprised?" His expression reflected a different sort of amazement—he seemed genuinely puzzled that I would even ask such a question.

"Jesus told us," he reminded me, "that this would happen."

CHAPTER TWELVE

A SECOND EXODUS FROM EGYPT

The news that my father had lost everything arrived at dawn one Saturday in early spring 1965. The bearer was Kassem, now the factory's night foreman. He rang our bell, and it was my father who opened the door. Seeing his boss look so crushed on guessing the reason for his untimely visit, the young foreman immediately burst into a fit of hysterical crying. "Did they take her then?" asked my father, meaning the factory. "The took her." "When?" "Last night. They wouldn't let me call you, so I had to come." Both men stood quietly in the vestibule and then moved into the kitchen while my father tried to improvise something by way of tea. They sat at the kitchen table, urging one another not to lose heart, until both men broke down and began sobbing in each other's arms. "I heard them crying like little children," was Aunt Elsa's refrain that day. "Like little children."
—Out of Egypt, A Memoir. Andre Aciman.

"All I can remember... is the element of fear," Joseph Abdel Wahed wrote to me, reflecting on the events of his 12th year—1948. "People in the streets would mock us with the famous Arab insult, *Ya yahudi ya ibn el kalb* [Jewish son of a dog], or even more ominously *Idbah el-Yahud* [slit the throats of the Jews].

"This really scared us because there was nowhere to hide. Many of us did not have travel papers and even if we did, the Egyptian authorities wanted to keep us as hostages and not let us out. After the revolution of July 1952, their attitude changed and they were only too glad to kick us out, but not before confiscating everything we owned—our businesses, farms, hospitals and homes and bank accounts."

Remembering a Lost World

The Jews who were driven out of Egypt during the tumultuous 20th Century call their traumatic departure the "Second Exodus," relating their experiences to the biblical Israelites' miraculous flight from Egypt. Most of these refugees, now in their sunset years, feel blessed to have escaped Egypt and grateful to have made their way to Israel and elsewhere, even though they left with little more than the clothes they wore and—if they were fortunate—one suitcase.

Joseph Abdel Wahed and Levana Zamir—who, like Joseph, is from Egypt—now live at opposite ends of the world. But for both of them, the events of May 14, 1948 were, indeed, catastrophic. That was, of course, the day when Israel proclaimed its independence and declared itself a nation, on its own land in accord with the UN partition resolution and plan. To put it mildly, the response across the Arab world was anything but congratulatory. Wahed was 12 years old; Zamir was 10. Although they weren't acquainted at the time, they both lived in or near Cairo.

These days, Levana Zamir speaks of her experiences in her breezy, sunlit Tel Aviv apartment, surrounded by tasteful décor highlighted by a collection of fine art in delicate watercolor hues. In a quiet voice she explains that she, her parents and her six brothers were once part of an affluent community that, for generations, had enjoyed the elegant lifestyle that she describes in her book, *The Golden Era of the Jews of Egypt*, published in cooperation with the University of Haifa.

Then catastrophe struck. "On May 14, 1948," Zamir recalls,

...we were sleeping. All of a sudden, exactly at midnight, people were knocking very, very hard on our door. We woke up and I saw 10 Egyptian officers in their black uniforms. I wasn't afraid because my parents were there and my mother was smiling to comfort me. But the soldiers opened everything. They went through everything. They were searching for something, but we never knew what.

The next day I went to school [she attended a Catholic elementary school]. The headmaster of the nuns came to me and said, "They took your uncle to prison!" My uncle lived in a big villa. He, my father and another brother owned one of the largest printing businesses in Cairo. I rushed home and asked my mother, "Is it true? Is he a criminal?" My mother told me, "He's not a criminal. It's only because we are Jews." So then it was even more a trauma for me. I thought to myself, "I am also a Jew! I too could go to prison!"

Eighteen months later, when her uncle was released from prison like many others—on the condition of permanent expulsion—Levana and her family fled Egypt, leaving behind their sequestered assets and possessions.

Zamir describes her childhood world—before those terrible events—in nostalgic vignettes, illustrated with fading photographs. It was a way of life cherished by her parents, an epoch of almost fairy-tale quality. The affluent Jews of Egypt, like those of Iraq, Iran and some other cosmopolitan Muslim countries, were well connected with royalty. They enjoyed beautiful villas, social prestige and the best of food and education, so much so that they were able to overlook their *dhimmi* status vis-à-vis their Muslim friends and neighbors. Nowadays, serving as president of the Israel-Egypt Friendship Association, Zamir works tirelessly to fulfill her dream of restoring warm ties between Egyptians and Jews.

Today Joseph Wahed lives in California, in a small town called Moraga, east of San Francisco. He keeps in touch with scores of other Jews from Arab lands and works with the Jimena organization he founded, seeking to provide recognition to those Jewish refugees and their families. He recalls,

> I was 12 years old in May 1948, living in Heliopolis [a Cairo
> suburb]. I remember the words of Azzam Pasha, the head of
> the newly formed Arab League, talking about the founding
> of Israel. He said, "This will be a war of extermination that
> will be likened to the Mongolian massacre and the Crusades."
> The very next day, the Egyptian army [and four other Arab
> armies] headed toward the new State of Israel to "throw the
> Jews into the sea." It was supposed to be a slam-dunk, but
> they lost.
>
> By then everything had begun to unravel and our previ-
> ously secure lives in Egypt had fallen apart. The Jewish sec-
> tion of Cairo, the Haret el-Yahud, was bombed [frequently]
> until 1949, killing and wounding many innocent Jews.
> Accompanying this were the usual assaults on our synagogues
> and on Jewish individuals. The authorities sometimes played
> a part in these assaults, especially the Muslim Brotherhood,
> which began in the late 1920s under the leadership of Hassan
> el-Banna. In 1967, about 400 Egyptian Jews, including my
> uncle and other relatives were thrown in concentration camps.
> They were treated harshly and forced to commit sexual acts.
> They were released in 1970.

Another man whose family fled Egypt, Yossi Ben-Aharon, now
lives in Jerusalem. A career diplomat, Ambassador Ben-Aharon
served as director-general of the Prime Minister's Office under
premier Yitzhak Shamir and represented the Foreign Ministry for
nearly a decade in the United States. In a recent interview, Ben-
Aharon made it abundantly clear to me that the explosive violence
against Jews in the Arab world following May 14, 1948 was no coincidence. He has collected a number of statements of lethal intent
made by Arab leaders, calling for the death and destruction of Jews
in their Arab homelands in case of the UN partition of Palestine.

"Immediately after the UN approved the partition resolution on November 29, 1947," Ben-Aharon explained, "Arabs attacked the Jews throughout the Middle East, including Palestine. Yet, since 1949, the Arab states, together with Palestinian organizations, have mounted an intensive propaganda campaign, based on a rewriting of history, in an attempt to shift responsibility for the Palestinian refugee issue onto Israel. They describe the events of 1948—and the estimated 762,000 Arab refuges—as an 'ethnic cleansing' by Israel." He continued,

> The facts of history point to the opposite: ethnic cleansing was perpetrated by Arab governments against their Jews, as witnessed by the fact that 850,000 Jews were forced to leave the Arab countries, while more than 4 million Arabs continue to live in geographic Palestine, including more than a million in Israel. Now, 60 years after the events, the time has come for the historical facts to be recognized and for justice to be done."

Joseph Wahed recalls, "Jews who were ethnically cleansed from the Arab world did not get one penny from the UN while the Palestinians have received over $50 billion [including funds from the European Union] since 1950. They still are receiving financial assistance."

The Jews who once lived in Muslim lands, like Zamir, Wahed and Ben-Aharon, have established new lives for themselves in Israel and elsewhere. But they have not forgotten. Hundreds of thousands of them were eyewitnesses to violent persecutions, deadly pogroms and forced expulsions that erupted instantaneously—as planned by Arab leadership—following the UN decision for the partition of Palestine and the founding of Israel.

In 1948, the number of Jews living in Egypt was estimated between 85,000 and 100,000. Today fewer than 50 Jews live in Egypt. Ben-Aharon concludes, "Responsibility for the resettlement of the Arab refugees from Palestine should be shouldered by the Arab governments and the Palestinian leadership. The rights and claims of Jews from Arab countries, both personal and communal, must be recognized and addressed properly and equitably. Only then can a climate conducive to mutual understanding and coexistence be fostered."

After my interview with Joseph Wahed, he and I have kept in touch occasionally by email. He has had some ups and downs with his health but continues to work tirelessly on behalf of the "Forgotten Refugees," to be sure their story is remembered and, if possible, not repeated. He recently forwarded to me a letter that he wrote to the *Wall Street Journal* in late 2011, in response to an article about Egypt's beleaguered Coptic people. He clearly recognizes the past abuse and expulsion of Jews as a precedent for the present persecution of Christians in Egypt.

> Dear editor,
> As an Egyptian Jew, I read with special interest Matt Bradley's article "Clashes between Christians, Police rock Cairo," Monday, October 10.
>
> This reminded me of what our Coptic neighbor told my family as we were being expelled from Egypt in November 1952: "After Saturday comes Sunday." He accurately predicted that the Coptic community also would feel the wrath and hatred of Egyptians, much of it inspired by radical Muslims.
>
> Mr. Bradley also commented that "Egyptians have long prided themselves on a shared sense of citizenship that straddles religious boundaries."
>
> Indeed, some individual Copts and Muslims have strong personal ties, but Mr. Bradley's statement is not based on historical fact; rather, it's based on a fantasy typical of Egyptian culture. Mr. Bradley needed to research why Egyptian's so-called "shared sense of pride" did not apply to the 80,000

Jews who once lived in Egypt and who were all kicked out.

There was no sense of pride when Egypt's nationality laws made it virtually impossible for Jews, and some Christians, born in Egypt to acquire Egyptian Nationality thus rendering many stateless. In addition, Jews were restricted from certain government Jobs.

Nowadays, Christians are being victimized by the Muslim community in Iraq, Pakistan, Gaza, Bethlehem, Lebanon, Nigeria and elsewhere.

Sadly, just like when Jews were being ethnically cleansed, there's the same stone silence from the U.N, Human Rights Organizations, religious leaders and the world's Christian community,

Joseph Wahed

As Joseph astutely points out, "First the Saturday People, then the Sunday People" is no longer just a slogan. It has become an observable reality.

Jean Naggar was one of the tens of thousands of Jewish Egyptians who had to leave their homeland between 1948 and 1972. Her family managed to weather the 1948 pressures, but was forced out of the country during Nasser's nationalization of the Suez Canal in 1956. Her memoir, *Sipping from the Nile,* is a colorful portrayal of her childhood and adolescence in a family that had enjoyed, like Levana Zamir's, a remarkably privileged life in Cairo and Alexandria for generations. In her late teens, the time came when the family's existence could simply not go on as it was; indeed none of them would ever again experience the carefree and (genuinely) multicultural way of life they had known before. She writes,

Endings are powerful moments, more compelling than beginnings. My life began to acknowledge the possibility of endings the day my eighteen-year-old self slumped in the soft Nile breeze and wept into the stone of the balustrade of the terrace outside my bedroom window, feeling both the retained warmth from the heart of the day and the dead cold underneath it. That day, preparing to move outward from the protection of my past, I tried to claim it, to imprint it on all my senses. That day I wondered how it would be to be gone *forever,* the word echoing strangely in my heart.

Now I know better. The past is never gone. It is the foundation on which we build the present, every day of our lives.

Like Jean Naggar, millions of Jews have, for centuries, started their lives over, and all too often not by choice. They have found their way into new surroundings, new nationalities, new languages, and in new and challenging circumstances. Even today, hundreds begin a new life in Israel each year.

Faith and New Beginnings

The Jewish faith speaks of beginning life again spiritually, and particularly in one sense by moving from a secular way of life into that of religious observance. A person who makes this choice and "returns" to the Jewish observance his or her fathers is often called a *Ba'al Teshuva* [a practitioner of return or repentance]. Many of these men and women are exceptionally observant of Judaism's laws and traditions, more so than those who have grown up in Orthodox homes and never departed.

New beginnings are also a deeply significant theme in the Christian faith. Believers speak of a "Second Birth" in which they are awakened to the spiritual world—another way of restating the words of Jesus, "You must be born from above" (sometimes translated "born again"). Coming into the faith is usually signified through baptism. Baptism in turn reflects a belief in the reality of Jesus' resurrection first, and eventually the passage "from death unto life eternal" for all who follow him.

One year, I went to the Church of the Holy Sepulcher to attend the Easter services there. I knew I would be watching and hearing a Christian Orthodox liturgy—the first one would be in Greek, then Coptic, followed by Syrian and others. These rituals would continue all night; I only planned to stay for the first one. When I arrived at nearly midnight, the old church—some of it dating to the Fourth Century—was so crowded that I had to set aside any spiritual notions I might have hoped to fulfill in the name of survival—this is to say staying on both feet in an upright position. It was hot and stuffy. And worse, there was thinly veiled animosity between some of the groups that had gathered—most obviously between the Russians and Arabs.

At times a group of clerics, robed in black and responsible for crowd control, pounded the pavement sharply with metal staffs to move the crowd back from the area along which the procession would eventually pass. The crowd surged back momentarily, then forward again, accompanied by a lot of grumbling in several languages—not including English. Everyone wanted to be in the "front row" to see the procession up close, but only a few would succeed: there were thousands upon thousands of people shoving and maneuvering their way toward the best view they could get.

Finally the procession began. The Greek Patriach, Theophilus III, and his various deacons, bishops and other clergy marched by in full regalia, attired in sparkling crowns and lavish robes. They marched around the Sepulcher three times, as is the tradition in the Orthodox Easter liturgy. From where I was standing, I could not see what happened after that. But after some time, the cry filled the church: *Christos Anesti!* Christ is Risen.

With one voice, the massive crowd responded, *Alithos Anesti!* Risen Indeed!

All at once, in the most amazingly sudden change of atmosphere I can remember, people began to embrace, strangers kissing strangers, and yes, Arabs and Russians alike sharing loving words and blessings. Small groups began to sing their traditional Easter songs in various languages. Thankfully, by then the competitive edge was gone. Now there was only celebration.

It was as if a tide of joy had washed across the massive church at the sound of the Celebrant's simple words. Hope had defeated despair. Faith had conquered disbelief. And above all else, in a reaffirmation of Christianity's most essential message, Life had triumphed over Death. That one message somehow spans denominational chasms and bridges differences of race, nationality and language. It is also reflected in the symbols of every Christian church.

I noticed many Coptic monks on the periphery of the crowd that night, waiting with their small community for the beginning of their own procession. These monastics, who serve beside the Holy Sepulcher itself, are particularly recognizable because of their distinctive black hoods. At the time I didn't understand the symbolism, but these *koulla* (Coptic), or *qalansuwa* (Arabic) hoods are decorated with twelve small crosses and one large one. I've since learned that the crosses signify that Coptic monks, like Jesus' disciples, recognize that they must leave everything earthly behind and look only to God—represented by the large cross. In today's troubled times, more and more members of the Coptic Christian community in Egypt are facing that very choice.

The period of time following the Arab Spring has not been kind to the Copts, who encounter ever-increasing threats, persecution and violence. Their ancient community, which according to tradition was founded in 60 CE by the Apostle Mark in Alexandria, comprises between 8 and 10 percent of Egypt's population, which now numbers around 83 million.

The Copt's bloodlines are even more ancient than the Christian faith, dating back to the Pharaohs, centuries before the Arab invasions in the 7th Century. As a religious minority in a Muslim majority state, the Copts have long faced discrimination under the *dhimmi* status spelled out in Islamic law. In recent years, however, they have suffered escalating attacks, as Islamist extremists have specifically targeted them.

The abuses Copts endure—incidents of forced marriage, rape, honor killing, extortion and murder—are rarely reported by Western media. Such dangers have now multiplied, beginning in late 2010. During the terrorist attack on worshippers in Iraq mentioned in the previous chapter, at Baghdad's Syriac Catholic Church of Our Lady of Salvation, masked assailants demanded the release of two Muslim women allegedly held by Egyptian Coptic Christians (a charge that had begun to circulate about a month before).

Al-Qaeda in Mesopotamia was quick to take credit for the 57 dead in the Baghdad massacre, and in the days that followed, they made continuing threats against the Copts. A scattering of news sources discovered and reported not only statements against Coptic churches, but also the targeting of specific Coptic leaders, whose names and addresses were published online. A fatwa emanated from *Shumukh al-Islam*, a radical Islamist website, again, affiliated with Al-Qaeda. More than 200 specific Copts were targeted for death, and some of them went into hiding.

Two months later, on New Years Day 2011, at least 21 were killed and 100 injured in a bombing at All Saints Church in Alexandria, Egypt. The *New York Times* reported, "Analysts said the weekend bombing was in a sense the culmination of a long escalation of violence against Egypt's Coptic Christians... But at the same time the blast's planning and scale—a suicide bomber evidently detonated a locally made explosive device packed with nails and other shrapnel, the authorities said Sunday—were a break with the smaller episodes of intra-communal violence that have marked Muslim-Christian relations for the past decade."

Coptic Christians and the Arab Spring

Then came something unexpected and startling—the upheaval in the "Arab Street" that seized the world's attention, first in Tunisia, but far more dramatically in Egypt. A global audience was transfixed, as hundreds of thousands of protestors—seemingly representing all sectors of the community, including Copts—demanded that President Hosni Mubarak step down as president after three decades. The demonstrations against Mubarak—infamous as a fierce ruler with an iron fist—were applauded around the world. Only a few cautious observers voiced concern, and among them were at least some members of the Coptic community. Their sensible question, "What kind of regime will come next?" was drowned out by enthusiastic applause for "freedom and democracy."

In the midst of the euphoric international outpouring, the Copts were attacked again. According to the Assyrian International News Agency,

> A massacre took place on Sunday, January 30 at 3 PM in the village of Sharona near Maghagha, Minya province. Two Islamists groups, aided by the Muslim neighbors, descended on the roof of houses owned by Copts, killing eleven Copts, including children, and seriously injuring four others. The two families were staying in their homes with their doors locked when suddenly the Islamists descended on them, killing eleven and leaving for dead four others family members. In addition, they looted everything that was in the two Coptic houses, including money, furniture and electrical equipment. They also looted livestock and grain.

For obvious reasons, this new violence magnified Coptic caution about the ongoing political revolution. Veteran reporter Arne Fjeldstad, in daily contact with Egypt's Christians, noted, "They are very uncertain about the future. As the crisis develops, their uncertainty is predominantly related to the influence of the Muslim Brotherhood and other even more radical Islamic groups. Of course there were Coptic Christian youth among the masses demonstrating both in Alexandria and Cairo as well as other cities. But so far this popular uprising has been dominated by the Muslim majority."

On February 23, *Compass Direct*, a Christian news agency, reported that one monk and six church workers had been shot when the Egyptian Army attacked the Coptic Orthodox Anba Bishoy Monastery in Wadi Al-Natroun, 110 kilometers north of Cairo. The attack was meant to destroy a defensive wall monks had built without a permit, to protect their property from raiders. It was reported that, in a similar incident, the army also attacked the Anba Makarious Al Sakandarie Monastery in Al Fayoum, 130 kilometers southwest of Cairo. Under an Egyptian law carried over from Ottoman times, state permission is required to build or repair church property, and such permits are rarely issued. Why the enforcement of this edict required gunfire to be turned on the monks remains unclear, but alarming YouTube videos bear witness to the incident.

On March 4, Copts in Egypt appealed for Egyptian Armed Forces protection when a mob of several thousand Muslims attacked their church in the village of Soul, about 30 kilometers from Cairo. The Church of St. Mina and St. George was set alight; the local fire department and security forces failed to respond to Coptic calls for help during the arson attack. According to a report from the Washington-based Coptic American Friendship Association, the mob, chanting "Allahu Akbar," pulled down the church's cross and blew up gas cylinders inside the building. The fire destroyed the church and everything inside, including ancient sacred relics. The motivation for the church burning was said to be a forbidden romantic relationship between a Christian man and a Muslim woman. This was aggravated, in the eyes of Islamist radicals, by the failure of the woman's father to restore the community's "honor" by killing his daughter. The infuriated mob murdered the father and another relative.

On March 9, Muslim rioters attacked Coptic Christians in one of Cairo's poorest neighborhoods, where the primary industry is garbage collection and recycling. There were 13 deaths and 140 injuries. The *Financial Times* quoted a Christian protestor named

Samia. "'We were staging a peaceful demonstration for the church, but they attacked us with firearms, stones and Molotov cocktails… The tanks made way for the thugs to come in…there was shooting until two o'clock in the morning. After that they burnt the houses and stole from them. They broke whatever they could not carry away. No fire engines or ambulances came. We had to take the injured to hospital in garbage trucks.'"

Another news source, *Al-Masry Al-Youm*, reported, "There has never been sectarian strife of this magnitude before. 'Some of them looked like they were the ex-convicts from neighboring areas, while others had big beards,' said Onsy a 27-year-old garbage man. Accounts from inside the neighborhood claim that the army had acted as a barrier in the beginning before turning their backs to the thugs."

In September, 2011, thousands of Muslims were incited by a Salafi imam during Friday prayers to attack a nearby church. The church had constructed a dome on its 70-year-old building—done, as required, with legal permission from Aswan's governor. But the imam was offended, and the mob he stirred up ransacked and torched the church. In the wake of the violence, the governor justified the attack by denying that he had given permission for the dome to be built.

The following month, when protesters (most of them Copts) gathered in Cairo's Maspero District to complain of ongoing attacks against Copts, including the recent destruction of churches, they were ferociously assaulted by the Egyptian military. On October 9, 2011, at least 27 protesters were killed. The military has since refused to take responsibility for the deaths, even though videos of the day's atrocities circulated widely on the Internet—including a gruesome scene in which military vehicles mowed down and crushed protesters—along with volumes of eyewitness testimony. These realities did not persuade the Supreme Council of the Armed Forces (SCAF) to change its fabricated story.

Just days later, Ayman Labib, a Coptic high school student, was beaten to death by his classmates on October 16, 2011 for wearing a cross. His teacher, who pointed out the cross to the class as well as a cross tattoo on the young man's wrist, reportedly asked the class, "What are we going to do with him?" Interviewed later, the 17-year-old boy's father said, ""They beat my son so much in the classroom that he fled to the lavatory on the ground floor, but they followed him and continued their assault. When one of the supervisors took him to his room, Ayman was still breathing. The ambulance transported him from there dead, one hour later." Two arrests were later made, but the teacher was not implicated.

Nina Shea writes, "There are growing concerns that Egypt's 10 million or so Coptic Christians are being targeted under the cloak of political chaos during these uncertain times... local Egyptian police have abandoned their posts in the provinces and thus many churches no longer have armed guards protecting them as they did following the Al-Qaeda-inspired church bombing of New Year's Day in Alexandria."

Egypt's neighbor Israel is paying close attention to the ongoing strife in Egypt. For one thing, many observers worry since the 2011 elections, that once the Muslim Brotherhood-affiliated party takes power, Egypt's Peace Treaty with Israel could be null and void. The status of the southern border is threatened, as well as the likelihood of increasing arms smuggling into Gaza.

"After You Jews, They Will Come After Us"

But there are also more personal reactions. For some Israelis, watching the abuses suffered by Coptic Christians stirs a feeling of déjà vu. Rachel Lipkin and her family fled Egypt in 1969, when her father was released from prison, after being forced to sign away all the family assets to the Egyptian government. During her father's three-year imprisonment (thousands of Jews were locked up after the 1967 Six Day War), Rachel still remembers the kindness of Coptic neighbors who regularly brought eggs, milk and bread to her mother. "I was just 11 years old at the time, but I clearly remember what they said. 'They are coming after you Jews,' they told my mother, 'and once they have driven you out of the country, then they will come after us Christians. We know this.'"

Lipkin, whose work involves monitoring Arab language radio and television broadcasts, has followed this story closely and does not anticipate a good outcome for Egypt's beleaguered Coptic Christians. As with the Jews before them, a sense of dread and danger among the Coptic Christians is steadily increasing. Following the example of their monks, who have taken a vow of poverty, they too may soon be forced to leave everything earthly behind, and to look only to God.

"Truth is strong, Love is strong, Hope is Strong"

In 2007, with several friends and colleagues, I attended a journalist conference in Istanbul, where a series of speakers addressed the subject "Fact vs. Rumor" and helped cast light on the increasingly murky situation in the Middle East.

One of the speakers was a Coptic bishop. I will leave him unnamed here because of the pressure that continues to threaten his work—and more to the point, his life—particularly since the "Arab Spring." At the Istanbul conference, he was a powerful presence to behold. There were a lot of "idea people" present there, including scholars who had studied the ever-shifting circumstances in the world as Islamism surged and, at times, took its toll on other ways of life. There were journalists, too, who wanted to understand the dynamics of present day tensions.

But this bishop bore in his body the scars of the conflict between Muslim radicals and Coptic Christians. Two separate road "accidents" had nearly cost him his life, and he was permanently crippled by the injuries he had suffered. He spoke with penetrating honesty and courage, without notes or prepared remarks. His conclusion captures his enduring spirit:

We are not a weak church, we are not a weak people, we are a strong people and we will survive. And the love in us, the love is much stronger than hatred. And with this love we can continue and go on and work...even though we are facing a lot of hardship, still we are not weak because, simply, truth is strong, love is strong, hope is strong. And that makes it possible for the Christians in Egypt to continue.

This courageous bishop continues to plead for Copts to stay in Egypt—they are, after all, its indigenous population. But if an avowedly Islamist regime eventually takes power, what then? Will the Copts—like the Jews before them—be killed or driven out? Even now tens of thousands of Copts have quietly left Egypt—those with money and connections are able to afford airfare, relocation, legal assistance and other costly but necessary services to begin their lives again elsewhere.

As for the others—those with few resources and even fewer options, except perhaps to flee on foot someday—where will a potential eight to ten million fleeing Copts and other Christians go? Will there be a future refugee crisis of enormous proportions? Is another Egyptian exodus yet to come?

Samuel Tadros, an Egyptian Coptic citizen himself and an expert on Coptic issues in Egypt, wrote in *National Review Online* about the results of the so-called Arab Spring in Egypt,

The most likely outcome...is a wave of emigration. Like the Jews before them, the Christians of the Middle East will be driven out of their homes, but, unlike the Jews, they will not have an Israel to escape to. The most fortunate will take the first planes to the U.S., Canada, and Australia, but a community of 8 million people cannot possibly emigrate en masse in a short time. The poorer Copts, the ones who face daily persecution, will be left behind. For them, the winter has already arrived, and it will be cold and long.

"Tell Thy Son in that Day..."

The story of the Second Exodus, during which thousands of 20th Century Jews fled Egypt and found a home in Israel, is a modern-day saga of triumph over tragedy. It is burned into the memories of those who experienced it. And it mirrors a much older and more familiar story: the first Exodus, which is celebrated during one of Judaism's most important holidays—Passover, or in Hebrew, *Pesach*.

Passover is a momentous Jewish celebration. First of all, it marks the ancient Jewish people's miraculous journey of deliverance from abuse and enslavement in Egypt, and their new beginning in Israel—the Land of Promise. Passover (*Pesach*) was of course significant in biblical times. In those days it was designated as one of three feasts that called for pilgrimage to Jerusalem, along with Pentecost (*Shavuot*) and Tabernacles (*Sukkot*). Passover's venerable tradition also serves to sanctify families as the center of Jewish life. The Jews left Egypt family by family. And it is family by family that they celebrate their freedom still today. The liturgy at Passover is not recited at the synagogue, but at the family Passover dinner—the *Seder*.

In Israel, I've been graciously invited to two memorable Seders. The first of these was strictly Orthodox and religious; the other was decidedly not. I don't recall the names of everyone at the table, or of the special foods, or of the exact sequence in which they appeared. But both of these occasions touched me and, despite their clear differences, left me with similar impressions—of the warmth and continuity of family rituals, and of the timeless story of freedom, which echoes around the world still today during Passover.

The Seder focuses on the biblical account in Exodus 12. There we learn about the Jews' plight, God's calling and ordination of Moses, Moses' confrontations with a stonehearted Pharaoh, the ten plagues that were visited upon the Egyptians, including the most horrifying judgment of all, the death of the firstborn. These plagues eventually changed the mind of Pharaoh—at least temporarily.

Once the vast procession of Jews had departed Egypt's border, Pharaoh changed his mind about letting them go. Why should he give up his invaluable work force? Disastrously, he ordered his army to pursue the fleeing slaves. The frantic soldiers tried to catch up with them in the midst of the Red Sea, which had been supernaturally parted, providing dry land for the Israelites' hurrying feet. The Egyptian Army was not so blessed; they were swept away and drowned when the parted waters suddenly broke over them like a tidal wave.

The epic Exodus tale of faith and freedom is recounted in the *Haggadah*—the "Telling"—which is the Seder's liturgy. The "telling," is based on the commandment "And thou shalt tell thy son in that day, saying: It is because of that which the LORD did for me when I came forth out of Egypt." (Ex. 13:8). Each Seder guest is provided a copy of the Haggadah. And every child old enough to understand participates in the reading and ritual.

When I arrived at my first Seder, of course I'd heard the Exodus story, but had little understanding of Passover's traditions. That dinner was held in the home of a scholarly and revered rabbi. He is, by all accounts, a fine teacher and a man exceptionally beloved by his family, friends and students. There were more than two dozen people seated around what looked like an endless table. Many of those around me were the rabbi's sons and daughters, grandchildren and extended family. But there were others as well. One was a single mother—a battered wife who had recently received help and guidance from our host, hostess and a nearby synagogue. Others were relatives from abroad. An Israeli woman of more than 90 years sat near me—tiny, bent with age, yet radiant with the joys of the feast. A Christian couple from Jerusalem joined us. And I was there, too, a friend of friends.

There are admonitions in the Torah that the Jewish people should be kind to foreigners in their midst. "Remember that you were slaves in Egypt," God instructed them. "That is why I command you to do this." Perhaps that's one reason I was made so welcome as a Christian visitor.

The rabbi wore a knee-length black coat and a black velvet *kippah*. His son, who had recently been ordained as a rabbi, was dressed in much the same attire. Every man wore a kippah. The women had focused their wardrobes on modesty and muted colors. There was a quiet dignity to the affair. And, for me at least, one of the most beautiful aspects of the meal—which lasted more than 4 hours—was the singing of the father and son together, who enlivened the liturgy with their resonant and perfectly harmonized voices.

It was easy to "disappear" into that room and to be a silent spectator. The lengthy dinner reflected the host's devotion to the details of the Haggadah and thus to the biblical story. In a sense, as the rabbi's wife and daughters cooked the meal (the amount of work they had done was almost unimaginable) they had brought to life, in the form of foods, the oral and biblical tradition of the Israelites' harried flight from their oppressors. We tasted of the bitterness of Egypt in the form of bitter herbs; we recalled the suddenness of the departure from Egypt with the matzo—as the Jews fled, there was no time for bread made with yeast to rise. We ate a paste of apples and nuts that represented the mortar that had once set in place the bricks with which they labored. We drank four cups of sweet, sacred wine. At the end, everyone sang together.

There was a sense of formality on that occasion, a careful adherence to custom and devotion and to important details. It was a little like a being in the midst of living biblical tableaux, performed by the offspring of those who had actually experienced the story.

My next Seder took place three years later, and it was as informal as the first was staid. The women were dressed colorfully, and the men casually. Only one older gentleman wore a kippah. He had, however, neglected to bring his own, and asked to borrow one. When he self-consciously donned the ceremonial white satin cap, he explained that he didn't want to speak of *Adonai*—the Lord—without covering his head.

The food was served with no fanfare, and once each serving was eaten—along with slightly haphazard but sequential readings from the Haggadah—the plates were removed and more food appeared. There was a great deal of laughter and happy conversation between the readings, and a few restless young men went out on the balcony for a smoke. Yet for all the differences between them, the two Seders were in many ways alike, featuring the same foods that held the same symbolism.

In fact, at that informal table were some whose families had come to Israel during the Second Exodus, not so many years before. No doubt they remembered well that recent flight from Egypt.

In the spirit of the evening, rather than the precise and melodious singing of the two rabbis, in this case the Haggadah was read aloud by the guests, one after another. Those who couldn't read it in Hebrew—including me—read it in English. By the time we were finished, the powerful old story had been told once again.

In attendance were those who are deeply involved in the functions of the present-day Jewish State. Their hearts and minds have long been tightly wound around discerning the best course for the young nation; their hope is to untangle its complex challenges. One or two at the table even recalled the Day of Independence in 1948. Perhaps they recognized the State of Israel as a promise fulfilled, or maybe for them it was an incomplete human dream, a work in progress.

But as the Haggadah's passages were read aloud, just as at the earlier Seder, the words recounted the same history. They expressed the same hunger for freedom, the same need for divine intervention and human obedience, the same deliverance, and the same hope for the future. And, as before, everyone sang together joyfully at the end.

"Every year," Rabbi David Hartman writes, "Jews drink four cups of wine and then pour a fifth for Elijah. The cup is poured, but not yet drunk. Yet the cup of hope is poured every year. Passover is the night for reckless dreams; for visions about what a human being can be, what society can be, what people can be, what history may become. That is the significance of *'Le-shanah ha-ba-a b'Yerushalayim"*—Next year in Jerusalem."

Next year in Jerusalem. For nearly two thousand years, every Seder has ended with those words. After the Jews were scattered among the nations following the destruction of Jerusalem and its Holy Temple in 70 AD, they returned to a cycle of homelessness, abuse, hunger, bloodshed and even slavery. From the beginning of the 1900s until today, millions of them have returned to Israel. Once again, they have arrived in the land of their forefathers as they did thousands of years before, family by family. In the Second Exodus from Egypt and other mass emigrations from other lands, they entered Israel by multiplied thousands, hoping and praying that the rest of their families would soon appear. Often they did, and now they are home at last. At those two Seders I sat with their sons and daughters, with their children's children, and together we celebrated life in the heart of Jerusalem.

For me, at least, it still feels like a miracle.

CHAPTER THIRTEEN

BEYOND BETHLEHEM'S CALM

"It's because he's a Christian that he has been accused. That's all. It isn't because he actually collaborated."

"Maybe it's because he's a Christian that he's willing to help the other side."

Omar Yussef was shocked. "I remind you that you were educated by the Frères. You studied at the very same Christian school as George Saba, the Christian school where I used to teach."

"Dad, I'm just saying that people will do things under circumstances like these that we would never expect from them in normal times."

"Like accusing all Christians of being traitors?" Omar Yussef leaned forward angrily.

*"That isn't what I meant. But, look, Christians are already on the outside of our society these days. Maybe they feel they owe less loyalty than a Muslim does."—**The Collaborator of Bethlehem** by Matt Beynon Rees*

J ust a few days before Christmas, as I walked around Bethlehem on a Sunday morning, the lyric "All is calm, all is bright" drifted into my mind. It was a calm, bright day— windy, with a ridge of purple rain clouds gathering on the horizon. There had been tension in the air during an earlier visit to Bethlehem, which had taken place not long after the Hamas takeover in Gaza. But now any sense of apprehension seemed to have vanished.

"Do They Think We're Stupid?"

I was in the company of "Stefan," an Arab Christian who

serves as a visitors' guide. He was quick to point out, as we passed through the checkpoint, his grievances against the Israeli security fence, the inconvenience of ID checks and the required work permits. As a resident of Jerusalem, he had free passage back and forth, but was still indignant about the checkpoint.

My question was probably a little too direct. "Isn't the checkpoint here to stop suicide bombers from getting into Jerusalem?"

"Bombs!" he growled. "Do they think we're stupid? If I wanted to take a bomb in I'd just go out of town another way, where there isn't a checkpoint." Then he added, "Look, I'm a Christian and we aren't bombers. But if we were, we wouldn't be crazy enough go through a checkpoint!"

"So it's possible to come and go from Bethlehem without passing through a checkpoint?"

"Of course! There are many ways in and out of Bethlehem. You just have to know where you're going."

Stefan was right. I later learned that the last two suicide bombers that struck Jerusalem had come from Bethlehem and had reached their targets through a then-unguarded back road. In fact more than half the terrorists who struck Jerusalem in 2005 came from or through Bethlehem. Reportedly, since its installation, the security barrier has decreased the number of suicide bombings by more than 90%.

Stefan talked a little about the difficulties confronting Bethlehem businesses. Once again he revisited the Israeli security issues—how merchants are suffering because of them. Then he went on to say that Muslims are moving into the city, "more of them all the time," he told me. "More and more Muslims are coming in," he repeated, "and more and more Christians are leaving. They're going out of business and leaving the country. It's too hard to make a living here."

An earlier visit to Bethlehem had fallen on a weekday when Manger Square was completely empty. I remember watching trash blowing across the pavement and a few birds squawking over a crust of bread. Now church bells pealed and there was hardly a parking place to found. Merchants were un-shuttering their shops. Men in *keffiyahs*—the familiar red-and-white checked Bedouin headdresses—and modestly scarved women strolled up the hill toward the market. Stefan and I, going in the opposite direction, made our way alongside families and clusters of friends. Each of us bent over to enter the Door of Humility, which leads into the Church of the Nativity.

Incense filled the warm air inside, and colorful lights and candles illuminated the Greek Orthodox service. I glanced around, recalling that terrorists had seized this church in May 2002. In a bitter and prolonged siege, Arab gunmen held dozens of Christian nuns, priests, monks and pilgrims hostage for weeks. In revulsion, the Christian captives had watched act after act of wanton destruction as the terrorists looted historic icons, confiscated gold and silver sacred vessels, urinated against the walls, defecated on prayer books and otherwise demolished and desecrated the holy site.

Now, several years later, ancient chants echoed, and downstairs, in the Grotto where tradition says Jesus was born, candles and lanterns blazed as a small gathering of Italian worshippers prayed. Next door, the Roman Catholic service was just beginning, and there was standing room only as the cross was carried in procession toward the altar.

The liturgy began and a spirit of reverence fell across the room, interrupted only by a handful of professional photographers scurrying around on the periphery of the crowd. While the Gospel was read and the response sung—the service was in Arabic—I reflected on this faithful Catholic congregation. *They may be leaving town,* I thought, *but somehow they haven't stopped worshipping together.*

Until recent years Christians had enjoyed relative prosperity in Bethlehem as well as in other West Bank municipalities. Today they are departing in record numbers while Muslims are moving into their houses and businesses. Do the newcomers imagine they will have better luck in the shadow of the security fence? Won't the checkpoints handicap their commercial efforts too? A closer look at the facts suggests that the fence and other Israeli security procedures are not the real reason Bethlehem's Christians are struggling, despairing and fleeing.

Christian Persecution "Every Day"

In 1948, Bethlehem was a largely Christian community, with Christians comprising an estimated 85 percent of the population. Today, although accurate demographics are extremely hard to find and verify, that percentage has shrunk to something closer to 12 per cent. Until the Palestine Authority took over the control of the city in 1994 following the Oslo Accords' "Declaration of Principles," Bethlehem thrived alongside Jerusalem. As Khaled abu Toameh pointed out in an earlier chapter, the roads in and out of the city were open to everyone, and residents freely traveled to and fro from shops, restaurants and markets. All that began to change during the First Intifada, from 1987-1993, with stone-throwing incidents gradually escalating into shootings, assaults, and torched cars.

Later, during the Second Intifada, which began in September 2000, and during which suicide bombings and other violent episodes were frequent and deadly, security became a matter of survival. These attacks ultimately led to the construction of the controversial security barrier, or "fence."

Rowan Williams, the Archbishop of Canterbury and no friend of Israel, wrote in late 2006,

> I have spent the last two days with fellow Christian leaders in Bethlehem...there are some signs of disturbing anti-Christian feeling among parts of the Muslim population, despite the consistent traditions of coexistence. But their plight is made still more intolerable by the tragic conditions created by the 'security fence,' which almost chokes the shrinking town...

He went on to speak of dramatic poverty, soaring unemployment and practical hardships. He failed to mention the loss of life or the perilous security challenges Israel continues to face. In actuality, the Archbishop's carefully crafted phrase, "some signs of disturbing anti-Christian feeling" falls woefully short of telling the whole story.

In 2006, the UK's *Daily Mail* reported on the struggle of two Christians from the Bethlehem suburb of Beit Jala who were facing continuous persecution for their faith. George Rabie, a cab driver, said that he had been beaten by a gang of Muslims visiting from nearby Hebron, angered by the crucifix hanging on his windshield, and that he experiences persecution "every day." Jeriez Moussa Amaro told the reporter that his two sisters Rada, 24, and Dunya, 28, had been shot dead by Muslim gunmen. "Their crime was to be young, attractive Christian women who wore Western clothes and no veil…" A terrorist organization, al-Aksa Martyrs Brigades, claimed responsibility for Amaro's sisters' murder.

Overt violence isn't the only difficulty faced by Christians in areas under the Palestinian Authority. Ramallah pastor Isa Bajalia, an American Christian of Arab descent, stated publicly that he had been threatened by a Palestinian Authority official, who had demanded he pay $30,000 in protection money to ensure his safety. On November 11, 2006 Fox News reported, "Pastor Isa Bajalia is legally blind, yet he was also told by the official he would be crippled for life. The trouble started after church members held a prayer session for several Palestinians. Bajalia says he has been under surveillance and receiving threats." Isa Bajalia has since fled Ramallah.

In July 2007, Rami Khader Ayyad, 32, a Palestinian Christian bookstore owner who had received repeated threats, was found stabbed to death in a street in Gaza City. "I expect our Christian neighbors to understand the new Hamas rule means real changes," commented Sheikh Abu Sakir, leader of Jihadia Salfiya, an Islamic outreach movement. "They must be ready for Islamic rule if they want to live in peace in Gaza."

The repression of what once amounted to two or three thousand Christians living inside the Gaza Strip is rarely mentioned in news reports. And who knows how many are left? I had a conversation with two Gazan Christians, who had fled their homes and were hiding out in the West Bank while hoping for asylum elsewhere. Their stories exposed the dangers Christian families face under Hamas, including extortion, rape, beatings and murder. For most of these Christian refugees, the topic of life under radical Muslim rule is forbidden—they simply won't talk about it for fear of endangering themselves or those they've left behind. And, if they think they are talking to a journalist, they are quick to distance themselves from anything that might sound supportive of "The Zionists."

Justus Reid Weiner is Resident Scholar of the Jerusalem Center for Public Affairs, and he has been researching persecution of Christians in the Palestinian territories for many years. In a recent Jerusalem briefing he reported, "The growing strength of Islamic fundamentalism within the Palestinian national movement poses problems for Christians, who fear they will be deemed opponents of Islam and thereby risk becoming targets for Muslim extremists. This is exacerbated by the fact that Hamas holds substantial power and seeks to impose its radical Islamist identity on the entire population within the P.A.-controlled territories."

Weiner later told me in an interview,

Under the Palestinian regime, Christian Arabs have been victims of frequent human rights abuses by Muslims. There are many examples of intimidation, beatings, land-theft, firebombing of churches and other Christian institutions, denial of employment, economic boycotts, torture, kidnapping, forced marriage, sexual harassment, and extortion. PA officials are directly responsible for many of the human rights violations.

Muslims who have converted to Christianity are in the greatest danger. They are often left defenseless against cruelty by Muslim fundamentalists. Some have been murdered.

"Islamic Mafia Accused of Persecuting Holy Land Christians" was the startling 2005 headline in the U.K.'s *Telegraph*. The writer, Harry de Quetteville, interviewed Samir Qumsieh, who operates a Christian television station in Bethlehem. Qumsieh spoke of "land grabs" as one of the challenges faced by the Christian population. "A criminal mafia and Islamic fundamentalists work together," he said. "Their interests meet to take our land away." Several Christians spoke of the persecution of a moderate Muslim imam in Bethlehem's biggest mosque, who was repeatedly threatened after giving a sermon calling for an end to anti-Christian discrimination and land grabs.

Quemsieh was arrested in November 2010 and jailed for five days by the Palestinian Authority for reporting about disagreements that had taken place between Palestinian President Mahmoud Abbas and senior Fatah operative Mohammed Dahlan. Quemsieh is, for obvious reasons, a hard man to reach for interviews these days.

"We Are the Sons of Abraham!"

One Saturday afternoon a friend and I went to Bethlehem to visit an old Syrian Orthodox priest named Abu Yaqub. We drove into the city along a different route than I had taken before, somehow skipping the main checkpoint—just as Stefan had described. We dropped the car off inside a gated compound. Because of its yellow Jerusalem license plates, it needed to be locked up and parked out of sight or, as my friend explained, it would probably get vandalized.

Just minutes later, a man of around 40 drove up—his car had green Palestinian plates—and he greeted my friend warmly. She seemed to know him well. His little boy was riding with him, a beautiful child with big, dark brown eyes and a shy smile. I noticed that the car had an olive wood cross dangling bravely from the rear view mirror. This driver took us on a rather breathtaking ride, careening through the narrow streets. Suddenly he made an abrupt U-turn. Then he made another one. I wasn't quite sure why we were driving so crazily. Was someone was following us? But then everyone started laughing—except me. That was only because I couldn't follow their conversation, which was in Hebrew.

My friend explained that our driver thought he'd seen the old man we were going to visit sitting with some other men alongside the road. But after taking a second look, he said, "No, it wasn't him after all." So he had screeched around and headed back in our original direction and sped on for a little longer. At last, mercifully, we parked.

I followed the others to the door of a large and fairly dilapidated house. We were soon welcomed inside. There we found the old man—Abu Yaqub—in his bed. The little boy rushed around bringing chairs to the bedside. Soon I found myself sitting in a plastic chair in the bedroom of a grizzled old man in rumpled, striped pajamas. His wife hurried in to serve us fruit juice and cake. I felt rather odd at first, vaguely wondering how I get myself into such strange situations. But before another minute had passed it seemed to be perfectly natural for us to be gathering in the old saint's bedroom.

As we talked, I learned that Abu Yaqub wasn't just a priest, he was a bishop—although it wasn't clear whether this was an honorary title or an official one. He was too ill to serve anyway—he was incapacitated by serious heart trouble, and had no insurance for treatment because he smoked. He claimed to have stopped, although his wife—a plump woman with a cheerful but slightly worried face—looked at him askance when he said so. In any case, there was no money for heart surgery, and he was probably too frail and weak to survive it.

Abu Yaqub spoke very good English, so nothing had to be translated during our conversation. At that time he was 78 years old. He had left Nineveh in Iraq 50 years before and settled in

Palestine. And he was quite a character. His father's family was from the ancient town of Ur and the old cleric proudly declared, "We are the sons of Abraham!"

"How are things with your family in Iraq these days?" I asked.

He shrugged, then explained that the community where he grew up had never had the least bit of trouble with Muslims.

"Why not?" I wondered aloud, thinking of the many horror stories I had heard about Iraq's Christians.

"Because if they create a problem we kill them! We are the sons of Abraham!" If his voice hadn't been so raspy, he would have been shouting. "And it didn't take the Jewish sons of Abraham long to take care of the Palestinians, either," he went on to say, with a wide smile.

He went on to talk about how he missed the days before Bethlehem was cut off from Jerusalem. "I had so many friends in Jerusalem—many of them were policemen. I used to go over to see them and we spoke Aramaic together. Nowadays they can't come here to visit me because they are Jews, and Bethlehem is closed to them. But I miss them very much!" Abu Yaqub had grown up in a region of Iraq where, until recently, the ancient Semitic language, Aramaic, was spoken by both Christians and Jews.

As a young man, he met his wife, Teresa, in Lebanon. She was from a family that fled Turkey in 1915, so we talked for a few minutes about the Armenian—and Greek and Syriac—genocide that her family had escaped. And that brought a story to the old man's mind.

He told us about a church in Iraq where he had served as a priest more than half a century before, which was dedicated to the Virgin Mary. On feast days, the whole community gathered and ate and drank at tables all around the church—Christian families and a number of Muslims, too. Yaqub had the keys to the church, and on one of those occasions five Muslim women, completely garbed in black, quietly asked him if they could please go inside the sanctuary to pray.

"I didn't understand why, but I unlocked the door. The women rushed inside, tore their head and face coverings off, fell on their knees and began to weep. They prayed and cried for a long time and then finally stood up and re-covered themselves."

I glanced at my friend, who looked equally puzzled. "Abu Yaqub," she asked, "Why did they do that?"

"An important question," he smiled. "I asked the group of them 'Why? Why do you weep? Why are you praying in a church?' One of them told me, 'We are really Armenians...'"

He explained that as little girls all five of the women had been kidnapped from their Christian families and forcibly married to Muslims. They were now middle-aged but had never forgotten their Christian faith. Then he reported something that was entirely new to me.

"Even now, thousands of Turks are being baptized as Christians. They are leaving Islam by the score." He said that at least one brave Syrian priest has been traveling from village to village in Northern Turkey, preaching and baptizing. "One entire Turkish village, which more than half a century ago was forced to become Muslim at risk of its inhabitants' lives, has returned to its Christianity."

Abu Yaqub died a couple of years after I met him. He was a delightful man with a warm and loving spirit. Just in telling a few stories about his life, he revealed how times have changed between Christians, Jews and Muslims—not only in Israel but throughout the Middle East. I've since learned that there were a few people in the old man's religious community who didn't like his forthright way of speaking, particularly about Israel, which he openly praised in such an affectionate way.

As I was leaving, I asked him and his wife what they feared most about the future in Bethlehem.

Without hesitation, they answered in unison: "Hamas."

The Case of Ahmad El-Achwad

Hamas is indeed a threat to many Palestinians in the West Bank—Christians, moderate Muslims and non-believers. And it is difficult to assess how active and powerful the organization is within cities like Bethlehem, Ramallah and Nablus or how much influence it undetectably exerts on the governing PA bodies, such as the police. On one occasion, my son Colin and I visited a refugee camp in Bethlehem. As we left, we passed a group of six- or seven-year-olds playing "war," cheering and shouting about their imaginary conquests. One of them was proudly carrying a small Hamas flag, and he smiled broadly and waved at us as we passed. He was a jovial little guy with a friendly face. He was delighted when Colin took his picture.

In the areas under PA control, all Christians are targeted from time to time, but no one suffers more than those who have converted from Islam to Christianity. Justus Weiner tells the story of Ahmad El-Achwad, a Christian convert who was first arrested on false charges of having stolen gold. "The only gold in his entire family," Weiner explained, "was his daughter's delicate necklace, which had been given to her for her birthday by her grandfather. And the family still had the receipt from the store where it was purchased."

No matter. Ahmad was imprisoned by the PA in a tiny cell and was frequently left unfed and was not even provided with water, sometimes for days at a time. The cruelties he endured had required him to spend a prolonged period of time in a hospital.

Weiner recalls, "When I interviewed Ahmad, he gave me photos of his injuries, taken while he was recuperating. It was clear that he had been tortured. He had suffered extensive and serious burns on his back, buttocks, and legs. The heated torture implement that was applied to his skin reminded me of similar medieval instruments."

After his eventual release from prison, Ahmad started a small house church in his residence where he gave out Bibles and Christian literature. Muslim Palestinians attended, and he freely shared with them the message of his newfound faith.

Over a seven-year period, Ahmad was arrested repeatedly, and his Bibles and Christian publications were confiscated. He lost his business, continued to receive death threats, and eventually found a way to move to Jerusalem in order to find work and safety. But whenever he returned to visit his family, his enemies sought him out. Once, a gang of masked thugs beat him. Later, his car was torched and his relative's residence was firebombed.

Predictably, Ahmad's story did not have a happy ending. Its unhappy conclusion came when, finally, he was shot dead by masked gunmen. Only for that reason can we use his real name. Meanwhile, his killers have never been brought to justice.

In Defense of a Vulnerable Sister

Another danger faced by Arab Christians is the rape of their young girls, which is all too common throughout the Muslim world, including areas in the West Bank. Christian girls are warned not to go out alone, and they often cover their heads so they appear to be Muslim—simply for the sake of self-preservation. Still, attacks happen. In one case, a young man was so angered by his sister's attempted molestation that he decided to confront her attackers. We'll call him "Habib."

The fact that I am using pseudonyms in most of these stories about Arab Christians should speak for itself—there is a serious safety issue for those who speak out about Muslim-on-Christian crime in the PA-controlled areas. Forthright people face the ire of Muslim radicals or of Palestinian opportunists who have no religious concerns but get political or financial benefits by harassing Christians. As I write this, Habib remains in a particularly vulnerable situation. And the woman who told me the story—we'll call her "Molly"—is at risk, too.

Molly, a pretty blonde from a western country, works with an organization that provides assistance to Christians on both sides of the Green Line. She returned to her Jerusalem home one evening and emailed me after a disturbing interview with a young man.

Molly had met with Habib at his grandmother's house just hours before, where he, his mother and an aunt were gathered.

"He's a skinny fella," Molly wrote, "but beyond his own physique he is skinnier than normal due to his injuries."

Habib related his story to Molly in some detail. His sister had been walking home from school one day when some young men in a car drove by, slowed down and let the young girl know exactly what they wanted. They tried to grab her and pull her into their car, shouting obscenities and threatening to rape her. After she managed to escape and make her way home, she told Habib what had happened. Infuriated by the incident, Habib figured out who the assailants were and tracked them down. He went to their neighborhood, knocked on the door of a house where they hung out, and told them to leave his sister alone.

After this confrontation, members of the group begin to track Habib's every move. He knew he was being followed, but tried to ignore the danger. One afternoon, Habib and his cousin went to a nearby forest to walk and talk and relax. Suddenly 13 young men, who had arrived in cars and on motorbikes, surrounded them. At first, they seemed only to be armed with sticks and a billy club. Then the knives appeared.

While his cousin was beaten and held back from interfering, Habib was stabbed 28 times. He was knifed on the head, neck, hands and the inner thighs (the attackers were trying to sever a main artery) and was left for dead. Once the assailants fled and the cousin was released, he frantically drove Habib to the hospital before he bled out. Habib received massive blood transfusions; his wounds were repaired, and his life was spared. But he still requires further surgery, to implant artificial veins in one hand and one of his legs. Habib is a wood carver, and without the full use of both hands, it is difficult for him to continue his work. Today he remains in hiding.

Why was Habib's sister attacked? Molly wrote, "It's an anti-Christian tactic, of course. But Muslims rape Christian girls and boys at least partially because if they tried doing it to a Muslim they know they might well be killed. They know that Christians are less likely to seek revenge. Many times the police allow the Muslims to operate as they do and they even stand up for them—no matter if clearly they are in the wrong. It's like a modern day mafia. Sickening! You add drugs to that mix and you have a very bad situation. But that's the reality in Habib's part of town."

Bethlehem and Beyond

Khaled Abu Toameh, who spoke to me in an earlier chapter about the relationship between Israel's Jews and Arabs, has written extensively about the problems Arab Christians face in the Muslim-majority Middle East.

> Palestinian Christians have... been feeling the heat, although their conditions remain much better than those of their brothers and sisters in Iraq and Egypt...In the Hamas-controlled Gaza Strip, the tiny Christian community is also living in fear following a spate of attacks by radical Islamic groups.
>
> The failure of the international community to pay enough attention to the dangers facing the Christians has encouraged radical Muslims and corrupt dictatorships to step up their assaults on Christian individuals and institutions.
>
> When Muslim fanatics cannot kill Christian soldiers or civilians in the mountains of Afghanistan or on the streets of New York, they choose an easy prey: their Arab Christian neighbors.

During the Christmas season in Bethlehem, Palestinian flags flutter above the busy marketplace surrounding Manger Square while Palestinian Authority policemen keep a close eye on tourists and anyone else they don't know. In a café, a tiny Christmas tree's ornaments gleam red and green as groups of men share a late morning meal of falafel, pita and hummus. Shopkeepers open their shutters early, hoping for enough business to make up for the slower seasons, when there's trouble in the air and foreign tourists avoid the city.

Just minutes away, along bustling Emek Refaim Street, Jerusalem's shoppers browse and chatter and drink coffee. Most of them are unmindful of the Christmas season. And many of them are also unaware of the relentless population exchange going on just ten minutes down the road. Amidst the calm, bright Christmas season, Bethlehem Christians continue quietly packing up their belongings and moving away. Muslims are moving in behind them, taking over their homes and businesses.

Why doesn't the world know or care? Most obvious is the fact that no one wants to blame all Muslims for the misbehavior of a few. But, more ominously, discussion of the plight of Christians in the PA territories is, as one journalist friend starkly put it, "Taboo." It is dangerous for local Christians to speak up because of potential retribution and, worse, the threat of being accused of collaboration with Israel. And it is politically incorrect for journalists and other observers to do so. If they do so, their work is discredited and stigmatized as "Zionist propaganda."

Abu Yaqub, the old priest I spoke to, remembered fondly his Jewish-Israeli fellow-countrymen from Iraq. He had been around long enough, and was politically unconventional enough, to openly declare that the people of Israel were his friends, and not his enemies. But new generations have come along during his lifetime, born in the years since the Intifadas, when the checkpoints and barriers were put in place.

Very few young Arabs have friends in Israel these days. For as long as they can remember, they've seen Israelis only as unsmiling soldiers, or watched them depicted on their television screens as hateful "settlers" or as other distorted caricatures of bloodthirsty Jews. Why would they trust an alien group of intruders, who, according to all they've heard and seen, hate them and want to harm them? This situation is only occasionally alleviated by non-

Israelis—people like Molly—who are able to come and go and speak in positive terms about the Israelis. And of course these visitors have to be careful, too.

Meanwhile, as the leaders of Arab Christian churches place the blame for the dangers facing Arab Christians squarely on the shoulders of Israel, they never hint that radical religious jihadis or an "Islamic Mafia" or other money-hungry, violence hardened criminals are extorting, threatening, falsely-accusing and sometimes murdering Christian Arabs. Such crimes happen repeatedly without the perpetrators being arrested, tried in a court of justice, or spending time behind bars for their crimes.

I began my first Christmas visit to Bethlehem with the beloved Christmas hymn, "Silent Night, Holy Night" playing in my head—*All is calm, all is bright.* At first glance, Bethlehem seems that way, at least on the surface. But as I reflect on my various visits, and on what I've since learned, I'm reminded of another song of the season, "It Came Upon a Midnight Clear" and one of its more obscure verses. For me, the stanza speaks well to the present troubles in Bethlehem—and beyond.

> *Yet with the woes of sin and strife*
> *The world has suffered long;*
> *Beneath the angel strain have rolled*
> *Two thousand years of wrong;*
> *And man, at war with man, hears not*
> *The love-song which they bring;*
> *O hush the noise, ye men of strife,*
> *And hear the angels sing.*

CHAPTER FOURTEEN

NATURAL ALLIES IN
A DANGEROUS WORLD

Once to every man and nation, comes the moment to decide,
In the strife of truth with falsehood, for the good or evil side;
Some great cause, some great decision, offering each the
bloom or blight,
And the choice goes by forever, 'twixt that darkness and that light.
…Though the cause of evil prosper, yet the truth alone is strong;
Though her portion be the scaffold, and upon the throne be wrong;
Yet that scaffold sways the future, and behind the dim unknown,
Standeth God within the shadow, keeping watch above His own.
—James Russell Lowell, 1819-1891

March 11, 2011 was a Saturday. Thanks to the quiet observance of Shabbat, there was little going on in my neighborhood. Like the observant Jews around me, I enjoy the peace and quiet of the Seventh Day immensely, and miss it when I'm away. But, not being constrained by tradition, I do log on to my computer, check my emails and glance at the news. And when I did so that Saturday, I immediately saw—thanks to a less-than-Orthodox Israeli news site—that something horrifying had happened.

By sundown, when everyone was back at work and the news was updated, the story became all too clear. A family of five—parents and three little children, including an infant, had been brutally murdered in Itamar (briefly described earlier), a settlement in Samaria. Before long, an assortment of photos of the Fogel family appeared on the Internet, posted by friends who were enraged by their murders. Ehud—"Udi"—and Ruth were the parents; Yoav was 11, Elad was four, and Hadas was a three-month-old baby girl. All had died in pools of blood, their throats slit. The tiny infant Hadas was beheaded.

Three Fogel children survived—Tamar, age 12, Roi, age 6, and Yishai, age 2. Thankfully, for some reason Roi and Yishai were not noticed by the killers. Tamar, who had been attending a youth event nearby, had found herself unexpectedly locked out—thanks to the murderers—and went to the next-door neighbor, Rabbi Yaacov Cohen, for help. He helped her get inside, and returned home. Tamar was alone when she discovered the grisly deaths. She screamed; Rabbi Cohen rushed back. They found Yishai sobbing, trying to wake up his father.

All of Israel was sickened and enraged. Tens of thousands of people showed up at the funeral. For days afterward, a heavy weight of sadness pressed against the whole country. Tamar promised, "I will be strong and succeed in overcoming this. I understand the task that stands before me, and I will be a mother to my siblings."

The following week, a flurry of photos appeared on line, depicting the happy and attractive Fogel family in earlier times, doing ordinary things in their home. These, of course, made the brutality all the more stunning. Then came the grisly images, with warnings attached, detailing the murder scene. Words fall short in describing the bloodstained walls, floors and toys that were left behind. One brief glance was enough. But like the images of the Baghdad church massacre, I have yet to remove the Fogel family's smiling faces from my computer.

Two Palestinian teenagers from a nearby village—both from radical Islamist families—unrepentantly confessed to the murders.

War against Zionists and Crusaders

When I arrived in Israel as a Christian visitor, I came with the conviction that an assault upon Jews is an implicit assault upon Christians, since it strikes at the root of the same ancient tree. In that light, I wanted to see for myself the predicament of Israeli Jewish communities under attack by Islamic militants. I saw it again and again, not only on the news, but in talking to survivors, or to loved ones left behind with their grief.

Today anti-Semitism is reviving throughout the world. Hardly a day passes without a report of a desecrated cemetery, a defaced synagogue, neo-Nazi violence or the more subtle forms of media-generated prejudice that blame the Jewish people for everything from the bad economy to every war in modern history. Annual reports compiled by the FBI indicate that about 65% of all hate crimes in the US are against Jews. It is not clear that this has an effect on Jewish life in the United States, but it does belie the hysteria over "Islamophobia," since hate crimes against American Muslims amount to only about 15%. In major Western European cities, Jews are threatened or attacked for their Orthodox attire or for wearing a Star of David or a yarmulke. In increasing numbers they are leaving western European cities where they are openly persecuted. Many are relocating in Israel.

Today's asymmetrical and protracted global jihad, specifically described by such well-informed spokesmen as Osama bin Laden and Mahmoud Ahmadinejad as a religious war, has not been declared only against "the West" as a geopolitical monolith. The targets are explicitly religious: "Crusaders," meaning Christians; "the descendants of apes and pigs," meaning Jews; and, of course, Zionists, meaning those who live in the State of Israel or those who support it. Meanwhile, thanks to media manipulation and resurgent anti-Semitism, world opinion increasingly frowns upon Israel, no matter who launches the first rocket, blows up the school bus, or beheads the baby.

But in keeping with the animus against "Crusaders," Jews aren't the only victims. In the weeks and months that followed my first introductions to Jerusalem, I saw that the "Holy City" is also a crossroads for Christians of every creed and confession, an ever-changing collage of pilgrims and sojourners. And more than a few of the Christian communities represented in Jerusalem suffer persecution under Muslim regimes. Mostly the victims themselves don't appear in Israel (although Sudanese refugees have arrived by the thousands, battered eyewitnesses to Khartoum's jihadist tyranny). It is those who know and love them who come and go, often bearing horrific news. Although I had come to Israel to better understand its Jewish community, soon I was learning more and more about Christians who suffer merely for being Christians.

During a single visit to a Jerusalem church, I heard three appalling accounts: A pastor described the brutal murder and mutilation of three Christian men in Turkey—he had attended their funeral just days before. A Finnish woman recalled the gruesome death of her best friend—a Christian physician whose throat had been slit by terrorists in Yemen. A fleeing couple spoke of the tiny and impoverished group of Gaza Evangelicals they had been forced to leave behind in the wake of the Hamas coup. Meanwhile, two writing assignments I'd taken with me focused my attention intently on the persecution of Christians.

A book I was writing at that time, *Baroness Cox: Eyewitness to a Broken World,* included Caroline Cox's personal interviews with victims. I was struck by the similarity of jihadi attacks in country after country, evident not only in body counts but in kidnappings and enslavement, bloodlust, rape, mutilation and torture. Often it was fellow Muslims who paid the highest price, but Christians were frequently targeted with special hatred.

At the same time, I wrote numerous country reports for *Religious Freedom in the World,* a survey by the Center for Religious Freedom at Hudson Institute. Once again, Islamists' bloody fingerprints were exposed. Again, most of the victims were Muslims who fell dangerously short of their co-religionists' expectations. Neither project cited abuses of Jews. Why? Because, with few exceptions, the Muslim world's Jewish communities have been slaughtered, expelled or have fled for their lives. Many of the survivors live in Israel.

In June 2007, during the journalists' conference I attended in Istanbul, both in sessions and in private conversations, reporters, editors, television broadcasters and other news people from the Middle East as well as from far-flung places like Indonesia, Malaysia, Nigeria, the Philippines and Pakistan, described their Christian communities' life-and-death struggles. A number of Muslim scholars and journalists attended too, expressing their dismay and a deep desire to see their religion moderated. After I returned to Jerusalem, one thing was clear. Although I hadn't intended to research or write about Islamist anti-Christian persecution, it was happening before my eyes.

Most recently I co-authored, with Paul Marshall and Nina Shea, *Persecuted: The Global Assault on Christians* (Thomas Nelson, 2013). We had to add two additional chapters to cover the mass of information our research had exposed on Islamist abuses and violence.

And of course, after stumbling across the story of the expulsions of Jews from Muslim lands, I continued to gather information about that unexpected discovery, which added the Saturday People, Sunday People dimension to these stories. That essential layer of history and human tragedy provides a gloomy backdrop for the present day's realities.

Surging Anti-Christian Persecution

The preceding chapters have provided a glimpse at the reasons Christians are fleeing Muslim majority homelands at an accelerated rate and in ever-increasing numbers. Some ancient communities are at risk of extinction. Are these Christians post-colonial detritus that simply need to, in Helen Thomas' immortal words about the Israelis, "go back where they came from?" Are they troublemakers who refuse to submit to majority rule? Or is something more significant happening?

I asked scholar Hillel Fradkin, Hudson Institute's senior fellow and Director of the Center on Islam, Democracy and the Future of the Muslim World about the departure of Christians from Islamic countries. He explained,

> The dwindling Christian populations in the Middle East and North Africa represent the decline and perhaps the end of the most ancient of Christian communities. This is often not appreciated, inasmuch as many people are used to thinking of the Middle East and North Africa as Muslim from time immemorial, and the present-day Christians as recent "colonial" implants - the result of 19th- and 20th-century missionary activity. But this is not the case. Prior to the Muslim conquests of the mid-seventh century, the large majority of inhabitants of the area were Christians, including many Arab Christians. Even Arabia had substantial Christian communities in such places as present day Bahrain, Yemen and the Najran area of western Arabia south of Mecca. This area also boasted Christianity's major theological centers—Constantinople of course, but also Antioch and Alexandria—and its leading theologians—above all Augustine, a native of North Africa.

At the time of the Muslim conquests, the Christian community was already divided into numerous sects from which many of the present day churches—Eastern Orthodox, Nestorian, Assyrian, Coptic, Armenian and others—in Muslim lands descend. These churches and their numbers have declined very slowly. In some cases hundreds of years passed before the majority of the population became Muslim. The most noteworthy case is Egypt, where even today the Coptic Church represents some 10-15% of the population. Modern Turkey lost its very large Christian community only at the end of World War I, when Turkish-speaking Christians were brutally expelled in exchange for Greek-speaking Muslims living in the Balkans, a story that has been nearly forgotten today, though more than a million-and-a-half Armenian Christians were killed.

Discrimination and persecution of Christians in Muslim lands are not limited to the Middle East. In Africa, Asia and the Indian subcontinent, Islamist aggression is also spreading and intensifying. Those who suffer rarely speak out for fear of inciting further bloodshed against family, friends, churches or villages. A few outsiders manage to visit and report; now and then the persecuted find a way to flee, and, even at risk of honor killings in their families, they may feel compelled to described the suffering they've endured. Those who cannot escape cling to lives of relentless anxiety, danger and necessary silence.

Major international media outlets infrequently mention the abuse or the victims. A dearth of detailed information makes it nearly impossible to precisely calculate deaths and casualties or to provide more than hints at what life is like in restricted countries. But what we do know, we should expose.

In Turkey

The ever-increasing influence of radical Islam in Turkey, under the leadership of Prime Minister Recep Tayyip Erdogan, has stealthily taken its toll on both Jews and Christians.

In 2004, not long after Erdogan's election, I joined a group of friends and colleagues, visiting the shattered Neve Shalom synagogue in Istanbul, Turkey, which had been nearly destroyed by a car bomber the previous November, killing 27 people and wounding 300. It was a scene of utter devastation—little was left of a large section of the building, so enormous had been the blast. And it wasn't the first time that synagogue had been bombed—terrorists had also attacked it in 1986 and 1992. The courageous leaders of the Jewish community told us that they would rebuild yet again, and would this time construct a wall that could withstand an even bigger bomb.

Meanwhile, Christian properties, some dating back to the early centuries of Christianity, have been seized over the years and declared government property, such as the 1,600-year-old Mor Gabriel Syrian Orthodox Monastery. Priceless Armenian churches lie in ruins; early Christian sites are left to erode beneath the elements or, worse, historic churches—such as the spiritually and historically revered Hagia Sophia at Nicaea—are turned into mosques.

The Christian population of roughly 90,000 has long been caught between radical Islam and Kemalist secular nationalism. Both extremes have little or no regard for Jews or Christians. The massacre of Armenian and Greek Christians between 1915 and 1917 was, in part, a response to a call for jihad. In 2010, *The Economist* quoted Mala Hadi, an Islamic sheikh in Diyarbakir, who admitted that "Collaborating Kurdish clerics pledged that anyone who killed an infidel would be rewarded in heaven with 700 mansions containing 700 rooms, and that in each of these rooms there would be 700 houris to give them pleasure."

To this day, the Turkish government continues to reject any acknowledgement of horrifying murders and death marches many have called genocide—events that encouraged Adolf Hitler to move forward with his plans for exterminating Jews. "Who speaks today about the Armenians?" he asked his generals.

There were several killings of individual Christians in Turkey—priests and a journalist—in the early 21st Century. Then on April 18, 2007, three employees of a publishing house that distributes Bibles were killed. The three victims—a German and two Turkish citizens—were found with their hands and legs bound and their throats slit at the Zirve publishing house in the central city of Malatya; it has been widely reported that the three were tortured and mutilated. There have been arrests, but the trials have been postponed repeatedly for political reasons. This does not surprise local believers. According to a spring 2011 report from the Turkish Association of Protestant Christians, the

Christian minority in Turkey suffers discrimination, slander, personal attacks and attacks against churches on a daily basis.

> John Eibner, CEO of Christian Solidarity International, wrote in May 2011,
> Unless Ankara is prepared to combat the widespread "Christophobia" that fuels violence and other forms of repression, the country's Christians are doomed to remain an oppressed and discriminated against minority, and Turkey's aspirations of democratic transformation and full integration with Europe will remain stillborn.

In Iran

A Jewish community of around 20,000 still exists in Iran. It is a closely monitored population, and the regime—which is the world's most overtly hostile to Israel, often calling for its extermination—offers few opportunities to its Jewish citizens while imposing pervasive scrutiny. Any contact between Iranian Jews and relatives or friends in Israel can result in accusations of collaboration with the Zionist enemy and can lead to arrest and imprisonment. A law was recently passed stating that any Iranians traveling to Israel now face prison terms of 2 to 5 years, as well as the confiscation of their passports for three to five years.

The Christian community, which amounts to .05% of the total population of nearly 70 million, is facing intensified crackdowns. In recent months, intending to intimidate and pressure them, hard-line authorities have detained, interrogated and eventually released Christians from several denominations and communities across various regions of Iran. The measures include attacks on private homes where Christians gather for worship. There are many stories of widespread Christian conversions among Iran's Muslims, which could account for the regime's obsessive surveillance and strong-armed tactics.

In one instance, in December 2006, secret police raided Christian fellowships in Karaj, Teheran, Rasht and Bandar-i Anzali. They confiscated computers, literature and Bibles, and arrested 15 Christians whom they accused of evangelism and actions against the state. All but one have been released, but only after forfeiting money, job permits and even house deeds as bail.

I wrote in the *National Review Online's* "The Corner," in March 2011,

> Rights groups are reporting new developments in Iran's anti-Christian crackdown, which has swept up nearly 300 Christian believers since June 2010. In late January 2011, Elam Ministries (a group that monitors Christian persecution in Iran) announced a "severe intensification of arrests and imprisonment of Christians in Iran."
>
> At about the same time, Christian Solidarity Worldwide (CSW) reported that five Iranian Christians had been sentenced to one year's imprisonment for "Crimes against the Islamic Order." Behrouz Sadegh-Khandjani, Mehdi Furutan, Mohammad Beliad, Parviz Khalaj and Nazly Beliad, all members of the Church of Iran, a Jesus-Only Pentecostal denomination, were found guilty by the Revolutionary Court in Shiraz. They have 20 days to appeal the sentence.
>
> 282 Christians were arrested in 34 Iranian cities from June 2010 until early 2011: "At least 15 of these Christians remain in prison, while others have been released, generally after posting large amounts of bail."
>
> According to Elam's report, Yousef Nadarkhani, pastor of a church in Gilan province, has been sentenced to death. He was arrested in October 2009 and is being held in Lakan prison while his case is appealed. He has been repeatedly prodded by the authorities to convert to Islam in order to regain his freedom. [Pastor Nadarkhani was unexpectedly released in

late 2012; his heroic Muslim lawyer, Mohammed Ali Dadkah, was arrested and imprisoned soon thereafter—for providing pro-bono assistance to a member of a religious minority.]

An earlier (August 2010) report from Elam described Iranian clerics' hostility to the country's Christian population. It quotes Ayatollah Seyed Hosseini Bousherhri, who blames the explosive growth of house churches on the enemies of Iran: "Today the global aggressors have accurately planned and invested resources for these purposes. This why in our country there is a strong inclination towards Christianity."

In Nigeria

Although there are a few thousand black Africans from the Igbo tribe who believe that they belong to one of the lost tribes of Israel, and despite their efforts at identifying themselves with Judaism, they are not widely recognized as Jews either in Israel or elsewhere.

Meanwhile, oil-rich Nigeria's 65 million Christians—nearly half its population—live primarily in the south of the country, and they are bruised and bloodied by repeated attacks on villages, churches and families. Referring to the instruction of Jesus to "turn the other cheek," a weary Nigerian journalist told me that his Christian community has "no more cheeks to turn."

There is a massive push among Islamists to apply shari'a law to the entire populace, Christian and Muslim alike. Twelve Nigerian states have already enacted shari'a; three more are moving toward it. The unbridled violence unleashed by bands of machete-armed thugs and jihadis with bombs and machine guns is horrifying. In 2011 alone, consider the following:

In January, in three separate incidents, 38 Nigerian Christians were killed by Muslim marauders—many of them women and children, most of them hacked to death. Sixteen were injured and several homes were torched.

In February, 23 were killed and 16 were injured in a Muslim raid.

In April, 321 Nigerian Christians were killed and 575 injured by sword or fire. More than 40 churches were burned.

In May, 17 were killed and three injured, including a Christian pastor and his wife and children.

In September, 28 were killed and 19 were injured—either shot or hacked to death.

In November 2011, 150 died and 200 were injured in bombing and shooting riots that destroyed several churches. Vatican Radio reported about the massacre, "The Nigerian Red Cross reports that more than 100 died in a series of attacks in northeast Nigeria's Yobe and Borno states launched by a radical Muslim group known as Boko Haram. The group wants to implement strict Shariah law across Nigeria... Its name means 'Western education is sacrilege' in the local Hausa language."

Of this massacre, the Pope said: "I am following with concern the tragic incidents that have occurred in recent days in Nigeria and, as I pray for the victims, I call for an end to all violence, which never solves problems, but only increases them, sowing hatred and division even among believers."

And still the protracted massacre continues. More than 250 Nigerian Christians have been killed in 2012, mid-year, by Muslim terrorists.

In Indonesia

While the Jewish community in Indonesia has diminished to only around 20, the scenic archipelago's Christian community, comprising around 13% of the population of more than 220 million, has traditionally lived in harmony with its majority Muslim neighbors.

But since the late 1990s there has been an escalation in Islamist activities. There are widespread reports of jihadis arriving from the Middle East to establish training camps. All this has led to extraordinarily shocking abuses and thousands of deaths—only a few of which were reported internationally.

The Associated Press reported on October 29, 2005 one of the most horrifying stories: the beheadings of three Christian schoolgirls. Six men attacked four girls—Theresia Morangke, 15, Alfita Poliwo, 17, Yarni Sambue, 15, and Noviana Malewa, 15—early in the morning as they walked to a Christian school in Poso district. The first three girls were beheaded; the fourth, Noviana Malewa, received severe injuries to her face and neck but survived the attack. The three murdered girls' heads were wrapped in black plastic bags. One was found on the steps of a Kasiguncu village church. The other two heads were left at a nearby police station. One of the bags contained a note, including the words: "We will murder 100 more Christian teenagers and their heads will be presented as presents."

Weeks later, two more schoolgirls—Siti Nuraini and her friend Ivon Maganti, both 17—were shot in the face. Nuraini died from her wounds; Maganti survived the attack. In recent years hundreds of Christian villages have been burned and thousands have died, some of them burned alive in their churches.

Since those horrific attacks, 18 other incidents have claimed the lives of 26 Indonesian Christians, and have injured more than 450.

More recently, in September 2011 six Christians were murdered in Maluku and 80 were wounded during a machete attack on a Christian village. Two weeks later, a bomb containing nails and bolts exploded during a church service in Solo. Two were killed and 20 were wounded.

In Afghanistan

Afghanistan is nearly without Jews. Only one remains: Zablon Simintov, who serves as the caretaker of Kabul's last synagogue. And, despite the best efforts of Allied Forces to remove the Taliban from power, extremist groups affiliated with them continue to violently oppose Christianity.

On July 19, 2007, Taliban forces in Ghazni province kidnapped 23 Christian humanitarian workers from Sammul Presbyterian Church in Bundang, South Korea. The workers were traveling by bus from Kabul to Kandahar. On July 25, the bullet-riddled body of 42-year-old Pastor Bae Hyung-kyu was found. A Taliban representative explained, "Since Kabul's administration did not listen to our demand and did not free our prisoners, the Taliban shot dead a male Korean hostage." A second hostage, Shim Sung-Min, was murdered days later, after refusing to convert to Islam. The remaining hostages were eventually released, reportedly amid promises from South Korea to withdraw troops and forbid further missionary travel to Afghanistan.

In August 2010, ten members of a Christian medical team, including six Americans, two Afghans, one Briton and one German, were dragged out of their cars and executed. Their Afghan driver was released after crying for mercy, and convincing the murderers that he could quote passages from the Koran. USA Today reported,

> Team members—doctors, nurses and logistics personnel—were attacked as they were returning to Kabul after their two-week mission in the remote Parun valley of Nuristan province about 160 miles north of Kabul. They had decided to veer northward into Badakhshan province because they thought that would be the safest route back to Kabul, said Dirk Frans, director of the International Assistance Mission, which organized the team. The bullet-riddled bodies— including those of three women—were found Friday near three four-wheeled drive vehicles in a wooded area just off the main road that snakes through a narrow valley in the Kuran Wa Munjan district of Badakhshan... Taliban spokesman Zabiullah Mujahid told the AP that the insurgents killed the foreigners because they were "spying for the Americans" and "preaching Christianity."

In February 2011, the story of a Christian who had converted from Islam—Said Musa—gained wide attention in the West because he was sentenced to death for apostasy. After powerful but quiet diplomatic efforts, spearheaded by the United States, he was released. At last report, a second Muslim-background Christian, Shoaib Assadullah, 23, remained on death row for the same offense.

In Saudi Arabia

One of America's key allies in the war against terror is so repressive that it is nearly impossible to determine how intense the religious persecution is within its borders. Although exceptions may occur, generally Jews are not permitted even to travel to the Kingdom of Saudi Arabia, much less to live there.

As for the predicament of Christians, in our book *Their Blood Cries Out: The Worldwide Tragedy of Modern Christians Who Are Dying for Their Faith*, Paul Marshall and I wrote:

> It is illegal to wear a cross or to utter a Christian prayer. Christians cannot even worship privately in their own homes. Worship is allowed occasionally on foreign company sites or in embassies or consulates, but even this is not secure... expatriates from less influential countries such as India, Egypt, Korea and the Philippines bear the brunt of the restrictions... as harsh as life can be for expatriate Christians, the worst adversity falls upon Saudi nationals who are Christians... A Christian Saudi citizen is assumed to be apostate from Islam, and therefore is automatically subject to death... To be a Saudi is to be a Muslim, with no exceptions.

The Iron Fist and the Unseen Hand

My father, a devout Christian, believed that he discerned the unseen hand of the Lord in the re-gathering of the Jews in their land during the 19th and 20th centuries, in the establishment of the State of Israel in 1948, and in the dramatic military victories that followed. There was an understanding in my childhood home that Israel's wars of 1967 and 1973 affirmed God's promises to his people, and demonstrated his blessings of peace and prosperity on them.

By the time I arrived in Israel—sadly without my father—it was all too obvious that Israel's state of war with her Arab neighbors was far from over. In summer 2006, Israel struck back at Hezbollah after its killing and kidnapping of Israeli Defense Forces soldiers. In 2009, the IDF launched Operation Cast Lead, attempting to end Hamas' firing of thousands of rockets from Gaza into civilian Jewish communities. And in 2010, Israel denied a Turkish "humanitarian" flotilla flagship, manned by terrorists, to break Israel's arms embargo on Gaza; nine assailants, who were attacking Israeli commandos with knives, chains and clubs, were killed.

In every case, there were not only casualties, but Israel was pilloried in the world's court of public opinion, where the international media's accusations of "disproportionate response" and human rights violations included distortions, lies and false evidence. Indeed, today's assaults on Israel encompass both bloodshed and libelous words.

And behind all of these assaults is another unseen hand: the iron fist of radical Islam.

Islam's hatred of Jews is nothing new—it can be traced to Mohammad's earliest military adventures, to passages in the Quran, as well as to more recent revivals of Muslim extremism. And now, as we've seen, another dark plot—directed against Christians—is unfolding in those same Muslim lands. With increasing frequency, Christians are being jailed, beaten, raped and murdered, under strikingly similar circumstances to those of the Jews half a century before.

Remarkably, and practically unnoticed, today there is only one country in the Middle East in which the Christian population is not declining but continues to increase: Israel. Home to nearly six million Jews, Israel also hosts an ever-increasing multitude of Christian creeds, confessions and cultures. Difficulties of course arise, but by and large the various traditions of Jews and Christians live together in peace and safety within the State of Israel. Israel also has a particularly upright reputation for making holy sites safely available to all pilgrims, tourists and other visitors.

Meanwhile, the Islamic Republic of Iran's radical Shiite mullahs still call for the destruction of Israel and for the defeat of the "Zionist-Crusaders." Before his demise, Osama bin Laden condemned "Control exerted by the Zionists and the Cross worshipers" and described the global conflict he espoused as "a struggle between two camps. One camp is headed by America, and it represents the global *Kufr* [infidels], accompanied by all apostates. The other camp represents the Islamic *Umma* [the total world-wide Muslim community] headed by its *Mujahideen* Brigades [holy warriors]." With or without Bin Laden and Mahmoud Ahmadinejad, and whether Al-Qaeda, the Taliban and similar groups' powers wax or wane, their bloodthirsty disciples continue to infect the world with hatred and hunger for blood.

Catholic Archbishop Timothy Dolan of New York said in late 2011,

> Internationally, all believers are in the crosshairs of fanatics around the world. Somewhere, someplace, somebody's being persecuted to the point of blood because of their faith, and we need to stand together in defense of those people. Jews and Catholics… need to face realistically the common threat we have from fanatics, especially in the Islamist community… It would take an ostrich not to see that religious fanatics have in their cross hairs Jews and Catholics. Perhaps you and I are going to be drawn closer together as we defend each other…

From the first century until today it has been true that Jews and Christians have hotly disputed religious disparities: messianic hopes, means of salvation, matters of law and grace. A number of our differences cannot and should not be compromised for the sake of mutual understanding, and we will continue to agree to disagree.

There have also been unjust accusations, ignorant assumptions, libels and atrocities; some continue even now. Meanwhile, it cannot be overlooked that the bloodshed suffered by Jews at the hands of so-called Christians over many centuries is a matter of historical record; it is no wonder that bitter mistrust continues to this day.

Yet whether we live in Israel, or are scattered among the nations of the world, to radical Islamists we Jews and Christians look astonishingly alike. In the eyes of those who despise us, whatever our differences, as Archbishop Dolan points out, we Christians and Jews stand together as one. And we stand in the face of an enemy that embraces death, not life.

Choosing Life

Hezbollah's spiritual leader, Sheik Hassan Nasrallah, has summed up concisely the motivation of radical Islamist killers: "We have discovered how to hit the Jews where they are the most vulnerable. The Jews love life, so that is what we shall take away from them. We are going to win because they love life and we love death."

The sword of Islam was forged in hatred's flames, and it is, indeed, wielded by devotees of death. But Jews and Christians have been offered a higher calling. In the words of Moses, that mighty warrior of God, "...I have set before you life and death, blessings and curses. *Now choose life, so that you and your children may live*" (Deut. 30:19).

Despite the constant death threats it receives, Israel is one of the liveliest places in the world. Israelis cherish life dynamically and celebrate it with zest at every opportunity. I've often wondered if this is because they have experienced so much more than their fair share of death. Thousands of Israelis are Holocaust survivors or the offspring of survivors. Shootings, stabbings, rockets, suicide bombings and other terrorist attacks have left innumerable grieving survivors. Meanwhile, Israel has faced three major wars and many more armed conflicts since its founding in 1948. More than 20,000 IDF warriors have lost their lives in these clashes. Often their families and loved ones remember their losses year after year in informal gatherings. Others hold formal annual services.

I attended such a memorial at Jerusalem's military cemetery on Mt. Herzl, which is also known as *Har HaZikaron*, the "Mount of Remembrance." Unlike most other private memorials, this one takes place annually and may sometimes appear on the Israeli news, because it pays tribute not only to one particular soldier, but to those who fought alongside him and what they accomplished. The occasion was a commemorative service for Lt. Col. Jonathan Netanyahu, "Yoni" as he is best known. It marked the 35th anniversary of the famous Entebbe Raid in which he lost his life—one of the most successful hostage recovery operations in military history.

Arriving at Mt. Scopus in a taxi on a July morning, I immediately noticed that heavily armed security guards were protecting the entrance. I was early and it was hot. There was no shady place to sit outside, so I walked past the guards, through the gates, and gave my name to a woman seated at a table with a printed list. It was a private event, and each guest was listed, along with identification numbers.

The woman carefully crossed my name off and directed me to a walkway behind her. I could see that the people in line ahead of me were being checked for explosives, after which they walked through a metal detector while their bags were x-rayed. It dawned on me that this was the tightest security I'd seen in the country since making the foolish mistake of scheduling a haircut at the King David Hotel while George W. Bush was ensconced there.

This time, just as I was about to begin the security screening, a woman came to my side and asked if was Lela Gilbert. "Yes," I said, and she escorted me into the cemetery. She removed a "reserved" sign from a seat, placed a plastic band on my wrist and invited me to be seated. Chairs were placed between and around monuments to fallen soldiers. A searing sun was almost directly overhead and there wasn't a cloud in the sky. Thankful to be near a large outdoor fan, I sat and waited and tried to recall as much about the Entebbe story as I could.

In late June 1976, pro-Palestinian terrorists hijacked an Air France flight in Athens; it had originated in Tel Aviv. Some 248 passengers and crew were taken at gunpoint; the assailants then flew the plane from Athens to Entebbe Airport in Uganda. All the non-Jewish passengers were released. A frightened group of Israelis and Jews was corralled into a sweltering airport terminal building where they languished for days. The hijackers' demands remained unmet, and the deadline for negotiations had passed. The hostages knew that, barring a miracle, they were awaiting their executions.

Meanwhile, in Israel, instead of attempting to meet the terrorists' terms for releasing the captives, after agonizing deliberations, the government—led by Prime Minister Yitzhak Rabin, himself an acclaimed warrior— chose instead to defy the terrorists and rescue the captives. A complex, daring and nearly impossible rescue operation was hurriedly hatched and rehearsed, led by a 29-man assault team comprised of the most elite and secretive Israel Defense Forces Special Operations group, *Sayeret Matkal*—popularly known as "The Unit."

On July 4, 1976—while America was celebrating its bicentennial with fireworks and anthems—a total of 100 Israelis and their equipment were clandestinely flown into Entebbe airport in three Hercules transport planes, covering more than 2500 miles at very low altitude, literally "under the radar" of the hostile countries through whose airspace they passed. One of the massive planes contained, among other vehicles, a black Mercedes Benz with Ugandan license plates, an exact duplicate of a prized vehicle belonging to Idi Amin, the brutal Ugandan dictator.

After landing the massive aircraft without runway lights, the commandos disembarked, a few of them riding in the Mercedes as it was driven out the back of the plane. First they cruised slowly and smoothly along the runway like a dignified military entourage, heading unhindered for the terminal where the hostages were held. Then in a lightening strike, they stormed the airport with guns blazing. They had exhaustively rehearsed every move, and they surprised and overwhelmed an alliance of Palestinian and German terrorists, rescuing 102 hostages. It was a nearly miraculous success. However, for the IDF, it came at a high price. The Unit lost its commander, Lt. Col. Netanyahu. He was shot dead, the only Israeli soldier killed in the raid. Mourned as a fallen warrior, he remains a national hero to this day.

As noon approached, the number of people seated around me grew, comprised of young soldiers, retired military personnel, friends of the family, and a row of reporters and photographers. Then, all at once, the crowd rose. There was a flurry of activity as the Minister of Defense, Ehud Barak—a much-decorated Sayeret Matkal commando himself—walked in. Next came the President of Israel, Shimon Peres, who had given the eulogy at Yoni Netanyahu's funeral 35 years before. A minute or two later came the IDF Chief of Staff Lt.-Gen. Benny Gantz, a distinguished looking rabbi, several Knesset members and others I knew I should have recognized. After greeting one another, and shaking hands casually with friends seated nearby, they all sat down in the row next to me.

Then, across the way, on the other side of the seating area, the Netanyahu family entered—including the family patriarch, Prof. BenZion Netanyahu, 101 years old, and his sons Benyamin ("Bibi), the Prime Minister of Israel, and Iddo, a physician and playwright. Both surviving brothers had also served in The Unit. They were accompanied by their families.

Israel's informality always amazes me. Nearly every person in the government's top tier of leadership was present, yet there was no pomp or pageantry in evidence. Only after I saw who was in attendance did I understand the need for such extensive security. Nonetheless, everyone's attention seemed unselfconsciously focused on the remembrance of a hero, and for many a friend and a brother.

The ceremony was relatively brief; a Psalm, a eulogy by President Peres, a tribute by Lt. Gen. Gantz, and a hauntingly chanted liturgy. Finally, the *Kaddish*—the Jewish mourners' prayer—was read by elderly Prof. Netanyahu, who was supported on either side by his sons. It was to be his last memorial for his lost son—he died the following spring.

As the memorial service ended, the family placed candles around the tomb. Once they had paid their respects, the rest of us quietly lined up and walked past, too. As is the Jewish custom, some people laid small stones on the gravesite as well—a customary way of saying that the deceased is not forgotten. There were a few tears, even among the young who couldn't have known Yoni. What they did know, very well, was that the man had fought and fallen not only for his own generation but for theirs, too.

Over to the side, as I was leaving, I noticed a group of youthful-looking soldiers, speaking unceremoniously with the Prime Minister, the Chief of Staff and the Defense Minister. I guessed that this was today's Sayeret Matkal, carefully chosen to carry on the battle.

Yoni Netanyahu's memorial service was a celebration of his life, not a glorification of his death. His vibrant dedication and devotion to his loved ones, his nation and his fellow soldiers continue to be carried out in his memory, earnestly and energetically. By all accounts, he was a beloved and charismatic man—remembered as an officer who led from the front, shouting "Follow me!" He is cherished and continues to be missed by those who knew him well. In fact, a collection of Yoni's letters, written to his loved ones and posthumously compiled by his brothers, has provided those who never met him with glimpses into his character and personality. In the book's introduction, the esteemed novelist Herman Wouk wrote,

> Yoni loathed war and fighting. To kill horrified him. Of such are the Israeli soldiers, and of such are modern heroes. Because he had to fight to save his nation's life, he made himself into a great fighting man. But he knew, as all men of sense know, that war today is an empty and dangerous lunacy, not a practical political technique. He was philosopher

enough to understand this truth, that so long as villains and maniacs would egg on and arm young Arabs to destroy Israel, he would have to be a soldier; and that if he had to he would die fighting for the Return and for peace. So consecrated, he flew off to Entebbe, and to his great hour.

Military heroes like Yoni remind us that freedom is not free, and that to love life means, paradoxically, to be willing to die for what we love the most—our loved ones, our faith, our nations and our liberty. Today, biblically-rooted Christians and Jews still share an understanding of freedom and morality. They build their lives on ancient biblical principles, founded on the sanctity of life, affirming that humans are made in the image of God. Such principles long predate Islam, and make us natural allies in a dangerous world. Our roots are firmly planted in common ground. We have chosen life, and we deplore the Islamist culture of death. We needn't fight our battles alone.

EPILOGUE

"You shall dwell in sukkot (huts) for seven days . . . so that you will know, for all generations, that I had the Children of Israel dwell in sukkot, when I took them out of the Land of Egypt; I am God, your God" (Leviticus 23:42–43)

"The sukkah makes us vulnerable. But, paradoxically, this vulnerability is our greatest power. We were vulnerable when we began our journey out of exile, and we will be vulnerable when we conclude it. But far from making us weak, this vulnerability allows us to embrace our unlimited source and unique destiny. In letting go of our dependence on the physical, on the 'roof,' we embrace our own true nature. We are partners in creation, divine beings made in the image of G-d."
—Shifra Hendrie, "Letting Go of the Roof" **(chabad.org)**

The roof of the sukkah is a fragile interweaving of palm fronds, through which the sky—clouds, starlight, sun and moon —can be seen. It provides little if any protection, which was manifestly clear as Sukkot began in 2012. On the last Friday night in September, I was at home reading and enjoying the sound of singing floating my way from several directions. Although the Feast of Tabernacles—Sukkot's other name—wouldn't begin officially until Sunday night, families were already gathering in their newly constructed "tabernacles." I could hear their songs, but they were soon drowned out by the voice of thunder, as an unseasonable storm rumbled through the Jerusalem skies, trailing rain showers that dripped and splattered through the roof of every sukkah in town.

Drawn outside by flashing skies and the scent of wet earth, I watched the raindrops splashing in my garden, wondering if thousands of dinners were being ruined. Thankfully, I soon heard singing again. People were too busy celebrating to be bothered by the early rains.

The following day, I joined my next-door neighbors, Joe and Orit Straus, in their sukkah, which was set up on their patio. It was fashioned of a freestanding metal frame, three panels of tightly stretched fabric shaping its "walls," with the house itself providing the fourth side. Images of Jerusalem, like illustrations from a Bible storybook, graced each end of the structure. It was simple but elegant.

I asked the Strauses and their other guests—two pretty girls from the US, spending their gap year in Israel, and a family friend—whether the storm had spoiled their dinner the night before. "No, it was definitely not a big deal..." one of them said. They were far more interested in discussing whether or not the rain had been—in biblical terms—a bad omen or a blessing. All the various arguments became even more inconclusive when it started showering again during dessert. I was on the side of the storm being a blessing. But I am, after all, from California where it supposedly never rains.

New friends—Ronny and Chaya Vance—invited me to their home the following night. The Vances live in a picturesque corner of the Old City's Jewish Quarter. Their sukkah, three stories up a circular staircase, was set in an outdoor garden area that features a venerable and verdant grapevine and one long table that could comfortably seat more than twenty. A Lubavitch rabbi explained why there were no visible decorations. "It's our view that those who sit in the sukkah are the ornaments," he said with a smile.

It was a peaceable dinner, with time for conversation and getting acquainted. But it wasn't so quiet a couple of streets away. Every square in the Jewish Quarter was jammed with people of every style and attire, dancing, singing, eating cotton candy and snacks. I could hardly move as I forged my way through the happy throng. I'd never realized before that the whole week of Sukkot was such an enormous party, carrying on night after night. On the way home that evening, I walked with another guest to the Western Wall, which was also packed with celebrants, elbowing their way through worshippers on both sides of the barrier that separates men from women. They were determined to tuck a prayer in the wall, or simply to press an outstretched palm against the cool, ancient stones as they prayed.

Another invitation took me back to the Jewish Quarter the following night. As before, no taxis or other vehicles were allowed in the streets surrounding the Old City, either for security reasons or crowd control or perhaps a little of each. Like the Israelites of old, hundreds of us literally made our ascent on foot through the city gates. Along with new friends, I entered a spectacular home with a huge sukkah overlooking the Temple Mount. From a two-level rooftop terrace, we stood gazing down at the Dome of the Rock. With music and laughter in the background, it was an unforgettable scene, especially when the moon rose, huge and clear, glowing with a lovelier golden sheen than the dome.

In 2012 I visited more sukkahs than in all my six years in Jerusalem put together. Every one was a small haven of sociability, grace and peace, each with a unique mood and style—visually and in the spirit of the conversation. And every occasion offered not only delicious cuisine, but also considerable food for thought.

On the last day of the Feast, I was seated at another neighborhood table, this one upstairs from my apartment, in Jeff and Annette Broide's outdoor flower garden. Like the surrounding array of colorful blooms, their sukkah was beautiful—decorated with hanging spheres of gold and burgundy glass, and framed with gracefully draped fabric in similar hues.

Although we'd met before, on this occasion I was able to speak at length to Amalia Oren, who was seated next to me. She is the Director of Social Services at Shaarei Zedek hospital in Jerusalem.

Amalia explained to me that it is an ultra-orthodox facility, strictly Kosher and carefully attentive to traditional Jewish rituals, including Shabbat and holidays. Although she is not religiously observant herself, she works hard to make sure that every patient's religious requirements are met, whether Jewish, Muslim or Christian.

This is important, because the hospital offers treatment to patients from all over Israel, 40 percent of whom are Arabs—from Israel or the West Bank. In fact, Shaarei Zedek provides free shuttle service throughout the country to dialysis patients or others in need of specialized care that is unavailable in their villages.

I asked Ms. Oren how Arab patients respond to receiving care in an Israeli hospital. "They are very afraid at first," she told me. "They imagine that we may be planning to kill them instead of helping them! So we have to calm them and make them comfortable." She went on to tell me that she had learned Arabic specifically so she could talk to the patients with ease, in order to befriend and encourage them.

Not only does the hospital accomplish the intensive cleaning and strictly leaven-free food preparation rigorously required by Jewish law during Passover, but they also serve dinners on a special schedule during Ramadan, the Muslim month of fasting. That way Arab patients who are permitted by their doctors not to eat or drink until sunset, along with their visitors, can break their fast at the proper time—after sundown. For this reason, the hospital's dining area keeps special hours throughout Ramadan. All of these efforts are financially costly but essential.

Sometimes, thanks to efforts like these, Arab patients begin to see Israel and Jews in an entirely different light after being treated in Israeli hospitals. Nonie Darwish—whose story I described in chapter 7—speaks of just such an occurrence. While her Egyptian family still lived in Gaza, Nonie's brother suffered a stroke so severe that he wasn't expected to survive. A family decision was made not to transport him to a Cairo hospital, but instead to admit him into Israel's world-famous Hadassah hospital at Ein

Kerem. To the family's amazement, he was treated superbly and with great compassion, and he soon recovered. For Nonie, a young girl at the time, watching this unexpected story unfold before her eyes, she began to seriously question what she'd been told about the ruthlessness of Israelis.

A few years after talking to Nonie about her brother's hospital experience, I met a man whose life was also in the process of being changed, thanks to the generous care of another of Israel's well-known hospitals. Umar Mulinde is a Christian pastor from Kampala, Uganda and a former Muslim. Daphne Netanyahu and I went to meet and interview him about the terrorist attack that had brought him to Israel for help.

As we entered his hospital room, we were immediately grateful that the friend who had arranged our interview had also sent us Mulinde's photograph. She had at least partially prepared us for the sight of the horrifying burns on his handsome face. We quickly learned that the blinded right eye, the scorched skin, the missing nostril, and the swollen lips—which made it difficult for him to speak—had not lessened Umar's passion for the mission he has set for himself: He is determined to tell his personal story of conversion from Islam and to proclaim his love for God and for Israel.

Umar was born into a devout Muslim family comprising many children and wives. His maternal grandfather is an imam; his father is a well-known Islamic leader. Today, however, Mulinde is an Evangelical Christian pastor who leads a Kampala church of more than 1,000 believers.

On Christmas night 2011, a terrorist made his way through the holiday crowds, and while shouting "Alahu Akbar" three times, threw deadly acid on Mulinde's face, chest and arm. The young pastor turned his head just in time to avoid being hit directly in the face; his right side bore the brunt of the injury. He was rushed to the hospital, but it was soon evident that the medical treatment in Uganda for such severe burns was inadequate. Mulinde contacted friends in Israel. They quickly transported him to Tel Hashomer

Hospital, where we met him. The attack on Mulinde had resulted from his conversion from Islam to Christianity—a capital crime according to Islamic Shari'a law.

Years before, a teacher in his university had convinced Mulinde that Christianity was true, but Umar had avoided openly converting. Nineteen years old at the time, he knew very well that declaring himself a Christian would mean being totally cut off from his Muslim family and friends, and thus from his future plans. Umar kept his religious views to himself.

Then a recurring dream began to haunt him: "My hands and my feet are tied. And I'm burning in fire. I am screaming. To my right a man with a shining face is telling me, 'Islam brings you this torture. Become a Christian and you will survive it.'"

Mulinde asked his grandfather the imam for advice, and listened carefully to his suggestions. But that night, after he returned home, the dream recurred. The next morning—Easter Sunday—Mulinde entered a Christian house of worship for the first time in his life. He announced to the congregation that he wanted to convert to Christianity. As he left the building, he was spotted by some of his Muslim friends, who promptly reported to the sheik that Mulinde had been to a church. Shortly thereafter, he was attacked and beaten up. Nonetheless, he began to speak publicly about his new faith, and he did so before increasingly large audiences.

"I am a new person. I have started a new life." He repeated these words a number of times during our meeting. Even though he was bandaged and his speech was slurred, it was not difficult to imagine Mulinde convincing great crowds of people about the source of the peace, confidence and love that he radiates. And some of that love belongs to Israel.

"When I was a Muslim I hated Israel. Don't know why. I knew nothing about Israel—not even where it was on the map. But after I became a Christian I loved reading the Bible—both the Old and the New Testaments—and I saw phrases like 'the God of Israel' and 'the people of Israel' repeated continually in the Scriptures.

What did that mean?"

In 2008 Mulinde made his first visit to Israel. He found himself with an Israeli guide and an Arab driver. He was shocked. "I didn't know that Jews allowed Arabs to live in Israel and to work. I believed that Jews were persecuting and hunting down Arabs." During his visit he saw that hotel workers were Arabs, living in safety and going about their business. He saw with his own eyes that "Israel is a democracy. And that this is a country of peace. I loved the nation and the people."

Umar Mulinde predicts that a great war between Islam and the Western world lies ahead. And it hard to disagree with him. For one thing, he understands the way his former co-religionists think. For another, "wars and rumors of wars" are on the minds and lips of nearly everyone in Israel, and have been particularly so over the last two or three years. This is, of course, because of the Iranian nuclear threat, as well as the surging upheaval of the "Arab Spring." Like everybody else, I am grateful to be dwelling in the calm eye of the storm. But ours is a fragile peace. How long can it last? Indeed, terror victims like Umar Mulinde and Petra Heldt and so many others are actually casualties in an already raging war. They are victims of the great jihad—holy war—that has long been declared by radical Muslims against Jews, Christians, other infidels and the West.

Dark days may well lie ahead. For very good reasons, Israelis have great confidence in their valiant IDF, savvy diplomats, cyber warriors, peerless intelligence agencies and hi-tech defenses, all of which are extraordinarily successful. Still, people of faith also believe that God will stand with His children. One of the primary purposes of the Sukkot tradition of building and dwelling in vulnerable, insubstantial booths is to remind Israel's people of their radical dependence on God during their 40-year trek through the desert. Only His hand saw them through. Today, Saturday and Sunday people alike trust that His power and glory will shield them yet again—accompanied by the sounds of their praise and celebration.

You can already hear joyful songs in Jerusalem's neighborhoods today. And the promises spoken by the Prophet Ezekiel offer the people of God even greater hope for tomorrow.

> *I will now restore the fortunes of Jacob*
> *and will have compassion on all the people of Israel...*
> *When I have brought them back from the nations*
> *and have gathered them from the countries of their enemies*
> *they will know that I am the Lord their God,*
> *for though I sent them into exile among the nations,*
> *I will gather them to their own land, not leaving any behind.*
> *I will no longer hide my face from them,*
> *for I will pour out my Spirit on the people of Israel,*
> *declares the Sovereign Lord."(Ez. 39:25-29).*

ACKNOWLEDGMENTS

I owe an enormous debt of gratitude to some very wonderful people, each of whom played an essential part in making my book possible—you allowed yourselves to be interviewed, befriended me, drove me, advised me, fed me, encouraged me, helped me locate people, wrote brilliant emails, read early drafts, kept in touch, allowed me to quote you, invited me to holiday dinners and otherwise provided indispensable help and hope and wisdom along the way. Some will have to remain anonymous. But to each of you whose name follows, a thousand thank yous.

Howard and Roberta Ahmanson, Neheda Barakat, Dr. Gabriel Barkay, Amb. Yossi Ben-Aharon, Jillian Becker, Ruthie Blum, Amanda Borschel-Dan, Lori Bryan, Nonie Darwish, Midge Decter, Katherine Embling, Arne Fjeldstad, Dina Gabay, Georgette Gelbard, Amb. Husain Haqqani, Malcolm Hedding, Rev. Dr. Petra Heldt, Pastor Chuck and Liz Kopp, Ricky Levitt, Rachel Lipkin, Malcolm Lowe, Rachel Machtiger, Linda Menuhin, Umar Mulinde, Iddo and Daphne Netanyahu, Amb. Michael Oren, Amalia Oren, David Parsons, Norman Podhoretz, Roz Rothstein, Jennifer Rubin, Uzi Rubin, Mike and Karin Runyen, Ilan Sibony, Khaled abu Toameh, Joseph Abdel Wahed, Justus Weiner, Levana Zamir, and Chana Zweiter. Portions of these chapters, in different forms, have appeared in the *Jerusalem Post* over the course of six years, and I am grateful to my editors there who permitted me to republish them.

I am particularly grateful to my colleagues at Hudson Institute, Washington DC—Ken Weinstein, Grace Terzian, Nina Shea, Paul Marshall and Samuel Tadros. And special thanks belong to Hillel

Fradkin, without whom this book would have been neither completed nor published.

My warmest appreciation to Roger Kimball, Heather Ohle and the team of professionals at Encounter Books for their hard work and excellence. As authors always say, any errors are entirely mine.

I so wish my father Caryle Hamner and my good friends Ed Steele and Rich Buhler were still in this world to share with me once again their own unique perspectives of Israel, and now to read mine.

Thanks to my son Colin Gilbert for the beautiful cover photographs. And much applause and many blessings to everyone in my beloved, supportive, patient and otherwise wonderful family —Dylan, Colin and Elizabeth Gilbert. You've never stopped encouraging me, advising me and believing in me, no matter what.

FOR FURTHER READING

Aciman, Andre. *Out of Egypt: A Memoir.* New York: Picador, 1994.

Amir, Eli. *The Dove Flyer.* London: Halban, 1993.

Amir, Eli. *Scapegoat.* Tel Aviv: Am Oved, 1983.

Aumann, Moshe. *Conflict and Connection: The Jewish-Christian-Israel Triangle.* Jerusalem, Gefen, 2003.

Becker, Jillian. *The PLO: The Rise and Fall of the Palestine Liberation Organization.* New York: St. Martin's Press, 1984.

Bowden, Mark. *Guests of the Ayatollah. The Iran Hostage Crisis: The First Battle in America's War with Militant Islam.* New York: Grove Press, 2007.

Brog, David. *Standing with Israel: Why Christians Support the Jewish State*: Lake Mary: FrontLine, 2006.

Companjen, Anneke. *Hidden Sorrow, Lasting Joy: The Forgotten Women of the Persecuted Church.* London: Hodder & Stoughton Ltd, 2005.

Companjen, Anneke. *Singing through the Night: Courageous Stories of Faith from Women in the Persecuted Church.* Grand Rapids: Fleming Revell, 2007.

Carlson, Carole. *Corrie Ten Boom: Her Life and Faith*. New York: Guideposts, 1983.

Carmi, T. Ed. *The Penguin Book of Hebrew Verse*. New York: Penguin, 1981.

Collins, Larry, and Dominique Lapierre. *O Jerusalem*. New York: Simon and Schuster, 1972.

Cook, David. *Martyrdom in Islam*. Cambridge: Cambridge University Press, 2007.

Cook, David. *Understanding Jihad*. Berkeley: University of California Press, 2005.

Dalin, David G., and John F. Rothmann. *Icon of Evil: Hitler's Mufti and the Rise of Radical Islam*. New York: Transaction Publishers, 2009.

Darwish, Nonie. *Cruel and Usual Punishment: The Terrifying Global Implications of Islamic Law*. Nashville: Thomas Nelson, 2009.

Darwish, Nonie. *Now They Call Me Infidel: Why I Renounced Jihad for America, Israel and the War on Terror*. New York: Sentinel, 2006.

Diamant, Anita. *Day After Night*. London: Pocket Books UK, 2010.

Efros, Israel, ed. *Selected Poems of Hayyim Nahman Bialik, Translated from the Hebrew*. New York: Bloch Publishing, 1948.

Gilbert, Lela, Nina Shea, and Paul Marshall. *Persecuted: The Global Assault on Christians*. Nashville: Thomas Nelson, 2013.

Gilbert, Lela, Paul Marshall, and Roberta Green Ahmanson, eds. *Blind Spot: When Journalists Don't Get Religion*. New York: Oxford University Press, 2009.

Gilbert, Lela, and Paul Marshall. *Their Blood Cries Out: The Worldwide Tragedy of Modern Christians Who are Dying for their Faith*. Dallas: Word, Inc., 1997.

Gilbert, Lela. *Baroness Cox: Eyewitness to a Broken World*. London: Monarch Books, 2007.

Gilbert, Martin. *Churchill and the Jews*. London: Pocket Books, 2007.

Gilbert, Martin. *In Ishmael's House: A History of Jews in Muslim Lands*. New Haven: Yale University Press, 2010.

Gilbert, Martin. *Israel: A History*. Santa Barbara: McNally and Loftin, 2008.

Jacobsen, David. *My Life as a Hostage*. New York: S.P.I. Books, 1991.

Karsh, Efraim. *Palestine Betrayed*. New Haven: Yale University Press, 2010.

Lagnado, Lucette. *The Man in the White Sharkskin Suit: A Jewish Family's Exodus from Old Cairo to the New World* (New York: HarperCollins, 2007).

Lewis, Bernard. *Notes on a Century: Reflections of a Middle East Historian*. New York: Viking, 2012.

Mallmann, Klaus-Michael, and Martin Cuppers. *Nazi Palestine: The Plans for the Extermination of the Jews in Palestine*. New York: Enigma Books, 2010.

Marshall, Paul A. ed. *Religious Freedom in the World*. Lanham MD: Rowman & Littlefield, 2008.

Meinertzhagen, Colonel R. *Middle East Diary:* 1917 to 1956. London: The Cresset Press, 1959.

Mintz, Ruth Finer, translator and editor. *Modern Hebrew Poetry: A Bilingual Anthology*. Berkeley: University of California Press, 1966.

Montefiore, Simon Sebag. *Jerusalem: The Biography*. New York: Knopf, 2011.

Morad, Tamar, Dennis Shasha, and Robert Shasha, eds. *Iraq's Last Jews: Stories of Daily Life, Upheaval, and Escape from Modern Babylon*. New York: Palgrave Macmillan, 2008.

Naggar, Jean. *Sipping from the Nile: My Exodus from Egypt*. New York: Stony Creek, 2008.

Nelihaus, Arlynn. *Into the Heart of Jerusalem: A Traveler's Guide to Visits, Celebrations, and Sojourns*. Santa Fe, NM: John Muir Publications, 1999.

Netanyahu, Benjamin and Iddo Netanyahu. *The Letters of Jonathan Netanyahu: The Commander of the Entebbe Rescue Force*. Jerusalem: Gefen, 2001.

Netanyahu, BenZion. *The Founding Fathers of Zionism.* Jerusalem: Gefen, 2012.

Oren, Michael. *Power, Faith and Fantasy: America in the Middle East, 1776 to the Present.* New York: Norton, 2007.

Peters, Joan. *From Time Immemorial: The Origins of the Arab-Jewish Conflict Over Palestine.* New York: Harper and Row, 1984.

Roumani, Maurice. "The Silent Refugees: Jews from Arab Countries." WOJAC, 2003.

Rosenthal, Donna. *The Israelis: Ordinary People in an Extraordinary Land.* New York: Free Press, 2003.

Satloff, Robert. *Among the Righteous: Lost Stories from the Holocaust's Long Reach into Arab Lands.* New York: Public Affairs, 2006.

Shabi, Rachel. *Not the Enemy: Israel's Jews from Arab Lands.* New Haven and London: Yale University Press, 2009.

Stillman, Norman A. *Jews of Arab Lands in Modern Times.* Philadelphia: The Jewish Publication Society, 2003.

Sultan, Wafa. *A God Who Hates.* New York: St. Martin's Press, 2009

Prof. Shmuel Trigano. "The Expulsion of Jews from Muslim Countries 1920-1970: A History of Ongoing Cruelty and Discrimination." Jerusalem Center for Public Affairs (JCPA), 2010.

Trofimov, Yaroslav. *The Siege of Mecca: The Forgotten Uprising in Islam's Holiest Shrine and the Birth of Al-Qaeda*. New York: Doubleday, 2007.

Yaari, Avraham. *The Goodly Heritage*: *Memoirs describing the life of the Jewish community of Eretz Y'israel from the seventeenth to the twentieth centuries.* Jerusalem: The Zionist Organization, 1958.

Zamir, Levana. *The Golden Era of "The Jews of Egypt."* Tel Aviv: World Congress on the Jews of Egypt, 2008.

INDEX

A

Abbas, Mahmoud, 87, 88, 115, 229

Abraham (patriarch), 111–112, 114

Abu Mazen. *See* Abbas, Mahmoud Abu Sakir, Sheikh, 227–228

abu Toameh, Khaled, 117–120, 226, 236

Abu Tor neighborhood, 32, 109

Abu Yaqub, 229–232, 237

Achwad, Ahmad el-, 233–234

Aden, Jews in, 159

Afghanistan, anti-Semitic and anti-Christian violence in, 161, 251–253

Ahmadinejad, Mahmoud, 6, 10, 17–18, 241, 255

Ahmanson, Roberta Green, 149–150

Al Adl Wa Al Ihssane, 180

Al-Qaeda: in Egypt, 211; in Iraq, 197; in Morocco, 176, 180, 184

al-Aksa Martyrs Brigades, 227

Al-Aqsa Mosque, 15–16, 58, 64, 65, 114

Algeria, Jews in, 160

al-Harizi, Judah, 58

Al-Hayat Al-Jadida, 58

al-Husseini, Hajj, 114, 157, 170

Ali, Rashid, 187-188

All Saints Church, Egypt, 211

al-Marwani Mosque, 65

Al-Masry Al-Youm, 214

al-Zawahiri, Ayman, 6

Amaro, Jeriez Moussa, 227

American Center for Law and Justice (ACLJ), 179

Amichai, Yehuda, 71

Amin, Idi, 258

Among the Righteous: Lost Stories from the Holocaust's Long Reach into Arab Lands (Satloff), 169

Amos (prophet), 100

Anba Bishoy Monastery, Egypt, 212–213

Anba Makarious Al Sakandarie Monastery, Egypt, 212

Anderson, Terry, 8–9

"Anne Frank of Baghdad." *See* Menuhin, Linda

Antiochus Ephiphanes, 75

anti-Semitism, 109–129;
concession-breeds-violence
theory, 118–120;
history of, 109–119;
Kaleidoscope program
and, 127–129; religion
as root of, 111–112;
resurgence in West, 9–10;
spread of, 241; taught in
Arab schools, 124. *See also*
Jews, Muslim hatred of
and violence against
apartheid: Abbas on not
allowing Jews in Palestine,
87–88; Carter's accusation
of Israeli, 73–74, 81,
82–85; Hedding on South
African, 77–82, 86; truth
of Arabs living freely in
Israel, 85–86, 88
Arab Spring, 120, 176;
Egyptian Christians and,
211–217
Arabs, treated in Israeli
hospitals, 265–268
Arafat, Yassar, 60, 62, 95, 171
archeological findings:
destruction of, 61, 65–66;
in Galilee, 136–137; at
Temple Mount, 66–68
Arens, Moshe, 88
Armenian Christians,
massacre of, 245
Assadullah, Shoaib, 253

Assyrian Catholic Church
of Our Lady of Salvation
(Baghdad), massacre at,
194–198, 211
Assyrian International News
Agency (AINA), 193, 212
Atheist Conservative
website, 196
Ayyad, Rami Khader, 227
Azoulay, Andre, 179
Azzam, Abdul Rahman
Hassan (Pasha), 204

B
Ba'al Teshuva, 208
Babylonian Captivity,
186–187
Babylonian Talmud, 186
Bae Hyung-kyu, 252
Bajalia, Isa, 227
Baka El Garbiya village, 128
Balfour Declaration, 113
Bangladesh, killing of
Christians in, 161
Banna, Hassan el-, 204
Barak, Ehud, 66, 80–81, 259
Barakat, Neheda, 120–123,
125–127, 128–129
Barbibay, Haim, 25
Bardash, Kory, 146
Barkay, Dr. Gabriel, 61–64,
65–68

Baroness Cox: Eyewitness to a Broken World (Gilbert), 242

Bat Ye'or (pen name), 32–33

Begin, Menachem, 103–104

Beker, Dr. Avi, 191

Beliad, Mohammad, 248

Beliad, Nazly, 248

Ben-Aharon, Yossi, 204–205

Benarroch, Mois, 167

Benedict XVI, pope, 250

Bernzweig, Aharon Reuven, 114

Bethlehem, 207, 223–238

Bhatti, Shahbaz, 155–156, 165

Bible references: Ezekiel 39:25–29; I Kings, 46; Jeremiah, 67; John, 56; Mark, 139; Numbers, 61; Psalm 137, 187; Psalm 84, 39–40, 43, 46–47, 59; story of Abraham, 111–112

bin Laden, Osama, 151, 152, 241, 255

Black Sunday Massacre, in Iraq, 194–197

Blind Spot: When Journalists Don't Get Religion (Marshall, Ahmanson, and Gilbert), 149–150, 151

Blum, Ruthie, 34, 47–48, 82, 91–92, 94

Boko Haram group, 250

Bousherhri, Ayatollah Seyed Hosseini, 249

Broide, Jeff and Annette, 265

C

Café Hillel, 122

Camp David Accords, 60

Carter, Jimmy: accusations of apartheid in Israel, 73–74, 81, 82–85; declares settlements illegal, 95, 104

Carter Center: Middle Eastern donors to, 82; resignations from advisory board of, 82–83

Chabad House, India, 151–153

children: Arab, 28, 124; Christian, 234–236; Israeli, 17, 29–30, 145–147

Choksy, Jamsheed, 196–197

Christian Solidarity Worldwide (CSW), 248

"Christian Zionists," 12–14

Christians: Jews distrust of evangelism of, 13–14, 42–43; Judaism and, 38; living in Israel, 254; as natural allies with Jews against radical Islam, 241, 261; Pentecostal and Charismatic, in Israel, 41–42

Christians, Muslim hatred
    of and violence against,
    154–155, 158–163, 241,
    243–244; in
    Afghanistan, 161, 251–
    252; in Bangladesh, 161;
    in Bethlehem, 223–238;
    in Egypt, 162, 208–217,
    244; in Ethiopia, 161;
    in Indonesia, 250–251;
    in Iran, 247–249;
    in Iraq, 192–199; in
    Kenya, 161; in Morocco,
    177–179; in Nigeria, 161,
    249–250; in Philippines,
    161; in Saudi Arabia, 253;
    in Somalia,161; in Turkey,
    242, 244, 245–247
Christmas, in Bethlehem,
    223–224, 236–238
Church of Iran, 248
Church of St. Mina and St.
    George, Egypt, 213
Church of the Holy Sepulcher,
    14, 68, 136–137, 209–210
Church of the Nativity,
    Bethlehem, 140–141, 225
Clinton, Bill, 60, 62
Clinton, Hillary, 92–93
Cohen, Yaakov, 26, 240
Commentary magazine, 91,
    170
Compass Direct, 178, 213

Coptic American Friendship
    Association, 213
Coptic monks, in Egypt,
    210–217
Cox, Baroness (Caroline), 49,
    242
Cruel and Usual Punishment
    (Darwish), 125
Cultural Intifada, Temple
    Denial and, 62, 68

D
Dadkah, Mohammed Ali, 249
Dahlan, Mohammed, 229
Daily Mail, 227
Dangour, Ronit, 189
Darna (restaurant), 181, 183
Darwish, Nonie, 123–125,
    266–267
David Project, 157
Days of Repentance/Days of
    Awe, 37, 41
de Quetteville, Harry, 229
de Souza, Raymond J.,
    160–161
death, Islamic culture of, 256,
    261
Deccan Mujahideen, 151
dhimmitude (inferior status of
    Christians and Jews), 32,
    117, 168, 203, 210
Dolan, Archbishop Timothy,
    255–256
Dome of the Rock, 64, 65

E

Easter, 208–209

Eckstein, Rabbi, 74, 76

Economist, The, 246

Egypt, 201–218; persecution of Christians in, 162, 208–217, 244; persecution of Jews and Second Exodus from, 159, 201–208, 217–218

Eibner, John, 247

Eisenhower, Dwight D., 170

Elam Ministries, 248–249

Elijah (prophet), 136

Embling, Katherine, 109–110, 117

Entebbe, Uganda, IDF raid to free Israeli hostages, 257–259

Erdogan, Recep Tayyip, 245

Erev Shabbat, 16–17

Eshoo, Fr. Mazin, 197

Ethiopia, anti-Christian violence in, 161

"Expulsion of the Jews from Muslim Countries,1920-1970: A History of Ongoing Cruelty and Discrimination" (Trigano), 156

Eyewitness to a Broken World (Cox), 49

Ezekiel (prophet), 270

F

Fadlallah, Mohammad Hussein, 8

Farhud pogrom, in Iraq, 187–188

Fatah, 133

fatwa, of *Shumukh al-Islam*, 211

Feast of Tabernacles, 56–57

fedayeen units, 123

Financial Times, 213–214

First Intifada (1987–1993), 226

"First the Saturday People, Then the Sunday People" (Muslim slogan), xi, 154, 159, 207

Fjeldstad, Arne, 212

Flavius Josephus, 76

flotilla, Turkey's 2010 "humanitarian," 254

Fogel, Ruth, Elad, and Hadas, 240

Fogel, Tamar, Roi, and Yishai, 240

Fogel, Udi, 97, 240

Foreign Policy, 196–197

"Forgotten Refugees," xi, 157–163

Fox News, 227

Fradkin, Daniel, 105–106

Fradkin, Hillel, 243–244

Frans, Dirk, 252

Furutan, Mehdi, 248

G

Gabay, Avraham and Rachel,
168, 170, 174. *See also*
Levin, Dina Gabay

Gabay, Zvi, 174–175

Galilee, 135–141

Gantz, Benny, 259

Gaydamak, Arkady, 29

Gaza: anti-Christian
violence in, 242;
Gaza Disengagement
and its aftermath, 131135;
Israeli settlers forced to
leave, 91,120; Israel's
supply of food to, 3–4;
Operation Cast Lead in,
141, 142, 144–146, 254;
rockets launched into
Israel from, 1, 2–5, 76–77,
120, 142–148, 254

Gethsemane, 136

Ghallab, Said, 173

Gilbert, Colin, 7, 140–141,
233

Gilbert, Dylan, 149

Gilbert, Elizabeth, 140–141

Givot Olam community,
97–99

Goebbels, Joseph, 84

Golan Heights, 139

Gold, Dore, 94–95

*Golden Era of the Jews of Egypt,
The* (Zamir), 202–203

Goldstone, Richard, 83–84,
142

Goldstone Report, 142

Goodly Heritage, The (Yaari),
113

Gordon, Jillian Becker, 196

"Great Arab Revolt"
(1936–1939), 114–115

Green Line, 94

Grinker, Yehuda, 173

H

Hadany, Israeli and Bridget,
31–32

Haddad, Heskel M., 170–171

Hadi, Mala, 246

Hafez, Mustafa, 123, 124

Haggadah (the Telling), at
Seder, 219, 220, 221

Hagia Sophia church, Turkey,
246

Ha'ivri, David, 95, 97–99

Hakim, Linda Masri, 164

Halevi, Judah, 50

Hamas: aftermath of Gaza
Disengagement and,
133–135; Bethlehem
Christians and, 228, 232;
call for death of Jews in
Charter of, 144; election
to majority in Palestinian
Parliament, 133; IDF
surgical strikes against,
140; Mahane Yehuda

market attack, 116–117; rockets launched into Israel by, 1, 2–5, 76–77, 120, 142–148, 254

Hamner, Caryle, x, 6–7, 253

Hanson, Victor Davis, 9–10

Hanukkah (Festival of Lights), 73, 87; story of, 75–76

Haqqani, Husain, 155–156, 165

Har Adar neighborhood, 94, 97, 99

Har HaZikaron (Mount of Remembrance), 256–257

Haret el-Yahud, 204

Hartman, David, 221–222

Hassan II, king of Morocco, 182

Hatikvah (Israeli national anthem), xiv, 16, 114

Hebrew, rebirth of Biblical, 51–52

Hebron: anti-Christian violence in, 227; pogrom in, 114, 118

Hedding, Cheryl, Charmaine, and Ethan, 86

Hedding, Guy Usher, 78

Hedding, Malcolm, 74–75, 86; on apartheid in South Africa, 77–82

Heldt, Petra, 33–34, 60, 82, 116–117, 269

Herzliya Conference, 157, 162

Hezbollah, 8, 9, 28–29, 139, 256

Hilltop Youth, 96, 97

Hirsch, Rabbi, 59

Hitler, Adolf, 157, 170, 173, 188, 246

Holland, protection of Jews in, 10–11

Holtzberg, Menachem and Dov Ber, 152

Holtzberg, Moshe, 152–153

Holtzberg, Rabbi Gavriel and Rivka, 151, 152–153, 154

Horowitz, Michael, 162

Hussein, Saddam, 192

I

India, anti-Jewish violence in, 151–153

Indonesia, anti-Semitic and anti-Christian violence in, 250–251

Institute for Policy and Strategy at the Interdisciplinary Center (IDC), 157

International Christian Embassy Jerusalem (ICEJ), 145

intifadas, 115; Cultural, and Temple Denial, 62, 68; First (1987–1993), 226; Second (beginning 2000), 74, 80, 97, 115, 119, 226

Iran: anti-Semitic and anti-Christian violence in, 247–249; call for destruction of Israel, 10, 254; financing of Hezbollah, 8

Iraq, 185–199; aftermath of U.S. invasion of, 192; anti-Semitic and anti-Christian violence in, 187–190, 192–199; Babylonian Captivity and, 186–187; Jewish emigration from, 159, 185–186

Iraq's Last Jews: Stories of Daily Life, Upheaval and Escape from Modern Babylon (Hakim), 164, 188, 191

Isaac (patriarch), 112, 114

Islam: culture of death and, 256, 261; founding of, 112; predictions of war with West, 269; radical interpretations of and hatred of Christians and Jews, 154, 256

Islamophobia, irony of hysteria over, 241

Israel: Arabs in hospitals of, 265–268; calls for eradication of, 6, 10, 17–18, 110, 254; Christian population in, 254; food supplied to all Gaza residents, 3–4; Iranians forbidden to travel to, 247; Jews building and rebuilding of in 20th century, 49–53; Jews repopulating of in 18th and 19th centuries, 49–50; love of life and, 256; public opinion about, 6–7, 9–10; religious freedom in, 85–86, 88

Israel National News, 179

Israeli Defense Forces (IDF): Entebbe and, 257–259; Gaza Disengagement and, 132; historic victories of, 30; Lebanon War and, 28–29, 84; military service required of Israeli citizens, 30; restrictions on, 29

Itamar settlement, 96–97, 239–240

J

Jacob (patriarch), 114

Jacobsen, David, 8

Jacquard, Roland, 152

Jenco, Fr. Martin, 8–9

Jerusalem: conquered by Muslims, 60; life in, 16–17; Moroccan Jews in, 181–184

Jerusalem Post, 34

Jewish Antiquities XII (Flavius Josephus), 76

Jews, as natural allies with Christians against radical Islam, 240–241, 261

Jews, Muslim hatred of and violence against, 150–160, 163–165, 241, 242; in Afghanistan, 161, 251; in Egypt, 159, 201–208, 217–218; in India, 151–153; in Indonesia, 250; in Iran, 10, 247, 254; in Iraq, 187–190; media coverage and, 110–111, 120–121; in Nigeria, 161, 249; in Saudi Arabia, 253; in Turkey, 245

Jihadia Salfiya, 227–228

Jordan, Jewish religious services prohibited in, 41

Joshua, memorial to, 98

Judas Maccabeus, 75

K

Kaleidoscope program, 127–128

Karnei Border Crossing, 3–4

Kashkush family, killing of, 191

Katz, Shmuel, 104

Kenya, anti-Christian violence in, 161

Kfar Etzion community, 93, 95

Kfar Nahum village, 138

Kfar Qana, Lebanon, 28

Kfar Tapuah community, 97–99

Khalaj, Parviz, 248

Khedouri, Sassoon, 188

Kibbutz Gevim, 142–144

Kidron, Asaf, 98, 99

Kiryat Shmona, 25–28

Koran. *See* Quran

L

Labib, Ayman, 214–215

Lantos, Tom, 193

Lebanon: American hostages in, 8; expulsion of Jews from, 159

Lebanon War, 12, 23; Kiryat Shomona's destruction during, 25–28; United Nations-brokered peace and, 26, 32. *See also* Gaza

Lehman, Esti, 147

Leibovits, Tova, 85

'Le-shanah ha-ba-a b' Yerushalayim"—Next year in Jerusalem," 221–222

Levin, Dina Gabay, 167–168, 170, 171, 174, 175

Libya, expulsion of Jews from, 159

Lipkin, Rachel, 215

Lowe, Malcolm, 34, 116

"Lying in Wait for Happiness" (Amichai), 71

M

ma'abarot (refugee camps),
172–173
Ma'aleh Adumin settlement,
105
Ma'ariv newspaper, 190
Machtiger, Rachel, 158
Maganti, Ivon, 251
Mahane Yehuda market,
Hamas attack on, 116–117
Malan, Daniel Francois,
78–79
Malewa, Noviana, 251
Mamann, Maurice, 26–27
Marshall, Paul, 149–150, 151,
162, 243, 253
Martynov, Yury, 106
Medad, Yisrael, 104
media, coverage of Israel:
international media, viii–xi,
28, 111, 134, 141–142;
Palestinian media, 58,
110; United States media,
2, 44, 134
media, in Israel: possibility
of military conflict and,
44; questioning of Leba-
non War outcomes, 31,
35; reporting on Moroc-
can incidents, 179–180
Mekouar, H.E. Aziz, 177
Menuhin, Linda, 163, 185–
186, 187, 189, 190–191

Messiah, Christian and Jewish
beliefs about, 23, 43, 45,
56, 70, 87, 136
Mohammad (prophet),
63–64, 154
Mohammad V, sultan of
Morocco, 175–176
Mohammad VI, king of
Morocco, 176–177, 179,
180, 181
Morangke, Theresia, 250
Morocco: anti-Jewish
incidents in, 170–171,
173, 179–181; bill to seek
compensation for émigrés
from, 174–175; Christians
persecuted in, 177–179;
government's relations
with Israel, 176; Jewish
emigration from, 160,
167–177; Moroccan Jews
in Jerusalem, 181–184
Mossad, 30, 171
Mount Moriah, 64
Mount of Olives, 136–137
Mount of the Beatitudes, 138
Moyal, Eli, 76–77
Mubarak, Hosni, 211
Mujahid, Zabiullah, 252
Mulinde, Umar, 267–269
Mumbai, India, terror attacks
in, 149–153
Musa, Said, 252

Muslim Brotherhood, 204, 215
Muslim Waqf, Temple Mount
 and, 61, 63, 65, 70

N
Nadarkhani, Yousef, 248
Nafisi, Amir, 18
Nafoura (restaurant), 198–199
Naggar, Jean, 207–208
Nahum, 138
nakba (catastrophe), 171
Nakba Day, 171–172, 185
Nasrallah, Hassan, 8, 256
Nasser, Gamal Abdel, 123, 207
National Review Online, 217,
 248–249
Netanyahu, Benjamin, 132, 259
Netanyahu, BenZion, 259
Netanyahu, Daphne,
 104–105, 267
Netanyahu, Iddo, 104–105, 259
Netanyahu, Jonathan "Yoni,"
 memorial service for,
 257–261
Neve Shalom synagogue,
 Turkey, 245
New York Times, 134, 211
Nigeria, anti-Semitic and
 anti-Christian violence in,
 161, 249–250
1967 War (Six Day War), 6,
 30, 115; aftermath in Iraq,
 189–190; settlement after, 93
1973 War, 30, 115

Nir, Noam, 179
North Africa, Nazism and,
 168–169. *See also specific
 countries*
Nuraini, Siti, 251

O
Obama, Barack, 127; "Cairo
 Speech" and criticism of
 Israel, 92, 93, 94, 100
"Ode to Zion" (Halevi),
 49–50
Olmert, Ehud, 23
Operation Cast Lead, 141,
 142, 144–146, 254
Operation Iron Dome, 146
Operation Lifeshield, 145
Oren, Amelia, 265–266
Ort Amit Technical High
 School, rocket attack on,
 145
Oslo Accords, 95, 118–119, 226

P
Pakistan: anti-Semitism in,
 153–156; Mumbai attacks
 and, 153–154
Palestine: Peace Not Apartheid
 (Carter), 73–74
Palestinian Authority (PA):
 Bethlehem Christians
 and, 226–237; Hamas
 and, 133; messages of
 death to Israel, 110

Palestinians: Israeli independence and, 171–172, 174; rejection of all compromise offers, 80–81

Parsons, David, 74–75, 77

Passover, 218–222

Pedatzur, Reuven, 146

Peres, Shimon, 95, 259

Peretz, Amir, 23

Peretz, Susan, 25–26

Persecuted: The Global Assault on Christians (Marshall, Shea, and Gilbert), 243

Philippines, killing of Christians in, 161

Plocker, Sever, 115

Podhoretz, John, 91–92

Podhoretz, Norman, 91–92

poems, 24, 47, 71, 107

pogroms: in Hebron, 114, 118; in Iraq, 187–188; in Morocco, 168–170

Poliwo, Alfita, 250–251

priestly benediction, 61

public opinion, about Israel, 9, 241, 254. *See also* media, coverage of Israel

Q

Qumsieh, Samir, 229

Quran, 60, 64, 112, 154, 155, 254

R

Rabie, George, 227

Rabin, Yitzhak, 95, 176, 182, 258

Rahho, Paulos Faraj, 193, 194

Ram, Ari, 139

Rambam Hospital, 12

Ran, Avri, 96, 99

rape, of Christian girls, 234–236

Reading Lolita in Tehran (Nafisi), 18

religious freedom, in Israel, 125, 254

Religious Freedom in the World survey, 242

Rome Statute, on apartheid, 84

Rosh Hashanah (New Year's Day), 35, 56

Ross, Dennis, 60

Rothstein, Roz, 15

Roumani, Maurice M., 158

Rubin, Uzi, 146

Runyen, Mike and Karin, 140–141

S

Sabih, Fr. Wassim, 194–195

Sadegh-Khandjani, Behrouz, 248

Samaria. *See* Itamar settlement

Samaria Regional Council, 96, 97

Sambue, Yarni, 251

Sammual Presbyterian Church (South Korea), killing of humanitarian workers from, 251–252

Samuel, Sandra, 152–153

Sassoon, Zuhair, 188–189

Satloff, Robert, 169, 175–176

Saudi Arabia, anti-Semitic and anti-Christian violence in, 253

Sayeret Matkal, Entebbe Raid and, 258–259

Schemm, Paul, 180

Sderot, 76–77

Second Exodus. *See* Egypt

Second Intifada, 74, 80, 97, 115, 119, 226

Security Fence, controversy about, 122–123

Seder, 218–222

Sephardic Jews, 48

Sermon on the Mount, 138

settlements, 118; Arab attacks on, 96–97; Givot Olam, 97–99; historical nature of, 92–95; Itamar, 96–97; life in, 104–107; Obama's criticism of, 92, 93, 94, 100; Tekoa, 100–104

Shabbat (Sabbath): atmosphere of, 21–24; ceremony ending, 101–103; preparation for, 16–17, 20–21, 43–44

Shabo family, killing of, 97

shahid (martyr for jihad), 110, 124

Shamir, Yitzhak, 204

sharia law, 32, 125; conversion to Christianity and, 268; in Gaza, 133; in Nigeria, 249, 250

Sharon, Ariel, 23, 91, 96, 97, 98; Gaza Disengagement and, 131, 132–133

Shea, Nina, 192–193, 215, 243

Shim Sung-Min, 252

Shumukh al-Islam fatwa, 211

Sibony, Ilan, 181–184

Simchat Torah procession, 57

Simintov, Zablon, 251

Sipping from the Nile (Naggar), 207

Somalia, killing of Christians in, 161

South Africa, apartheid in, 77–82, 85

St. Paul, 38

St. Peter, 139

StandWithUs, 15, 25, 29

Stein, Kenneth W., 82–83

Straus, Joe and Orit, 264

Sudan, 242

Sukkot (Feast of Tabernacles), 53, 55–56, 263–270

Suleiman the Magnificent, 136

Sutherland, Thomas, 8

Syria: expulsion of Jews
     from, 159; persecution of
     Christians in, 162

T
Tadros, Samuel, 217
Taj Mahal Palace Hotel,
     India, 149–150
Tekoa community, 100–104
"Tel Aviv, 1925" (photograph),
     52
"Tel Aviv Inauguration"
     (photograph), 52
Tel HaShomer Medical
     Center, 1–2, 12, 267–268
Telegraph, 229
Temple Mount: archeological
     findings at, 66–68;
     Camp David Accords and
     location of temple, 59–60;
     Christianity and Judaism
     absent from, 58–59; illegal
     archeological excavation
     of, 61, 65–66; importance
     to Christians and Jews,
     45–47, 57, 65; Temple
     Denial and split sover-
     eignty, 61–65; Temple
     Denial's spread, 68–70
ten Boom, Betsie and Corrie,
     10–11
ten Boom, Willem, 10–11
Their Blood Cries Out:
     The Worldwide Tragedy of

Modern Christians Who
     Are Dying for Their Faith
     (Marshall and Gilbert),
     162, 253
Theophilus III, 209
This Goodly Heritage (Yaari),
     49–50
Thomas, Helen, 243
Time Magazine, 152
Tisha B'Av, 14–16, 58, 70
Trigano, Shmuel, 156
Tunisia, expulsion of Jews
     from, 160
Turkey: anti-Semitic and
     anti-Christian violence
     in, 242, 244, 245–247;
     "humanitarian" flotilla
     ship and, 254
Tutu, Desmond, 81–82

U
Uganda, IDF raid to free
     hostages at Entebbe,
     257–259
United Nations World
     Conference on Racism, 81
United States: hate crimes
     against Jews, 241; media
     in, 2, 44, 134; scholars
     and Temple Denial, 62
"U.S. Policy on Israeli
     Settlements" (Gold),
     94–95
USA Today, 252

V

Vance, Ronny and Chaya, 264

Vatican's Special Assembly for
the Middle East, 160–161

W

Wahed, Joseph Abdel,
201–202, 203–204,
205–207

Wall Street Journal, 206–207

War of Independence (1948–
1949), 30; Arabs leaving
homes after, 186; persecution of Jews after, 171–172,
204; settlement after, 93, 94

Warren, Charles, 66

Weiner, Justus Reid, 228–229,
233–234

Western Wall (*HaKotel*):
Rosh Hashanah and,
38–41; Sukkot and, 57,
265; Tisha B'Av and, 15;
Yom Kippur and, 44–45

Williams, Rowan, 226–227

Wilson, Charles, 66

World Organization of
Jews from Arab Countries
(WOJAC), 158, 164

Wouk, Herman, 260–261

Wye Plantation talks, 96

Y

Yaari, Avraham, 49–50, 52,
113

Yehuda, Eliezer ben, 51

Yemen, anti-Semitic and
anti-Christian violence in,
159, 242

Yom Kippur (Day of
Atonement), 37–38;
atmosphere of, 47–48;
end of, 48–49

Z

Zamir, Levana, 202–203

Zelouf, Alda, 191

Zionist movement: Balfour
Declaration and, 113;
Christian Zionists, 12–14;
Iran and, 247; journalists
and, 228, 237;
Morocco and, 171,
180–181; Muslim
hatred of, 151, 240–241,
254–255; Psalm 137 and,
187; settlements and, 95;
Temple Mount and, 70

Zirve publishing house,
Turkey, 246

Zweiter, Chana, 127–128